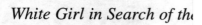

White Girl in Search of th

Pauline and H. A. in Cape Town, *c.* 1945.

White Girl
in Search of the Party

PAULINE PODBREY

*For Margaret and Michael
with fondest best wishes*

Love

Pauline

London 6.3.94

Hadeda Books
Pietermaritzburg
1993

The quotation on page 140 from 'Do not go gentle into that good
night' by Dylan Thomas, published by J. M. Dent & Sons Ltd. in
The Collected Poems 1934–1953, is reproduced here with permission.

ISBN 0 86980 904 0

Hadeda Books is an imprint of the University of Natal Press.
These publications reach out beyond the academic community
to the wider reading public. Like the bird for which they are
named they have a wide distribution and a loud voice.

Typeset in the University of Natal Press
Printed by Kohler Carton & Print

For my daughters – Sandra, Karen and Jennie

Contents

Illustrations

All illustrations are from the author's own collection.

Author's Note

No doubt some will contest my version of events and to them I can only submit that everything I have written here is how I remember it. I have tried to be as truthful as possible but I must confess that in a few places I have altered names to save distress or embarrassment. Invented names are denoted by the sign ° at their first appearance.

To those who have helped me by reading the manuscript, pointing out errors and spurring me on, my grateful thanks. Among them are Lily Herzberg, Pauline Kahn, Wolfie Kodesh, Roz Ainsley, Sandra Ashton, Karen and Jennie Naidoo, Bruna Cordatti, Joe Podbrey. Thanks also to Margery Moberly for being such a delightful editor to work with.

But it is Terry Callaghan, my present husband, who bore the brunt of my efforts yet who never wavered in his support and encouragement. He it was who checked my grammar and who acted as peacemaker/intermediary between me and my computer when, as often happened, we nearly came to blows.

How is the gold become dim!
How is the most fine gold changed!

Lamentations

1933–1943

Durban

S LOWLY, ponderously, the SS *Watussi* nudged her great bulk into the
Durban harbour and, with much creaking of ropes and chains, settled
herself in the docks. It was February 1933 and we had arrived. We were the new
immigrants and this was our promised land.

This ship had been home for six weeks, ever since we left Hamburg, but our
journey started even earlier; it began in Malat, the little Lithuanian *shtetl* where
we'd waited for Father to send for us. From Malat we travelled to Kovna, the
capital, where my brother and I had been born, and we were put up for the night
by Mother's wealthy relatives. We knew they were wealthy because they had a
bathroom, the first we had ever seen, and my brother Yossele was transfixed
with wonder at the sight of such technology. When no one was looking he stole
into the bathroom and turned all the taps full on. He watched as the water
reached the top of the bath and began to overflow, the shower thundered in the
corner and the lavatory chain produced a most resounding tumult when pulled.
Our hosts found him before the whole house flooded but they were greatly
relieved when we left for Hamburg the next day.

When we reached the transit camp in Hamburg we were greeted by a
formidable German woman in clinical white overalls who gave us to understand
that she was in charge. We were the transients and she was used to dealing with
emigrants, refugees, travellers, people who could not afford hotels. Her deep,
harsh voice needed no amplifier; it reverberated in the furthest corners. Every
minute of our two-day stay here was organized and controlled. We were
instructed when to go to sleep and when to wake, how to make up our bunk beds
and where to sit for our meals. It was a place untouched by dirt, chaos or human
warmth.

Boarding the *Watussi* and breathing in the icy, salty North Sea air opened
vistas of a new and freer world for Yossele and me. We raced along the
windswept decks and chased each other through vast dining rooms, lounges,
games rooms, up and down carpeted stairways, in and out of cabins and

bathrooms. 'Children, Children, stop it; you must be good, you must listen to me,' Mother alternately ordered and pleaded. It made no difference. We'd heard it too many times before: just another boring old refrain, and so we continued to run and play and hide as though the vast ship had been designed for our delight.

Now here we were in Durban, about to be re-united with our father whom we had last seen four years ago when he left us to seek, if not his fortune, at least a job.

Many East European Jews without money were being driven by growing unemployment to seek refuge overseas. Thousands had already left to escape the oppression and persecution to which Jews were subjected throughout eastern Europe. A goodly number of the young and idealistic departed for Palestine where they were to build a national home for the Jews; among them were Father's younger brother, Itzhak, and Mother's younger sister, Chava. For most of the rest, America was the land of opportunity; it beckoned with promises of freedom, employment and the good life. When they could no longer enter the United States, the former haven whose borders were now closed to the poor and hungry and oppressed of the world, would-be emigrants looked about for another destination and many chose sunny South Africa, the country where the streets were paved with gold, or so it was bruited about by those left behind.

That was not why Father emigrated. He wasn't seeking gold and he wasn't a bolter. He was a Bundist, a member of the left-wing Jewish movement which maintained that Jews had a right to live where they were born and it was their duty to make their homelands safe, secure and dignified for all their inhabitants, not only for Jews. Fortunately for us, Father lost his job when the depression hit Lithuania and seek as he might, there was no work available. Because one must live and provide for one's family, Father packed his bags and left his country. Subsequent events in eastern Europe proved that this was the wisest decision he ever made. It took him four years of abstemious, monastic living in South Africa to save our fares. Now, as we lined the deck, together with the other anxious immigrants, we peered down at the clusters of men below us, incongruously suited in heavy dark serge and felt hats. We were trying to find, among the tense, upturned faces, the one who was our dad.

'Four years is a long time to be separated,' my mother once said to °Mrs Kabalsky, in the days when they were still friendly, weeks before, when the Kabalskys were sharing our cabin. 'You're lucky,' Mrs Kabalsky had sighed. 'We had to wait seven years.' 'If I were Mr Kabalsky,' my mother later confided to °Mrs Cogan, 'she'd still be waiting.' But that was after Mother had to bribe the cabin steward to remove Mrs Kabalsky and her two sons from our cabin, when the smell of decomposing food hidden under their bunk beds could no longer be tolerated and all her pleas to Mrs Kabalsky to desist from this habit

The sign ° denotes an invented name.

of squirrelling away bits of food, fell on deaf ears. 'In case the children get hungry at night,' was Mrs Kabalsky's plaintive excuse. Years of worry about where the next meal was coming from proved a more powerful impetus than the assurance of breakfast, dinner, lunch and tea as well as the unexpected luxury of ice cream every day at eleven o'clock. In the end, when Mrs Kabalsky's tentative smile no longer served to mollify Mother, the cabin steward agreed, for a consideration, to find them another cabin.

Among our fellow passengers was a party of German nuns who were going to Africa to save heathen souls for Jesus. In their long black cloaks and wide, starched headgear framing little white faces, they reminded me of a picture I had once seen of a flock of outsize penguins. I would gaze from a distance as they clustered in a corner of the deck to knit and read and chatter and at first their strangeness unnerved me – nuns and priests had always been a species of alien life it was better to avoid. If I saw one walking down the village street I would cross the road or flatten myself into a doorway. It wasn't fear exactly but it was just as well to avoid contact with anyone as unaccountably threatening as these people who inhabited a world so totally divorced from what I knew to be ordinary, natural, everyday. The priests in their tall hats with their long, flowing beards and the nuns in their enveloping cloaks out of which their pale little faces peered, these were the people who typified the chasm that lay between us normal Jews and the extraordinary, strange, menacing Goyim. So when one of these nuns held out her arms and made as if to catch me one day as I ran along the deck, I shrank away in fear. Then I saw her laughing and when I looked into her face I was surprised to find that she was young and pretty. She seemed almost ready to join in our game.

'I'm °Sister Mathilde,' she told me. 'What's your name?'

'Peske,' I mumbled under my breath.

'Oh,' she said, 'then I'm going to call you Pessale.' I looked at her in amazement. How could a nun know the Yiddish diminutive of my name? 'You needn't look so surprised,' Sister Mathilde laughed. 'I've known lots of little Jewish girls and I know what their mothers call them when they're good.'

We became friends and I spent many hours sitting at Sister Mathilde's side, watching her stitching away at her embroidery and listening entranced to her tales. She was deeply moved by the cruelty and injustice meted out to Africans by the whites and her mild blue eyes would widen with indignation as she related these stories.

'Do you know,' her voice dropped to a whisper, 'when a white man wants to reach for something, he makes a black man kneel down and then steps on his back?' I didn't know but I shared her revulsion. I too hated injustice and wished I could do something about it. Of course I couldn't become a nun but I resolved to find some other way of expressing my sense of outrage. Now, as I gazed down from the height of the deck I was searching for kneeling blacks with white men on their backs. There weren't any but I did see black men straining under heavy sacks while white, florid men in big hats lounged about, smoking and talking, making no effort to help the ones who were doing all the work.

I'd seen a black man once before: he'd come to our *shtetl* with a travelling circus and proved to be the main attraction. We children followed him wherever he went, timidly keeping a distance between us and speculating on how he managed to achieve that colour. 'It's just painted on with shoe polish,' Motke declared. He pointed at the black man and shrieked with merriment. 'Look, he's forgotten to paint his hands, they're pink inside.' I had joined in the laughter, relieved to find that I did not have to embrace such an outlandish concept as a black man. My nine-year-old world was already bulging with enough unanswered questions and unresolved enigmas that demanded explanations and that needed sorting out. I wasn't looking for another 'Why' and 'How'; I already knew how hard it was to find any answers. Yet here were black men, lots of them, many more than whites, and no one seemed to find it strange or disturbing. Everyone seemed to accept it as unremarkable.

MOTHER was tense, standing between my brother Yossele and me, searching for Father. Suddenly her grip tightened; 'Look, there he is, there's your father.' I strove to match the dim image of my memory with the unfamiliar figure below at which Mother was pointing. He was peering up at us, anxiously searching, as we gazed down at him. Then he focused on Mother's waving hand and he lifted his hat in the air, shouting, 'Henneh, Hennale, *kinderlach*!' We disembarked and I allowed myself to be hugged and kissed by this man who was my father and then we were driven off to a big house where Uncle Sam lived with his family.

Uncle Sam was a relative and a *landsleit*, a countryman, and he was also my father's employer. Lily, his elder daughter, did not trouble to hide her resentment at having to give up an afternoon's tennis to entertain these 'greenies', these straight-off-the-boat foreigners who couldn't even speak English. Pauline, the younger daughter, was solicitous and kindly. As soon as tea was finished she took Yossele and me by the hand and led us away to her room where several of her friends were already waiting. Soon they were all engaged in a lively debate on what to call us, on what our new names should be, while my brother and I stood by, speechless and wondering. In her limited Yiddish Pauline explained that we needed proper English names: Yossel and Pessel would not do. Yossele was easy, it had to be Joseph which then became Joe. As for me, it was a toss-up between 'Bessie' or 'Pauline'. They took a vote and the Pauline faction won by a narrow margin.

From Uncle Sam's grand residence we moved on to the modest house in Ridge Road where Dad had rented two rooms for us from Mrs Piccione. Our new landlady was short and plump and busy and warm-hearted. She and Mother shared a kitchen for the four months we lived there without a harsh word between them. The two women laughed a lot and talked to each other in mime and signs and animal noises. When Mother wanted lamb, not beef, she would crouch low and shake her head: 'No, no, not moo moo; baa, baa,' and the two of them would giggle and clap their hands. Mr Piccione was as taciturn as his wife was voluble and we saw him rarely but their sons, especially Ronnie, the eldest, took great delight in teasing and tormenting Joe and me. 'Not sin-ging,' he would jeer at my attempts at English: 'Can't you say "singing"?' In the evenings nostalgic fellow-immigrants would come to drink lemon tea with strawberry jam and ask for news of relatives left behind in the old country. Then Dad would lift me on to a chair and I'd sing Yiddish songs for our guests. This usually brought tears to their eyes and made Dad very proud.

The first big purchase my parents made was a Singer sewing machine, not a treadle which was more expensive but a hand machine. By the end of the first week Mother was sewing brassieres for the ladies of the neighbourhood, introduced by Mrs Piccione who worked hard at drumming up business. Mother charged 2/6d per garment and when she wasn't cooking or cleaning she was always at her machine. Dad's salary of £11 per month from Uncle Sam wasn't enough to pay for food and rent and for the instalments on the shiny bedroom and dining room suites which Dad had bought on hire purchase. Her friends in Malat had mocked at Mother when she decided to take up a course in corsetry and brassieres a few months before our departure. 'You're going to the land of gold and diamonds,' they reminded her: 'What do you need this for?' Mother didn't argue, she just went ahead with her course. '*Ich ken meine schreire*,' was all she'd say, meaning that she was familiar with her goods: in other words, knowing my father, she could anticipate correctly that even in the *Goldene Medina* her earning power would count for more than pin money.

One day an African came to the gate looking for work. Mother told him there was none, and then as he walked away sent Yossele and me to call him back. 'He looks hungry,' she said and motioned him in. He refused to enter the house and squatted outside where Mother presented him with a doorstep sandwich and a huge mug of tea. The Picciones turned away in open disapproval clicking their tongues. Father, the acclimatised South African, was visibly embarrassed.

IN THE Piccione's garden was a handsome mango tree and this I often climbed to commune with God. He and I had become acquainted fairly recently but now I could tell Him my innermost thoughts and confide my secret doubts and longings. Not that I actually spoke the words – with God one didn't need to. God could read people's thoughts and understood exactly what one wanted to say. Having grown up in a family where Father called himself an atheist and Mother a 'don't know', I had taken God's absence for granted until we went to stay with Grandma the year before we left Lithuania. Grandma was not tall but her regal bearing gave her stature as she swept through the house, the street, the *shtetl*, swishing her long black skirt. She ordained the lives of her family with a no-nonsense firmness that left little room for argument or opposition. I never heard her raise her voice nor did I ever hear anyone contradict her.

Grandpa was 'Moshe der Eisenkremer', the ironmonger, and he spent his days in his shop at the front of the house, selling chains and nails and saddles and spades to peasants who came in from surrounding villages and with whom conversation was conducted in a series of grunts. He didn't speak to me much, either, but I would sit for hours on a stool in the corner of the shop watching him, wondering what he was thinking. 'What's the child doing there?' Grandma would grumble. 'She'd be better off helping in the house.' 'Let her be,' Grandpa would mumble back and it pleased me to believe that Grandpa liked me and wanted me around, even though he never told me so. They had three sons who had all left home: the eldest, Reuben, had followed my father to South Africa but had settled in Johannesburg, a long way from Durban. Itzhak, the youngest was the *chalutz*, the pioneer, who went to Palestine in the early twenties to dig the land, drain the swamps and become the first farmer the family had ever known. Their only daughter, Chaie, a plump, pouting beauty, lived with her well-scrubbed husband Yankel and their two pretty children in a wing of Grandma's house.

I loved being there, surrounded by grandparents, aunty, uncle and cousins and I particularly enjoyed Pesach, the bustle, the excitement, the anticipation, the holiday which had passed almost unnoticed in our own household. In Grandma's house, before the First Seder, all the children in the family were invited to join Grandfather in searching the house for any traces of leaven that might have been overlooked. This was great fun, peering into corners and under sofas, following Grandfather round the house, pretending to discover bread-crumbs in unlikely places. By the time we took our seats around the long, damask-covered table, in our new clothes and with our shoes and hair squeaky clean, we could endorse Grandpa's declaration to the Lord that every crumb had been removed but if any had escaped our notice, they were to be declared annulled and worthless, 'as the dust of the earth'.

An empty seat was always left for Elijah, and Grandpa – whose status during the rest of the year was somewhat ambiguous – now took his place at the head of the table, bolstered by cushions and pillows for his comfort, and led the prayers. Apart from Yankel, the former *Yeshiva* scholar, and Grandfather himself, none of the rest of us could understand the archaic Hebrew of the prayers but that did not spoil our enjoyment. Yossele had been coached to ask the traditional question: '*Ma nishtano ha'laila haze . . .*' (Why is this night different from any other night?) A lengthy reply followed, explaining how we had been brought out of bondage in Egypt and why it was important to remember the event, even though it happened many years ago. The litany stretched on and on but by the time the children started getting restless the singing began and we all joined in.

> The kid, the kid, an only kid,
> That father bought for two *zuzim* . . .

How intoxicating the evening proved to be! How enchanting the memory of warm, enveloping family, of thrilling liturgy and the exciting sense of occasion, of participation, of belonging. But it was not only the ceremonial that won me over to God. I search my memory but cannot recall any single event that transformed me into a passionate believer, a true and faithful follower of the one and only God. At no stage did Grandma say: 'There is a God and you must worship Him.' She had no need to. Her faith needed no rocks or miracles or declarations; it just was. And her certainty, her unquestioning confidence, impressed me powerfully with all the force of a newly discovered faith. I dedicated myself to God and promised Him that I would keep His command-ments, be ever faithful and never tell a lie. When we returned to our own home it pained me to see that we mixed our *milchike* and *fleishike*, our milk and meat dishes, that on our door there was no *mezzuzah* and certainly no prayers were recited at any time of the day. My attempts to discuss these matters with Mother met with a smile and an airy dismissal. 'I really haven't the time to worry about these things,' she'd say. At night, before falling asleep, I'd explain to God that Mother didn't understand what she had to do but that He shouldn't punish her because even though she wasn't religious, she was good.

Being on easy terms with God also enabled me to rid myself of an unpleasant recurrent dream which had dogged my sleeping hours for years, or so it seemed to me. In this dream I was invited by a group of sinister looking adults to go into a room where a surprise was promised me. The surprise turned out to be a corpse, lying on a high bed in the middle of the room. I screamed in terror and ran while the adults pointed their fingers and laughed at me. I wrestled with my terror for years and hated going to sleep for fear of my nightmare. Then I hit on an obvious solution, I would appeal to God. 'Please God,' I prayed, 'don't let me dream that horrible dream,' and to my delight He didn't. In time I added a few other unpleasant themes that I would rather not dream about and, provided I remembered to identify each in my thoughts before falling asleep, God saved me from dreaming about them.

My horror of death and corpses began when I was much younger, in Kurkl, when our ancient neighbour died. Her two spinster daughters followed the body to the cemetery with much wailing and gnashing of teeth; they covered their heads in soot and tore their garments to the accompaniment of shrill and raucous crying. It was a deplorable spectacle, a vulgar ritual which repelled and embarrassed and served only to banish all feelings of sadness and sympathy.

What made it worse for me was Mother leading me to visit the neighbours just before the funeral. I did not see the corpse in the next room but a glass of water with a sponge in it, placed on the windowsill, caught my attention. 'What's that for?' I asked Mother. A woman standing nearby overheard my question and took it upon herself to explain. 'It's for the soul to wash itself before it leaves the house,' she told me. I kept my eyes glued on the glass; I would not be distracted for an instant; I had to see what the soul looked like and how it would wash itself. But after a while Mother grasped my hand and pulled me away before I could catch the soul at its ablutions, leaving my morbid curiosity to feed on itself.

I was four or five years old and we were still living in Kovna, when Mother led me one day to a big hall in a part of town that seemed a long way from home. She held me firmly by the hand as we approached the building and at the entrance we were motioned inside by two uniformed men guarding the door. Inside we found many other mothers with children sitting on hard benches round the walls. The children looked scared and the mothers seemed full of foreboding as they gripped the hands of their offspring. An unnatural hush hung over the hall but it was suddenly shattered when there appeared, from the door opposite the entrance, two blood-bespattered nurses half leading, half carrying a child of about my age, covered in blood. The child's mother rushed forward, gathered her daughter in her arms and hurried off with her, to the accompaniment of a loud wailing from the children left behind in the hall. 'Next,' called the nurse and a mother stepped forward, dragging her protesting child to hand her over to the nurse with the blood-stained uniform. I waited in horror and sure enough, soon it came to my turn. Mother disengaged my grip on her arm and led me to the tunnel of blood.

'No, Mummy, no, don't leave me,' I begged as I was forcibly dragged away from her, taken inside a small room where I was strapped to a chair and held down by two nurses. A doctor wielding a long, sharp knife, came towards me and blocked out the light. I, too, was bleeding and whimpering as I was handed back to my Mother. I never discovered why I had to undergo this torture. What had I done to deserve such punishment? Why had my Mother deserted me when I needed her? No one ever explained to me and I still don't know what operation was performed on me and all those other desperate children. It wasn't to remove my tonsils because I still have those. What else called for such drastic, indiscriminate surgery? My mother never referred to this incident and in time I managed to erase it from my memory so successfully that I didn't even need to ask God not to let me dream about it.

I CONTINUED my role of go-between between my parents and God after we arrived in South Africa. 'They're really good,' I'd assure Him from my perch in the mango tree. 'They just don't think it's necessary to prove it.' And God, being all-seeing and all-powerful, would surely understand this; after all He could look into people's hearts and read their thoughts. To compensate for my parents' shortcomings, I re-dedicated myself to His service; I would be good and honourable; I would tell the truth, always, no matter what the cost to myself or to others. My eleven-year-old soul yearned for a chance to prove itself to God. I longed to serve a higher being, to grasp at absolutes, to be totally at one with God and His universe. But, as time went on, it grew increasingly difficult to sustain my beliefs under Father's mockingly tolerant debunking. 'Faith is not enough,' he'd declare. 'With faith alone man can believe anything – and he does. People have worshipped horses, the moon, cats, all sorts of things. What one needs is proof, scientific proof, and what proof have we of the existence of God?' A question I found difficult to answer but I persisted in arguing.

'If there is no God, how will we know the difference between right and wrong?'

'We'll know because we're human beings. Man has a conscience and a brain and he's got to learn to rely on himself.'

'But Dad,' I protested, 'not all people are good. A lot of them are bad; they're cruel and wicked and they do terrible things to each other. What's the good of them relying on themselves?'

But Father had no doubts. 'I don't believe that given the choice, most people wouldn't behave decently,' he declared. 'It's the structure of society that's rotten. It rewards greed and selfishness.' Uncharacteristically, Father was making a speech. 'It's not a question of individuals sacrificing themselves, giving up everything to help others. That's charity, or religion or what have you. It doesn't change anything, it only makes the giver feel good. What we need is the sort of society that doesn't put a premium on wickedness; we need a decent, human, socialist society. Change society and you'll change human nature, including the nature of the capitalists themselves; which doesn't mean,' he added, 'that they won't fight like tigers to cling on to their privileges.'

Father's logic was seductive and the more I thought about it the more reasonable it seemed. All the same, I was more than reluctant to abandon God. The succeeding weeks and months brought me closer to Father and as I listened to his wry comments about religion and humanity, my faith in God began to falter. Many hours of anguished communion followed in which I pleaded with God to make Him see my dilemma. 'Please God,' I begged, 'I want to believe in You. Give me some sign that You're there.' God remained stubbornly silent and eventually I decided to put Him to the test. He knew how I longed for a bicycle; would He please perform a little miracle and make one appear right there, in front of me? After all, for God that would be a small thing to do; for me it would change my life. I waited and waited but my bicycle never materialised and gradually but inexorably my faith dimmed and died.

Now as I climbed the mango tree, bereft of God, I gazed at the vastness of the sky above me, at the brilliance of the myriad, uncountable stars and I agonised over the purpose of life and our existence on earth. If there was no God and our earth was just a speck in the universe did we human beings count in the great universal design? Was there a plan, a pattern? If there was, then who made it? And if there wasn't, then what did it matter if we disappeared without trace? Would it change anything? Why should the death of a human being matter more than the death of an ant or a bee? And if it didn't matter, why didn't we just lie down and die? Why spend a lifetime creeping towards death and annihilation when we could reach it quickly and cleanly right away?

This was the closest I had ever come to cosmic despair, no less overwhelming for being immature and childish. My self-induced nihilism was real and terrifying, it brought me to the edge of the abyss of nothingness, a fearsome place to be. Happily, it didn't last long. Soon life and curiosity proved more enticing. I was searching for a new philosophy to fill the gap that God had left and I embraced with enthusiasm Father's dictum: man must rely on himself, on his own sense of right and wrong. I tried to cultivate a heightened sense of moral sensibility and decided that self-imposed codes of conduct could and should be every bit as binding as those brought down from Mount Sinai.

My preoccupations with the timeless issues of morality, the meaning and purpose of life, were strongly reinforced by the discussions that took place in our living room at that time. My father had managed to bring together a group of like-minded friends in the political wilderness that was Durban. When my exhausted mother had retired to bed and my brothers and I were supposed to be fast asleep, these men would launch into their polemics, continuing into the small hours. I would creep out of bed and surreptitiously curl up in a corner of the balcony where I could overhear them. They were passionate, earnest and dedicated to their cause which I soon discovered was Communism. Here, I realised, were men who cared about the world and who wanted to change it. I too would be a Communist when I grew up.

M Y SCHOOL years at the Berea Road Juniors were not happy but the first term was the worst. As I had no English it was assumed that I was backward and so I was placed in Class 2 with the seven-year-olds. At eleven I was a big girl and I towered over my classmates. Stinky Miller was instructed by the teacher to act as my interpreter but he was a shifty, mean little boy who would crib my arithmetic and then join my tormentors in the playground. In dumb rage I'd lash out when the jibes and jeers got too much for me; then the teacher would intervene to berate me for hitting out at children so much smaller than myself. 'A big girl like you, aren't you ashamed of yourself?' I couldn't explain how they had provoked me so I just grew angrier and more isolated. How I wished I could go back to Malat to my friends and my old school and the lessons which were interesting and sensible and oh, so intelligent, compared with this infantile nonsense. Before Malat there was Kurkl, the little village where I enjoyed prestige and status as a leader of our gang even though I was a girl. There, when sides were picked for hopscotch or rounders I took my rightful turn at picking first. Here nobody thought of appointing me leader. Worse than that, they didn't even like to have me in their team; I was only included, grudgingly, and with bad grace, when all the others had been picked. I was the idiot outsider.

It occurred to me that this is how the Minkoff kids must have felt in Kurkl when the rest of us tried to exclude them from our games. At the time none of us had any scruples about chasing them away because they were bedraggled and barefoot and smelly and everyone knew their father was a horse thief and their mother a slut. They would follow us to the fields, keeping a cautious distance behind, the elder boys humping their younger brothers and sisters on their backs. 'Go away,' we would order them, as one might a pack of mangy dogs, 'Go home.' But like a pack of homeless animals the Minkoff kids would pause, eyes cast down, and wait, dumbly. They never questioned the justice of the role we had assigned them; they never argued or answered back. Shmulke, the eldest, didn't even protest when we ordered him to show his *pinkele*. He would pull down his dirty short pants and stand snivelling, sucking at his thumb while the rest of us poked at him, laughing and jeering. Then I'd be ashamed that I could be as bad as that and I'd be overcome with pity and remorse. To make amends I would then offer to carry one of the brood on my back, suppressing my revulsion at their unwashed smell.

By the time we left Lithuania I'd attended school in three different languages. In Kovna, when I started, I went to a Yiddish school and my education was conducted in the same tongue that I spoke at home. Then Father was transferred and we all moved to Utian where there was no Yiddish school, only a Hebrew one. After the initial strangeness I soon accepted this new language and within months I was quite at ease with it. Once again Father was transferred and this time we found ourselves in a little town where the only junior school was in Lithuanian and so I had to learn a third language. This too, was not insuperable; what impressed me more was the stress laid on patriotism, the obligatory rendering every morning of a song in which we pledged to get Vilnius back from Poland which had seized it in 1920. '*Mes be Vilnius ne nurimsin*,' – our childish voices rang out loud and clear and after the Second World War Vilnius was returned to Lithuania. Then, in the six weeks that it took to reach Durban on the *Watussi* I picked up much more German than I realised; it has served me well. Now, in South Africa, I was confronted with my biggest challenge – English. As before, in our previous schools, my brother and I were packed off in the morning and it was assumed we would get on with it. There was never any question of coaching, cramming or private tuition and in our case it worked, after the first three or four traumatic months.

In my second term at the Berea Road Juniors I could understand much more than I could express and I soon learnt that Miss Widgely, our class teacher, didn't like children. I didn't know she liked Jews even less. When she caught Stinky Miller cheating one day, she screwed up her thin lips and stabbed at us with her forefinger.

'You Jews,' she snorted, 'you're always cheating.' I was outraged and speechless; I'd never cheated in my life. How could she accuse me so unfairly? That evening, when I told my father, I was choking with indignation.

'What exactly did she say?' Father wanted to know, getting ready to do battle.

'Well,' I said, 'Perhaps she said, "You Jewish children must stop cheating", or, oh, I don't know, I can't remember the exact words.' Father removed his jacket and placed it over the back of his chair.

'How can I go and argue with the woman if I don't know what she said?' he turned on me and there was relief in his voice. Not only was his English inadequate to dispute with teachers but he developed a stutter when excited. He knew and I knew that he would have been worsted in an argument.

YEARS before, when we lived in Kurkl, I had my first encounter with Jew-baiting. I tackled the problem directly and, to my mind, satisfactorily. I was leading Yossele home from school on a cold winter's afternoon. At five years old he was pale and puny while I, at seven, was big, healthy and strong, his natural protector. Janis, the village bully, his little henchman in tow, saw us coming across the field and called out to Yossele, 'Dirty Jewboy.' Startled, Yossele took his thumb out of his mouth and protested, 'I'm not.'

'Yes you are, and you killed Christ.'

'I didn't, I didn't,' Yossele cried. I invited Janis to shut up but he wouldn't. He kept on tormenting my little brother and laughing at his distress so I picked up a stone and threw it at him. To my great surprise it reached its target and Janis howled with pain as he ran off, clutching his head.

That evening we had a visit from our Rebbe who said that the priest had been to see him because Janis's mother had complained about what I had done to her son. The Rebbe spoke seriously to my mother and wagged his finger in my face. 'What are you trying to do?' he demanded of me. 'Do you want to start a pogrom?' I was neither sorry nor contrite. I was sure that Janis had learnt his lesson: he would not again abuse my little brother. I had learnt mine: it's best to fight back when you are attacked. But the Rebbe and my mother, instead of demanding from the priest that he stop his flock from Jew-baiting, were apologising to him and turning on me. It was my first lesson in the ghetto mentality: the fear, the fawning, keeping your head down, keeping your nose clean. How I hated and despised it.

Years later in Durban I'd detect a wheedling tone creep into Mother's voice when addressing officialdom no matter how insignificant, as when applying for a trading licence from a junior clerk at the Town Hall. 'You don't have to be beholden to him,' I told her. 'He's just doing a job of work. He's not doing you any favours.' Mother would pat my shoulder and smile and refuse to be drawn. I was constantly embarrassed by Mother: her broken English, her foreign accent, her inability to read and write the language, her speaking Yiddish in public and her ingratiating manner to petty bureaucrats made me ashamed of her and ashamed of myself for feeling like that about my mother. I also held it against her that she was nice to people she didn't like and preferred not to make a fuss.

POVERTY is relative – until it becomes absolute. We never went hungry and we always had enough to wear but our diet was monotonous and our clothing purely functional. I never thought of ourselves as poor and I do not remember ever comparing our possessions with those of our neighbours. As children do, I took it for granted that our life was the norm, that money was scarce and pennies were precious.

'Can I have twopence, Dad?' I would ask, not very often.

'What do you need it for?'

'For sweets.'

'For sweets!' Dad would exclaim and then he would start to tick off on his fingers. 'For twopence I can get, a newspaper.' One finger. 'Half a packet of Needlepoint cigarettes.' Another finger. 'A ride in the bus.' Finger three, and on and on until I stopped listening and walked away, suitably chastised for my lack of appreciation of the relative value of things. 'And you want twopence for sweets!' was how the catechism always ended, to my chagrin.

When we moved to our flat above the shop at the corner of Berea and Essenwood Roads, our next-door neighbours were the Van Heerdens. Mr Van Heerden was a sergeant in the police and their children were our playmates. They were poor like us but Mother was amused to find that, as part of their economy drive, each child was rationed to two pieces of lavatory paper. When Mother returned from the hospital with the new baby Mrs Van Heerden came in to help her. Then Mother found that a £5 note – a present for the baby – was missing from the room where only Mrs Van Heerden had been and knew that she had stolen it.

'What are you going to do about it?' I demanded.

'Nothing,' Mother answered. 'You don't complain to policemen about their wives.'

'H'm,' I snorted. Typical of her, compromising, scared, no principles.

The appearance of my brother Maurice, fourteen months after we arrived in South Africa, took me completely by surprise. No one had told me to expect him and I hadn't noticed the changing shape of Mother's body. Like everything else about my parents, I took her bulging belly for granted. My new baby brother, Maurice, captivated me completely. I loved him with an all-consuming adoration that only a helpless infant can evoke. This didn't prevent my hating the daily task imposed by Mother of taking him out in his pram, up and down Essenwood Road, before leaving for school.

I WOKE one morning to find blood on my pyjama pants and showed them to my mother. 'Mum, look, how did this happen? I haven't cut myself.'

'You must go to bed and stay there for two days,' Mother ordered. Then she tore up some flannelette sheets and gave them to me with two big safety pins and an elastic band. She showed me how to adjust them. 'Make sure you wash the cloths properly after you've used them and put them away where you'll find them next month and every month after that.'

'But Ma,' I wailed, 'I'm not sick. I don't want to go to bed. I've got to go swimming today.'

Ma was adamant. 'You can't swim today or any other day when you get your periods.'

Feeling perfectly fit and very foolish I spent the next two days in bed. That was my introduction to womanhood.

'It happens to all girls,' was the only explanation Mother offered.

'I AM sending you two to boarding school,' Father announced one day. 'You've got to learn to speak English properly and you can only do that when you're away from home.'

Neither Joe nor I had any concept of what 'boarding school' meant but we listened with interest as Father described how progressive, advanced and modern Mrs Stevenson's school was, in East Griqualand, near Kokstad. 'It's on a farm,' he told us 'where you'll enjoy a good, healthy life and live with the Stevenson children and other pupils.' He'd spent a week at this farm and decided that it was just what we needed although it would make a big dent in his slender income.

For Joe and me the year we spent there was made up in equal parts of revelation and deprivation. What we lost in academic achievement we gained in other accomplishments. We learnt to ride horses, make friends and cope with enemies. Mr French showed us how he handled venomous snakes and extracted their poisons. Once, when he was exhibiting a newly captured boomslang, I, in my ignorance, entranced by its primeval eye and earthy stillness, crept up behind the teacher and gently stroked the skin of the cold, prickly, beautiful serpent. Out of the corner of his eye Mr French caught me at it.

'How dare you play with death?' he stormed at me. 'Our lives depend on my grasp; I haven't removed its venom yet and you're interfering, you stupid girl.' I apologised and promised not to do it again, but secretly I exulted that I was able to come close to such a strange and mysterious being. The brittle touch of the snake on my fingers lingered with me for a long time and I'd shudder with a sense of hidden power every time I recalled it; I thrilled with a sense of deep affinity to this marvellous creature. This empathy with a snake was not something I could talk about without exposing myself to ridicule; I hugged the secret to myself. I could not share it even with Hope Barrable and Maggie Stevenson, the two senior girls whose intellect I admired and whose company I craved.

The tall, stooping teacher whom we called Uncle Bill played the piano and taught us country dancing. We learned to sing patriotic ditties of another country and another age and we sang them with gusto, unconcerned with their irrelevance to our lives:

> Home Boys Home, For it's Home We Ought to be.
> Home Boys Home, in the Old Country,
> Where the Oak and the Ash and the Weeping Willow Tree,
> For they all Grow Green in the Old Country.

The 'Old Country' that Uncle Bill assumed was ours – and it therefore followed that we must long for it – was, of course, England, a land that none of us had ever seen. It was a conceit common among English-speaking South Africans, but particularly Natalians, to refer to England as 'home', even though very few of them had ever been there. They strove to cultivate an accent which they fondly believed to be that of the English home counties, and to cling to English customs like tea and cucumber sandwiches, sundowners and cricket.

One of our teachers loved nasturtiums and she embroidered this flower on pillowcases, face-cloths, table-mats, antimaccasars. Mr Venter, our Afrikaans teacher, was a big unco-ordinated man with a perpetual good-natured grin. He didn't teach us much Afrikaans but he joined us at night when we crept out of our dormitories and ran to swim in the river by moonlight and dance magic dances round an old leafless tree. Mr Stevenson, husband of our headmistress, was a farmer. On Mondays he would pack his old Ford with seven, eight, nine Africans, and drive them down to the coast, to Port Shepstone. I don't know how his passengers survived the journey through the hot, dusty veld, but he came back in the evening with an empty car. The trip was not intended as a joy ride; he was selling labourers to the white farmers at so much per head. 'Slave trading,' my father called it when I told him about it afterwards.

Mrs Stevenson, our headmistress, was a remote figure, worshipped by her five children who formed the core of the school population. We were expected to emulate this adoration and extend it to embrace Mrs Stevenson's Pekinese, Nanky Poo. This dog was allowed to roam freely over the dining-room table, picking off our plates whatever titbit caught her fancy. We wondered why Nanky Poo bothered: her diet was far superior to ours. We envied Nanky Poo her liver, fish and other dainties; we had to make do with vegetable soup, bread and potatoes, and even these were doled out in restricted quantities. I cannot remember a time when we weren't hungry. We begged our parents for tuck boxes. All our pocket money went on food at the tearoom on the road to Kokstad, on buns and bananas, sweets and cold drinks. Our special treats were Marie biscuit sandwiches filled with tinned sardines and oozing with condensed milk.

It was at this school that I first learned about illicit love affairs between adults and how to pretend that one didn't know about them. It was here, too, that I was invited to share a bed with one of the older girls who introduced me to the strange uses of a candle between the sheets. I found the practice extraordinary and distasteful but I bore with it rather than risk being dubbed immature and accused of being inhibited. What I could not pass unchallenged was a casual remark by one of the Stevensons one day that my father was a short man. 'My father's not short,' I corrected them, wondering where they could have picked up such an extraordinary idea. 'He's a tall man', I declared, convinced that I was only stating a fact that should have been obvious to all of them who had met my father. When I returned home and discovered that Father was indeed quite short, not much taller than me, it came as a great surprise. I suppose all children believe their fathers to be ten feet tall; the shock of discovering a father of average height or less comes with the revelation that maybe Father is not even a hero. It's a sad day. It's a day of sudden growth out of childhood but not necessarily into adulthood.

Joe's time at the boarding school was not happy. Just how miserable it was I didn't discover until many years later; he kept his distance from me, eager to be accepted as one of the boys and determined to fight his own battles without interference from his big sister. This wasn't always possible. When I came across my little brother one day, inspanned in a dog cart in which were wedged the two big boys, Colin and John, each with a whip which they were threatening to use on his back if he didn't pull hard enough, I saw red. Enraged at such blatant bullying and worried that the strain would prove too much for Joe who was puffing and panting with his exertion, I flew at the two big boys, tipped them out of the dog cart and flayed about with my fists until they both disappeared. When I went to help Joe out of the shafts in which he was harnessed, he turned on me and battered me with his fists. 'Why don't you mind your own business?' he cried in fury. 'Why don't you leave me alone?'

During one of the summer holidays the Stevenson children came to Durban and Mother invited them for lunch. 'They're vegetarians,' I reminded her.

'What's that?' Mother wanted to know. When I explained Mother shook her head in disbelief and carried on preparing chicken soup with *kneidlach*.

'You can't give them that,' I protested.

'Leave it to me,' Mother answered and sure enough, each visitor was served with a steaming bowl of her home-made chicken soup.

'That was delicious,' John said as he accepted a second helping. Mother looked at me challengingly, daring me to speak. 'You see,' she told me afterwards, 'I told you they wouldn't know the difference.'

B Y THE time I reached the Durban Girls' High I had finally caught up with my age group but I was still the odd girl out, even though by now my English was as good as that of my classmates, if not better. The gaps in my education were large holes where subjects like History, Geography, Maths were jumbled together, disjointed, unconnected, irrational. Afrikaans was regarded with disdain which no one was expected to take seriously in the Durban of the '30s. For the extra language we had a choice: serious, intellectual Latin with Maths, or frivolous, feminine French with Domestic Science.

'H'm,' snorted Father: 'Of course you'll do Latin and Maths. Cooking's not a subject.' Which left me with no French and precious little Latin beyond *Amo, amas, amat*. Father always maintained that the most important subject was Arithmetic: 'Language was invented to explain numbers,' he asserted and occasionally, through the fog of barely comprehensible Maths classes, I would catch a glimpse of the marvellous possibilities of Algebra and Geometry, the pure, crystalline logic, the hidden certainties waiting to be discovered – but not, alas, by me.

Miss Ward was our History mistress, a desiccated little old lady who droned on endlessly about one Kaffir War after another. One afternoon, walking into the classroom, she found us in high spirits, laughing boisterously. 'Gels, gels,' she covered her ears, a pained expression on her face: 'You sound like the kaffirs down the road.' In the hush that followed I took a deep breath and stood up.

'Please Miss Ward,' I tried to speak normally but my throat was dry: 'the natives don't like to be called kaffirs, do they?' There was a flutter in the classroom as girls turned to look at me. Miss Ward adjusted her pincenez and peered at me over them, taking her time. Then she demanded: 'Are you chastising me?' 'Yes, Miss,' I answered, and gulped. Scared as I was I felt an enormous relief at having spoken. Unlike that time in the primary school when the teacher had maligned the Jews, now I could express myself well enough to protest, and I knew I would despise myself if I remained silent.

Miss Ward took a deep breath and drew herself up to her full 5'2". 'You are right,' she said. 'I apologise.' Such magnanimity filled me with admiration; I never learned to like Miss Ward but I did respect her after this incident.

The only class I loved was Literature, and that was thanks to Miss Gardiner, our English mistress with the funny, twisted mouth. I, too, wanted to smile like that, lifting one corner of my lips in what I believed to be a sardonic grin; I'd pose in front of the mirror, practising. Thanks to Miss Gardiner the English language became a magic door to marvellous undiscovered regions. She introduced me to a love affair with books which has lasted all my life and which is perpetually self-renewing. I read voraciously, indiscriminately, greedily, with an appetite that grew with what it fed on: books and poems, advertisements and articles, Angela Brazil and Leo Tolstoy, Mary Webb and Sinclair Lewis, Flaubert and Thackeray, Gorki and de Maupassant, Aldous Huxley and Knut Hamsun, Jack London and Charles de Coster, Dostoievsky and the Brontës. At first I stumbled over words and passages which I could not understand but I was too impatient to interrupt my reading in order to consult a dictionary. I went on reading and gradually, then more rapidly, more and more words unveiled themselves for me and revealed themselves in all their glory. Exploring the intoxicating world of literature became an adventure, full of wonder and enchantment.

'You'll spoil your eyes if you go on like that,' Mother warned but I was hooked, a book junkie for life. How, I marvelled, did these writers understand me and my emotions so well? They knew me better than I knew myself, they plumbed depths that I didn't know existed, illuminated corners of my mind that were hidden and unsuspected.

'Isn't it extraordinary,' I once said to my cousin Chana after reading Anna Karenina, 'that Tolstoy is able to get under the skin of a woman. How can he, a man, know what it feels like to be a woman, to identify so completely with her emotions, sensibilities, feelings, reactions?'

Chana replied, 'It's not a question of having these feelings or even of understanding them. We all have them but it takes a writer of genius to express them.' Yes, of course, it's the words, the words, the magic of words! I delighted in the language but I found myself questioning the mores and attitudes in the books I was reading, wondering how, for instance, a great humanitarian like Leo Tolstoy could depict with obvious approval Karenin's refusal to divorce Anna and to set her free; such a distortion of religious morality, it led to so much pain. And why must the woman always suffer? By what right did the man determine when and if a mother could see her son? And how contemptible was the society that welcomed the male lover in its midst but punished and ostracised the woman who loved too well. In the end, after Anna's tragic suicide, we knew that her lover's life would be disrupted and that he would be smitten by sadness and remorse – for a while. We also knew that soon he would regain his will to live and continue to enjoy his cards, horses, parties. In time he would find a new love and Anna would dwindle to a memory, poignant but faded. One genre that I could not come to terms with was the detective novel or thriller. In these books people were killed and bodies lay around but no one ever wept for them. Why was no one ever loved or mourned? All they cared about was *whodunit*, a purely intellectual exercise, without a flicker of emotion. It seemed all wrong to me.

F ATHER, an atheist, decreed that I could not attend Scripture classes; he was not going to allow them to pervert my young mind 'with all that nonsense'. This suited me and I spent the Scripture classes sitting outside on the verandah, reading novels. There I was joined by the McGregor twins, whose father also forbade their attendance at Scripture classes because, in his opinion, the lessons weren't sufficiently dedicated to a literal belief in the Holy Book. The three of us spent the afternoons minding our own business and reading our own books and I didn't know that our fathers were even acquainted until one day Father arrived home rather breathless to tell us of an exchange he'd had with Mr McGregor in the corner shop. I don't know how the argument started but it ended with Mr McGregor waggling his finger at Father and demanding,: 'So what do you call yourself?'

'I'm a Jew', Father replied and then, in turn, asked: 'And what are you?'

Mr McGregor pushed out his chest: 'I'm a Scotsman, and proud of it.'

'Oh yes,' Father answered. 'But are the Scots proud of you?' This incident delighted and impressed me. Not only was my Father a wit but he proved that it was possible to be a proper Jew without religion.

In his youth, in Lithuania, as an active Bundist, Father had turned his back on religion, Zionism and Hebrew. He believed in Yiddish as a living language, spoken by the common people, with its own literature and culture, something to cherish. The Bundists also believed that Jews should strive to make whatever country they found themselves in a safe and civilized haven for all minorities, not only Jews. The Zionists, in contrast, despised Yiddish and any interest in local affairs. All they sought was to build their own homeland in Palestine and to encourage as many Jews as possible to emigrate. The Bundists could lay claim to the moral high ground but the next two decades tragically proved how right the Zionists were in urging Jews to leave eastern Europe. Even Birobidzhan, in the Soviet Union, which was set aside to become a Jewish homeland, turned out to be a chimera, a dream without substance.

B Y THE time my fourteenth birthday came and went, I longed more and more to grow up and to turn my back on my silly, irrelevant school. I was impatient to become a grown-up, a person who can do things, change life, shape history.

'Its all very well if you're a man,' my friend Jane grumbled, 'then you can do what you like. I wish I'd been born a boy.'

'No,' I insisted: 'I'm glad I was born a girl. Girls are just as good as boys. I'm going to prove it.'

But I didn't know how. I spent long lazy afternoons after school stretched out on my bed, daydreaming, weaving fantasies, longing for I knew not what. I was Anna Karenina, pale, langorous, dying for love; I was Jo, of *Little Women*, bossy, practical, in charge; I was Becky Sharp, shrewd and calculating, or Joan of Arc, burning for a Cause; I was 'She' who must be obeyed and also poor Emma Bovary, silly, misguided but sensual, passionate, desperate for life. These were women who made things happen and with whom I could identify; these were women of character, worthy of respect in their own right, not because they were wives or lovers of famous men; unlike the Little Nells of this world and all the other Dickens female characters who were passive, soppy, sentimental creatures.

My body tingled or smouldered: alien forces hovered over every limb, invading my inner self with strange desires; I ached with pains which I couldn't identify. My skin was icy cold or burning hot; I hugged myself to embrace the unexpected darts of pleasure which penetrated my thighs, stomach, breasts. How could I be dancing on top of the world one minute and lie buried deep in the bowels of the earth the next? I longed to be touched by someone, possibly Larry, the boy next door, but when he stretched out his hand as if to do so, I'd toss my head and turn away disdainfully. Love that was pure, romantic, untainted, that was what I longed for, not the groping and kissing and messiness that some of my friends permitted, even encouraged. Keats, Wordsworth, Tennyson, they had an inkling of my needs but it was Shelley who really understood me:

> Away, away, from men and towns,
> To the wild woods and the downs,
> To the silent wilderness, where the soul
> Need not repress its music
> Lest it should not find
> An echo in another's mind.

Shelley and I, kindred souls. But Shelley was dead and who in the world was left who could guess at my soul's desires? The music of words, the surprise and delight of a felicitous phrase, these haunted me and I would repeat them to myself as one hums a well-loved ditty. I didn't disdain clichés or platitudes, I didn't know they existed; everything was new and exhilarating. I was the explorer of new worlds, a sailor on a clear white paper sea where island words kept popping up, waiting to be discovered.

'She walks in beauty, like the night', I would mutter to myself, or 'Where sheep may safely graze,' and 'Like a ghost she glimmers unto me'. The phrases were random and irrelevant but they rang like bells in my head and I loved the sound. 'Alone and palely wandering', 'dappled things', 'Had we but world enough and time', 'The people, yes, the people'. ''Twas brillig, and the slithy toves / Did gyre and gimble in the wabe', 'Sing me at morn but only with your laugh' and so on and on and on.

Then I fell in love with Peggy, our leggy Head Girl, and when our paths crossed in the school corridors, I'd tremble with ecstacy. We never exchanged any words and she was unaware of my existence but I was content to worship from afar. It was bliss to see her swinging a stick on the hockey field or wielding a racquet on the tennis court; her performance as Rosalind in the school production of *As You Like It* became for me the definitive interpretation of this play and the green feather she wore in her cap epitomised jaunty female chic.

JANE Meadows was good-humoured, even-tempered, cheerful, all the things I was not. She wasn't bothered by burgeoning sensuality or conflicts of conscience. No slave she to inexplicable demands of an awakening womanhood. I envied her equanimity and admired her composure and we became best friends. When she invited me home for tea I found myself in a new and unsuspected world. Set in the higher reaches of prosperous Essenwood Road, the house she lived in was big and cool and scented with lavender polish and roses. The black servant who brought in the silver tea tray, dressed in purple turban and starched white jacket, addressed Jane's mother as 'Madam', not 'Missus' as my mother was called by our servant.

Mrs Meadows poured the tea into translucent china cups before adding the milk and passed me cucumber sandwiches which were so dainty that one bite was big enough for each but my hostess took two or three nibbles per minute segment. She pronounced each word with precision and moved with slow and easy grace. In this calm, leafy suburb no one hurried or shouted or laughed too loudly. The gardener in his short blue pants directed an even spray on the manicured lawns. The hedges of 'Yesterday, Today and Tomorrow' with their sweet-smelling flowers of purple, blue and white, nestled obediently within their well-defined limits.

What Jane thought when she came to tea with us she never told me but I did wish that my Mother, rushing in and out of the shop to attend to us, did not pile her plate quite so high with thick slices of home-made fruit cake and insisted less on her having another slice. With Jane in our living room I was suddenly aware of the continuous jangle of the traffic outside and the whinging noises from the radio in the flat next door. They'd been there all the time but I'd never noticed them before; Jane's demure presence in our house made me wish that we, too, lived with more grace.

'Can't we have some pictures on the walls?' I asked Dad a few days later.

'No,' he answered. 'Real paintings we cannot afford and cheap copies we won't have.'

So our walls remained bare as did my Mother's throat and arms. If she could not afford real jewels, she would have none, Father decreed. He despised the phoney, the ersatz, the imitation – that was for the vulgarians, not for him. Mother's plain gold wedding ring was all I ever saw on her hand until after Father's death. In matters of taste or conscience, or when principles were involved, Father held sway; Mother was free to decide on the humdrum matters, like how to make ends meet.

Jane and I were walking down West Street one day after school, swinging our satchels, when we met Mr Singh, an Indian commercial traveller who called at our shop. Mother thought he was 'a nice man'. 'It's hot to-day, wouldn't you like a cold drink,' she'd say, offering him a bottle of ginger pop with a straw. To see an Indian, drinking in the shop, raised some eyebrows among our white customers but later, when we got to know him better, Mother would invite Mr Singh to have tea with us at the table, in full view of the customers, and this, they felt, was going too far. Everyone could see that he was drinking out of the same cups that we were using and we were all sitting at the same table. Mother chatted easily with him, choosing to ignore the hostile looks and occasional snide remarks of customers.

'Really, Henneh, you don't do things like that here,' her friend Malke remonstrated when she came in and saw this one afternoon. Mother only laughed and changed the subject. I marvelled at her patience, I would have picked an argument.

Now, in West Street, here was Mr Singh, dressed as usual in a sober grey suit and highly polished shoes. He raised his hat as he passed us and said, 'Good afternoon, Miss Podbrey.'

'Oh, hullo,' I muttered in some confusion: I wasn't used to being called 'Miss.' When he'd passed us, Jane grabbed my arm.

'You shouldn't have answered him, the cheeky coolie, fancy talking to you in the street.'

I stared at her. 'Don't be silly, how can you not answer if someone greets you?'

'My mother would wallop me if she caught me talking to a coolie in the street.'

So, I thought, her strict upbringing and good manners did not extend to 'coolies' or 'kaffirs'. Rudeness to them did not count; on the contrary, it was decreed in their code of behaviour.

MY OTHER 'best friend' was Helen, the youngest of three sisters whose mother set high standards in language, deportment and feminine decorum. Martha, the eldest, was slow, kind, heavy, with thick glasses. Her calm female passivity passed for dependability. Although the family was completely divorced from all things Jewish and had never been near a *shul*, Martha had made up her mind to marry 'a nice Jewish boy'. The middle daughter, Thora, had one passion in life and that was tennis. She covered the court like a restless spider, all arms and legs. Helen was the prettiest; she cultivated a giddiness and a fetching little giggle which always emerged when I tried to talk to her about the differences in the treatment of whites and blacks. 'I wish you'd stop being so silly,' she'd say with a flutter of the hand. Their mother didn't approve of me and although she was too considerate to show me the door, she did hope that I wouldn't fill her daughters' heads with my dangerous nonsense, as I overheard her telling a neighbour. Nor did she approve of her sister's daughter, Melanie. In her case Helen's mother feared a different kind of corruption. She worried that Melanie, with her painted nails, rouged cheeks, languid air and her ability to fascinate boys – even when she wasn't trying – would set a bad example to her own daughters.

Melanie was a 'loose' girl who would come to no good, her aunt predicted sadly. I could see that she had 'It' and I envied her, but how did the boys know that, I wondered, as I watched them turn to look at her when the two of us walked down Berea Road. Was she sending out secret signals? Was that half-smile intended to beguile, even when turned on me and not on the passing strangers? How did they know, I wondered, that I, too, wasn't a 'loose' girl? Why didn't they look at me when the two of us were together? She had mysterious powers that I wished I could emulate. I, too, would have loved to have 'It' but if I did, would that mean becoming as silly as she was in all the important matters? Does one have to choose, I asked myself, between being a seductive, attractive female or having opinions about books and politics and being able to argue with people on an equal basis? Do intelligence and integrity, to which I aspired, necessarily preclude femininity and sensuality, for which I longed? It was clear that in the whole of Durban there was no one who shared my preoccupations or who sympathised with my outlook or my interests. Was I destined to spend my life searching for a fellow human being who didn't exist?

Then I met Herman and I realized that here at last was a real friend. Herman didn't mock when I told him why I wanted to be a Communist even though he called himself a Zionist Socialist. He listened to me patiently as I expounded my beliefs, hopes, fears. Here, for the first time, was someone who understood me and who was prepared to sympathise with opinions which until now had been dismissed as misbegotten or dangerous nonsense. He found time to help me with my homework, talk to me about politics and point me to new and exciting books. It was Herman who introduced me to Heine and sent me copies of his poems. He told me about Freud and lent me the *Interpretation of Dreams*.

When his family moved to Johannesburg, Herman wrote me letters which were beautiful and tender and which excited my imagination. I awaited them eagerly and read and reread them. At last, I told myself, I'd found real platonic friendship and confounded the cynics who said there was no such thing. I felt betrayed and dismayed when Herman, now in uniform, turned up on our doorstep three years later, threw his arms round me and demanded to know how soon we could get married. Mother approved of Herman and was very disappointed when I told her that I could no more think of marrying Herman than I could consider taking my brother for husband.

IN 1937 Father decided to leave Uncle Sam's scrap metal business and work for himself, or rather, to work for many bosses instead of one. Various small shopkeepers and traders, knowing Dad to be good at his job and honest, employed him as their bookkeeper. But father despised his bosses and told them so, often. In his outspoken opinion they were crude and ignorant, *grobbe jungen*, and he was not prepared to countenance any slight from them, real or imagined. One by one his clients left him and those who remained did so mainly out of sympathy for Mother. Father began to spend longer periods in bed: not ill exactly but certainly not well. Mother would bring him meals in bed and cups of tea with slices of her home-made cake. She would rise at five o'clock and leave the house before any of us were awake to get to the Indian Market in Warwick Avenue. There she would stock up with fresh fruit and vegetables for the shop and load them on to a ricksha, but, unlike the other shopkeepers, she herself never travelled in a ricksha, returning, as she went, by tramcar.

'But, Henneh,' her friend Malke pointed out, 'Look how long it takes you to get to the Post Office and then to take another tram to Umgeni. Besides, how can you trust the ricksha boy to take your stuff home? How do you know he won't run off with it?' He never did. Often the ricksha puller would arrive at the shop before Mother, having trotted the six or seven miles, much of it uphill, clutching in his hand the scrap of paper with our address. Even without a fat white woman like Malke sprawled among the fruit and vegetables, the ricksha 'boy' would arrive panting, with sweat pouring off him. Not surprisingly, the average life expectancy of a ricksha puller was about 26 years. Mother would wonder aloud: 'How can a human being let another human being drag him through the streets?' It was not a theoretical or philosophical question, nor even a matter of principle. It was just something she could not do; it went against the grain.

By the time she returned from market Father was awake so she'd make his breakfast, take it to him and hurry into the shop, ready for the early morning rush of customers for bread, milk, tea, fruit, cold drinks, cigarettes. She also made sure that my brothers and I ate our porridge and that I had made the sandwiches for Joe and me to take to school. Little Maurice, too young for school, wove in and out under the table and got under everybody's feet.

Like every white family in South Africa, even the poorest, we too had a black servant. They came and went very frequently, were always called Jim and had even less English than Mother. Day after day they came, young and not so young, Zulus from the countryside, knocking on the back door or standing mutely at the gate, palms pressed together, seeking work. Some days there'd be two or three, more often five or six, each one carrying a wooden stick and a bundle of his clothes, in a never-ending procession.

'*Umsebenzi*?' 'Work?'

It usually fell to me to refuse them. 'No, no work today,' and they'd move to the house next door and the one after and so on down the street. These were men who'd never seen the inside of a white man's house. When one was chosen, he'd be issued with an apron and told to peel potatoes, boil water, clean the lavatory. When he stared dumbly, uncomprehending, 'madam' would click her tongue in irritation at the stupidity of these natives. At parties and rummy evenings, white 'madams' would outbid each other with tales of 'her' Jim's crassness and simple-mindedness. A new 'language' sprouted in Durban kitchens, not one with which to communicate but with which one could give and the other receive, basic orders. 'Kitchen Kaffir' or 'Fanagalo' employed a very limited vocabulary of bastardised Zulu, English, and, in our home, Yiddish. It was a debasement of language which mirrored the poverty of the human relationships between the people using it.

I believed myself to be free of prejudice, fair-minded, unsullied by racism. Then an insignificant little event occurred which forced me to re-appraise my self-image. Mother saw me one morning, running about the flat in my underwear.

'Put on some clothes,' she ordered. 'Don't walk around half naked.'

'But Mum,' I answered: 'There's no one here.'

'Yes there is,' she said; 'The "boy"'s here.'

With a shock I realised that I was behaving like any other white girl to whom blacks were invisible; they didn't exist as men, they were servants, non-human, sexless. I was ashamed of myself. I, too, was becoming corrupted; yet my mother, who laid no claim to the higher reaches of moral philosophy, saw quite clearly that our 18-year-old 'Jim' was entitled to the same consideration as any other young male.

T HE '30s were getting on, and so was I. At 15 I was beginning to suspect that life was passing me by. Father's poor health and diminishing income and Mother's struggle to provide for us fuelled my impatience to be up and away, to relieve them from keeping me, to stop wasting time at that boring old school, to earn money, to join the Communist Party, to start putting the world to rights.

The exciting political discussions in our sitting room of earlier years had long since faded out. Of that circle of impassioned radicals who embodied for me the core and very soul of the Communist Party, only one remained in touch, the Durban barber, Mike Diamond. Mike was cheerful, garrulous, devoted to the Cause, and not much concerned with ideology. His shop in West Street continued to be a distribution centre for the Communist Party paper, *Inkululeko*, meaning 'Freedom', the *Guardian* published weekly in Cape Town, and various left-wing magazines. One could even find the occasional copy of *New Statesman* on his shelves. Later on appeared the forbidding organ of the Communist International, with its less than snappy title: *For a Lasting Peace, for a People's Democracy*. The editors disdained captions and paragraphs, presumably on the assumption that serious Communists did not need such frivolity; it was considered to be obligatory reading.

Cadaverous, hungry Ronnie Fleet was back in Johannesburg. He had been sent by the Central Committee of the Party in Johannesburg to help Durban re-organize and as often as not he would drop in at supper time so Father would invite him to stay and eat with us. Mother grumbled that he seemed to be making a habit of it and Father would adopt a placatory tone and explain to Mother that on the wages the Party paid him, Ronnie couldn't afford to eat and how could we stand by and let the man go hungry?

Hatchet man Lazar Bach had left for the Soviet Union and disappeared without trace, although he was the most loyal and inflexible follower of Stalin, ready to trample down anyone suspected of 'deviationism'. He was a small man with cold eyes which glinted past me and registered only distaste if I crossed his vision. Not because he disliked me, (How could he? He didn't know me.), but because to him I was an irrelevance, a distraction. His Communism was a grand mathematical structure, a game of chess where it didn't matter how many pawns fell in the struggle for final victory. Did he connive with his masters in the Comintern in his own destruction? Did he, like the leading Bolsheviks killed in the purges, confess to crimes he had not committed for the sake of the greater good of the Party? Did he accept in the end that he, too, was a pawn and therefore expendable? We shall never know because, like millions of others, his end was unrecorded and his grave unmarked.

Sidney Adler retreated into his corner tearoom and concentrated on earning a living; he had attended these evenings as if on sufferance, not to contribute but to listen. He accepted his *petit bourgeois* status with resignation and the others regarded him with tolerance laced with contempt. Willie Kalk faded from view. These figures whose words had intoxicated me in my early 'teens and whose views and opinions loomed large on my consciousness, were now a dim memory, no longer real people, just shadowy figures from the past. But although the people had faded, their ideas lived on; the talk of those evenings, the arguments, discussions, debates had imprinted itself on my mind, had been absorbed by me with passionate intensity. It didn't occur to me to question the absence of any women, or, even more bizarrely, the fact that not a single black man was ever present; they were, after all, the main targets of the discussions. The hours spent at school, helping mother in the house, and playing with the Van Heerden kids next door were but a prelude to the evenings when I could crouch unobserved behind a sofa or on the balcony beside the open door, listening hungrily to the men talking inside. This, to my mind, was about real life. In my twelve-year-old opinion these were great men, revolutionaries, Communists, people who, alone among their fellow men, had seen the light. These were the sighted in the land of the blind.

Eddie Roux had also left Durban, but him I remembered clearly with great affection. He was no shadowy figure; he stood out as a person of warmth, understanding, sympathy. No matter how heated the argument grew, Eddie never raised his voice or shouted abuse. He talked quietly, reasonably; and he also listened. There are not many men I have known – perhaps four or five – who have added lustre to my life, whose presence enlarged my vision, who made existence meaningful, more joyful. Eddie was one of these. I was fortunate to have known him then, when I was very young and later, when I, a cocksure twenty-two-year old, was crass enough to argue with him about plant genetics, his speciality.

Eddie was visiting us in Cape Town with his wife Winnie and daughter Alison and we argued heatedly about many things because by now Eddie had shed his earlier blind devotion to all things Soviet, whereas I was still a firm believer. I was convinced that the Soviet Union was leading the world in all spheres, art, science, industry, the emancipation of nationalities, women, agriculture. In his usual mild-mannered way Eddie suggested that the Russians were not always right. For instance, the geneticist Lysenko was mistaken in his theories about the transmission of acquired characteristics. I, knowing nothing of the subject, asserted positively that Lysenko must be right; had not Comrade Stalin and the whole Central Committee of the Communist Party of the Soviet Union endorsed his findings? They couldn't be wrong! I knew that Eddie was a scientist and a leading authority in his subject and I also loved him but by then Eddie had been expelled from the Party so how could I side with him against the great Stalin!

Many years earlier, in our Durban flat above the shop, Eddie found me one evening, crouching on the balcony outside the room where the men were talking politics, eavesdropping on the discussion when I should have been in bed. He did not holler 'Ho, ho, ho, what have we here?' as some of the others would have done. With his slow, gentle smile he asked: 'Do you find the discussion interesting?' I nodded eagerly and was reassured by his lack of condescension. 'In a few years' time you'll be able to join us,' he told me, leaving me buoyant and full of hope.

It so happened that it was also through Eddie that H.A. Naidoo joined the Communist Party. One day in the early '30s, the young H.A. and his friend, George Ponnen, were walking down West Street when they were brought up sharply by a strange sight. A white man was standing on the street corner, selling newspapers. This was something they had never seen before and out of curiosity they bought a copy of the Communist Party paper, *Umsebenzi*.

'Why don't you come along to the meeting tonight?' the white man invited them. Intrigued, they did so and were again surprised to find the same white man on the platform. He was the main speaker, Eddie Roux. That same night both H.A. and Ponnen enrolled as members of the Durban branch of the Communist Party and immediately afterwards H.A. was nominated Party secretary. He protested his lack of experience – it did not seem to him sufficient training to have acted as secretary of the Indian Youth League – but Eddie assured him that he would soon learn. H.A. also made it clear that he knew nothing of Communist Party theory or practice.

'You must start studying Marxism/Leninism,' Eddie told him. He undertook to lend him and Ponnen the necessary books and he also arranged to give study classes as long as he remained in Durban. That was when H.A. and Ponnen relinquished the ambitions they had nurtured to further their careers. They stopped attending night school at the Durban Technical College and instead of studying bookkeeping and business skills, they concentrated all their energies on the theory and practice of Marxism/Leninism and on mastering the practical arts of how to conduct meetings, keep records, issue cards, safeguard the finances.

A few months later, when H.A. was himself addressing a meeting in the same hall where he'd first heard Eddie speak, he recognised among his audience the bearded figure of George Bernard Shaw. During his visit to South Africa Shaw had earned the opprobium of the whites by declaring that South Africa's problems would only be solved by intermarriage between the races, by the dreaded word, miscegenation. After that he was shunned by the white population and maligned by the white press. He spent most of his time in Durban strolling around the Indian area of Grey Street.

'We are greatly honoured to have this distinguished visitor here tonight,' H.A. announced and he invited Mr Shaw to come up to the platform and say a few words.

But Mr Shaw declined; 'Tonight,' he replied, 'I've come to listen to you, so just carry on.'

IN THE early '30s, the South African Communist Party, riven by internal strife, had almost disappeared, especially in Durban. It was not helped by the destructive meddling from the Communist International of Moscow. The few dedicated leaders like S.P. Bunting who had the courage to contest the Moscow orders were expelled from the Johannesburg Head Office and they were replaced by time-serving bigots like Lazar Bach. The Industrial Commercial Union of the African workers, the ICU under the leadership of Clements Kadalie, which, in the '20s had swept the country, diminished and faded away. We were in the political doldrums. I was unaware of this history. All I knew as I was growing up was that I had to find the Communist Party, the only torch of liberty. I was 15 years old when I asked my father, 'Where is the Communist Party in Durban?'

'There isn't one,' he snapped at me. 'The Party is dead.'

Father had become a sad and disappointed man but his greatest disillusion was yet to come. The Soviet trials of 1936/37 left Father a man shipwrecked in a sea of doubt. I saw him age as he followed the press reports in stunned disbelief. With growing incredulity he read the 'confessions' of the accused. His heroes of yesterday, Rykov, Bukharin, Zinoviev, men who had shaped and led the 1917 Revolution, comrades and intimates of the great Lenin, now stood in the dock abject and humiliated, confessing to the worst crimes in the Soviet calendar: to being saboteurs, spies, paid lackeys and running dogs of British and American imperialism, even of serving the Nazis.

'It's not possible,' Father almost wept. 'I can't, I won't believe it.'

A decade earlier, when Leon Trotsky had been denounced as a traitor and banished from the Soviet Union, Father had found it hard to accept but preferable to believing that Joseph Stalin and the whole Soviet leadership were liars and rogues. He tried to draw consolation from the official Soviet argument, that it was necessary to consolidate its own borders and build up its defences against the enemies who surrounded it before it could lend its energies to fostering international revolutions, as, they claimed, Trotsky demanded. At least it had a theoretical substance, specious though it proved to be. Now there was no ideological debate, no pretence about the correct interpretation of Marxism or how best to bring about a just Communist society. All that emerged from a reading of the trials was the vicious vituperation of Vishinsky, the prosecutor. There was no evidence against the accused, only a stream of invective. Father suffered as he grappled with the equally unpalatable alternatives. If the accused were innocent then the trial was a farce, a trumped-up, vicious lie and where did that leave Comrade Stalin and the rest of the Soviet leadership?

There were days when Father would lie on his bed with his face to the wall, shaking off Mother's hand on his arm, refusing to eat or drink. When he finally surfaced, Father's face was greyer and more deeply lined. He'd reached the bitter conclusion that Stalin was the one who had betrayed the Revolution and that something was very rotten in the state of Russia. I felt sorry for father ut also impatient. I had not grown up with the names of Trotsky, Bukharin *et al* ringing in my ears. 1917 was history. What mattered was *now*. The Japanese had invaded Manchuria and the Italians had overrun Abyssinia. And now, daily, with a sense of passionate commitment, I followed the events of the Spanish Civil War and wished I were old enough to fight in the ranks of the International Brigade. Dolores Ibarruri – La Passionara – was my heroine and 'Non Pasaran' was my slogan. I collected money for the Republican cause, sold stickers and posters, and sang the songs of the fighters for freedom. From all accounts available to us, the Soviets were the only ones giving succour to the Spanish Republicans. They couldn't be all bad.

I had not yet found the Communist Party, but I was getting nearer. I was discovering other people in Durban who cared about Spain and Ethiopia and Manchuria and it didn't strike me as odd that they cared more for these far-off places than they did for the Africans, right here, at home. They were anti-Fascists, they argued for the need of a United Front against Nazism, they supported the struggle against imperialism. This was not the inner core of incorruptible, dedicated Party members whom I was still seeking – but I was encouraged. As my horizons expanded and my enthusiasm grew, so Father's bitterness and disillusion with his lifelong beliefs became more irksome. I didn't want to hear about Soviet betrayal; I thrilled to the stories of Soviet help for the Republican fighters – who else was helping the legitimate Spanish government while Hitler and Mussolini were arming Franco and sending in troops to fight on his side? If only I could find the Communist Party and take my place alongside the real fighters for freedom!

'If the Party came to power and you were ordered to shoot me because they told you I was a traitor, would you do it?' Father asked, during one of our arguments. His question exercised my mind. I dug deep into my conscience. Party membership meant obedience, discipline, absolute loyalty. If the Party accused Father of being a traitor, then he was a traitor. I could never disobey a Party order. Personal considerations must never be allowed to stand in the way. The good of the Party takes precedence over all because the Party means the People.

'Yes, I would,' I said, swallowing hard.

Father looked at me, sadly. He said nothing and turned away. He never forgot. Years later, when I had grown up sufficiently to be ashamed of my remark, he reminded me of it. He then said, 'Well, I suppose I had only myself to blame. It could only be from me that you'd inherited such diehard attitudes. I suppose you believed that was being honest, didn't you? I also used to think so when I was your age.'

When I heard that a Socialist parliamentary candidate was standing in

Umbilo, I hurried to offer my services. Duncan Burnside was a tall, lean Scotsman with a wry sense of humour and an attractive smile who had left the Labour Party to fight on the Socialist ticket. The Labour Party, like the United, National, or Dominion Parties, admitted whites only but that wasn't the reason for Burnside's breakaway. The colour question did not loom large in his campaign either, but at least he talked about the rights of workers, even if this did mean white workers only. Surprisingly, he was returned, and when he got to Parliament, he livened up that place with his wit and *bon mots*. But his election victory proved to be a short-lived burst of working-class consciousness. In the following election he lost his seat.

ONCE again we moved house, this time to a flat on South Beach so that Mother could be nearer her new shop at the Point. Every day I'd hurry home from school and change into my bathing costume. Then I'd mix myself a milk-shake of grenadillas, cold milk and sugar, stirring until it curdled deliciously. After drinking this concoction I'd hoist my little brother, Maurice, on my hip and hurry down to the beach. As I came near the beach I'd slow my step and assume an air of calculated nonchalance, strolling down to spread my towel where all the other young had spread theirs. Lugging little Maurice to the beach with me wasn't entirely an act of sisterly devotion. I did love him, dearly, but it was also true that with his long blond curls, which Mother refused to cut, his big round eyes and his endearing chubbiness, he attracted a lot of favourable comment and made it possible for boys whom I would otherwise not have met, to introduce themselves by asking: 'Is he your little brother? What a darling little chap!' In no time we'd have a crowd of boys round us, chatting and joking and there was never any problem in finding someone to mind the child while I went in for a swim.

Now there are shark nets on Durban beach but in my day there were only lifesavers with binoculars who kept a lookout for the man-eaters and blew whistles when they spotted one coming in too close. Then they would run to the water's edge waving their arms to warn everyone to leave the water. It amused me to tease them by pretending I hadn't heard or seen them and instead of swimming in to shore I'd strike out towards the open sea. Then they would have to come in after me and it gave me a perverse delight to see such brave men frightened. 'How dare you play with death?' they'd shout at me, but whether from a lack of imagination or a belief in my own immortality, I never did believe that any shark would get me. 'Not me, it could never happen to me,' I'd think. Even when a shark almost brushed against my thigh it still did not occur to me that I would ever be attacked.

Not until that day when we came upon an accident on the non-European beach. A crowd had gathered round a young Indian boy who had been dragged from the water a few minutes earlier. His right thigh was a ragged stump from which the blood was still pouring, turning the sand around him crimson. A shark had bitten off his leg and as we watched the colour slowly drained from his face. By the time the ambulance arrived, he was dead. It burned itself into my consciousness; there, but for the grace of God, lay I.

I stopped teasing lifesavers but I continued to swim. Death had swung into my line of vision and through its ugly, misshapen self had tried to frighten and disarm me, to stop me from enjoying life ever again by filling and overspilling my heart with compassion; death meant to dull my brain with a diet of despair, despair and pity and an overwhelming sense of futility. It mocked me with its proof of the fragility of youth and by its careless, contemptuous destruction of life. For a while it seemed as if death might win. I was dazed with shock and could not rid myself of the memory of that mutilated stump and ashen face. It was not something to discuss with others; they wouldn't understand, they might even laugh at me. 'For goodness sake, Pauline,' I could hear them in my mind, 'stop being so morbid, it's nothing to do with you.' In my imaginary conversation I argued that of course it had to do with me but I couldn't explain why, not so as to convince them.

After a few days my depression started to lift. I was young and strong and the life force reasserted itself, coursing freely through my veins. I returned to the sea and plunged into the waves. Nothing, not even death, could dim the elation of running into the breakers to catch them on the upsurge and then to soar, high and higher, until one's outstretched arm almost touched the clouds overhead. Then, as the huge waves curled up into themselves, in the second before they dissolved below with a thunderous crash, the ecstacy of hurling your body into the wave, abandoning yourself with total submission, to be carried shorewards as and how the omnipotent sea determined. With luck and good timing one could cover the whole distance to the water's edge on the back of one wave and then, when the sea had left you breathless and panting, as though tiring of the game, you'd jump up, toss your soggy hair out of your eyes, turn and run back, to take up the challenge once again.

'DOES this belong to your little brother?' I turned to see a tallish stranger, older than most of us, holding out a red beach ball belonging to Maurice. 'Thanks,' I said as I reached up for it, intrigued by his grown-up self-confidence but also irritated by his superior smile.

'My name is Mannie Peltz,' he announced as he lowered himself next to me without an invitation. 'What's yours?' I told him. I looked him over and my annoyance gave way to smugness; it was, after all, flattering to be singled out by a good-looking adult — he must be at least twenty-five.

After that first encounter, we'd meet quite often on the beach and talk about serious things. He didn't laugh at me when I confessed that I was really a Communist, determined one day to find The Party. Nor did he argue or dismiss as nonsense my revolutionary opinions and radical views. He encouraged me to talk and it soon emerged that Mannie, too, was a Communist. He promised that one day soon he would take me to a meeting. This was the first Commmunist I'd met outside my father's small circle and my spirits soared to find that I was not alone in the political wilderness that was Durban.

The night Mannie took me to my first Communist Party meeting, he warned me not to broadcast the fact. I told Mother I was going 'out' and ran before she could question me further. I waited in the street outside our house for Mannie to pick me up at the pre-arranged time and as we drove into the poorer, seedier Indian district, I became more and more elated; at last I would link up with people who thought like me, friends, comrades. Near the railway station we drew up at a derelict tenement building. The small dark room we entered measured up to all my expectations. It was lit by one fly-spattered, unshaded bulb which left most of the room in shadow, making it hard to identify the black and brown men occupying the wooden benches. These were men exhausted by their labours; many were still in their overalls – they'd come to the meeting straight from work and they sat with shoulders hunched, elbows on knees and heads cradled in their hands. It occurred to me that the Party could exact no greater tribute than the attendance of these tired, hungry men who chose to come and listen to the Party message before going home to wash and eat and rest.

Mannie introduced me to the Indian chairman: 'This is Comrade H. A. Naidoo,' he said and I shook hands with the handsomest man I'd ever seen. He stood at his table with an easy grace, narrow-hipped, taller than me, dark-complexioned with black, wavy hair and smiling eyes set well apart. His chin was as confident as a man's chin needs to be, without aggression, and his full, shapely mouth suggested kindliness and humour. His shirt was spotless and his well-cut suit contrasted sharply with the faded clothes of those around him but seemed just right on him. He stared at me with unconcealed curiosity. We shook hands and it occurred to me that this was an unusual man in more than appearance. Here was a black man who had no need of postures or assertions in his dealings with any group; he could afford to be perfectly at ease across the colour barrier, feeling neither hostile nor inferior. He was relaxed, friendly and fully in control, of the meeting and of himself. Little did I guess that evening that this was the man I would one day marry.

H. A. Naidoo's interest in me was to be expected – I was conspicuously the only white girl in the room; in fact, I was the only girl there – until the other white woman arrived; Bettie du Toit, the main speaker of the evening. Bettie was not only white, she was also an Afrikaner, one of the tiny minority of the

Volk who had thrown in her lot with the 'enemy', the blacks. I knew nothing of her background but could easily imagine that it must have taken a lot of courage to break away from the rule of the *dominie* and the church elders.

'Comrade du Toit,' the chairman announced, 'is here from Johannesburg. She has just returned from a visit to the Soviet Union and she will give us her impressions.'

Bettie rose, smilingly acknowledging our applause. She was neat and trim and everything about her sparkled, her black hair, her red lips, her dark eyes. Her white linen frock was newly pressed and on her feet were high-heeled sandals – altogether a most unlikely Communist activist, I thought. Yet, here she was, telling us about the marvellous life in the Soviet Fatherland and the need for a strong Party in South Africa so that we too, could wield workers' power, without regard for the colour of a man's skin.

'People often ask me,' she said, with a flirtatious toss of her head, 'What is the difference between a Communist and a Socialist.' She waved her hand dismissively: 'Duncan Burnside is a Socialist,' then she paused for effect. 'But I am a Communist.' Her definition of the difference was not entirely satisfactory but I joined in the enthusiastic applause and wished I could get to know her better. However, I knew that I had to get back home quickly or there might be trouble.

There was. As we drove up to our house I saw Father standing in the middle of the road with his arms outstretched, commanding Mannie to stop right there.

'What do you mean by bringing my daughter back at this time of night?' he demanded. I tried to calm him. 'Dad, we've been to a meeting and it's only just gone ten.'

'She'll have time enough for meetings when she's older,' he shouted at Mannie. 'She's only fourteen; she should be doing her homework, not running around at meetings.'

'I thought she was older,' Mannie looked discomfited. He threw me a baleful glance.

'And don't let me catch you taking my daughter out again, you hear me?' Father shouted. Mannie grated into gear and disappeared into the night. We didn't meet again until three years later. My lifeline to the Communist Party was severed but my plans for the future were reinforced. I knew what I would do, as soon as I grew up.

AT FIFTEEN I left the Durban Girls' High without any regret, after scraping through the Junior Certificate exam. 'What are you going to do now?' Father asked. My ambitions were tempered by the realities of life. I would have loved to be an architect, to build tall buildings and graceful bridges, to unite peoples over rivers, across borders. But I knew that called for years of study at university. It was out of the question, a pipe-dream! To be a journalist would be marvellous. To travel all over the world, to move in the epicentre of international events, to tell everyone what really happened, to expose the evil-doers and rouse the conscience of mankind. 'I'd like to become a reporter on the *Daily News*,' I said diffidently. I didn't really believe it was possible. 'You don't stand a chance of getting in,' Father pronounced. 'The competition is much too fierce.' My faith in Father's judgement was absolute; I didn't even bother to apply for a job on the newspaper. But I longed to write.

An opportunity arose a little while later when I was sufficiently moved by a news item to write a letter to the editor and was gratified to see it published. The news which stirred me into print was a report that Paul Robeson, the great American black singer with the voice of molten gold, had expressed his determination not to play 'Uncle Tom' roles in films again, after his part as the 'good native' in the Hollywood movie, *Sanders of the River*. Important roles for black actors in the Hollywood of the '30s were scarce enough; to reject them on moral grounds was to demonstrate real integrity. I had no illusions that Paul Robeson stood in need, or would ever be aware of, my encouragement but it pleased me to think that my first venture into journalism was a letter of support for a black man whom I admired so much. Many years later, when Paul Robeson finally managed to get his passport from the US authorities and arrived in London, it was my little Jennie who was chosen to present him with a bouquet at the airport. At a house party a few days later he made us all feel good by telling us that he felt completely at ease among South African whites, which was more than he could say for white Americans, even including the liberal ones. It appeared that we, from backward, racist South Africa, had retained our common humanity; we behaved like normal, natural people.

My second venture into journalism was my successful application, in competition with many other teenagers, to review the film *Carnet du Bal*. Foreign films were still regarded as an exotic oddity and the distributers felt that the extra publicity boost would not come amiss. My critique of this fine film was immature and superficial and this was pointed out to me some years later by my German boyfriend, Gunther. He was right. I was equipped neither by age nor experience to appreciate this sophisticated, sensitive film. Sadly, my amateur attempts at writing were not enough to impress Father sufficiently about my potential as a journalist and so it was decided that I attend the Durban Business College for a six-month course in typing, shorthand and bookkeeping, the usual lacklustre solution to a girl's problems. I accepted it without enthusiasm but also without demur; I knew that even that modest investment in my career was a drain on the family finances. And anyway, shorthand and typing were irrelevant. I would be a revolutionary.

At the end of six months when I could barely type, let alone do shorthand or bookkeeping, I applied for and got a job at the Durban Saw Hospital. 'Hospital?' Mother queried. 'Ach, no, Mum,' I told her. 'It's a place where they sharpen knives and saws and scissors.' 'Hospital indeed!' she snorted.

The owner of the Saw Hospital, felicitously called Mr Sharpe, was a shuffling, elderly gentleman with droopy shoulders who laboured at the back of the shop, mostly out of sight. In the office with me, perched on a high stool from which she could monitor the comings and goings, was the boss, Mrs Sharpe, a large lady of stern demeanour and bristling moustache. 'Now, Pauline,' she'd order whenever she caught me glancing through the window, 'keep your mind on your work.'

The J. & B. Electrical Fitters next door employed a number of lithe young men who steered their little vans in and out of the courtyard with much screeching of brakes and deft manoeuvring of steering wheels. One of these devil-may-care drivers caught my fancy. I never did find out his name but I liked his cheeky grin and the careless way in which his cap was perched on his head. When he glanced up and saw me looking down, he'd smile and wave. Then I would compose the muscles of my face into a cold stare and turn haughtily away. I was the maiden in the tower and I must watch my demeanour; I was inviolate, cool, distant; there must be no suspicion that I might be 'loose' or 'fast'. Now, looking back, it strikes me as incomprehensible that I should have been so concerned with my virginal reputation while at the same time being quite prepared to challenge every other notion of social behaviour. I was willing and eager to break the taboos about mixing with non-whites but I would have been mortified if I thought that boys snickered about me.

The day I received my first wage packet was a red-letter day. Here was £4 that I had earned, mine to do with as I pleased; it was freedom, independence, self-respect. I ambled slowly down West Street, savouring the warm feeling of my own money in my handbag. I'd never enjoyed such wealth. Dreamily I planned; I'd give Mother a pound for my keep, buy a pair of new shoes, put aside my tramfares for the month . . . I walked slowly, glancing into shop windows, not focusing on anything in particular until suddenly my eye was caught and held by a display which I had not seen before. It was a newly opened bookshop with a dazzling array of books, books, books. Here were books in shiny black, elegant gray, imperious red and modest blue and yellow, some with pictures on the covers and others almost superciliously disdainful of any decoration. I gazed and gazed at all of them together and each in turn until sudenly my eye settled and was held by the cover of one particular book entitled *A New Anthology of Modern Verse*. It was a plain rose volume with neat black trim and gracefully etched on the centre of the cover was the slim outline of a figure in full flight, bearing a torch, the torch of knowledge, of freedom. The price tag announced 8/6.

'Oh well,' I thought, 'no harm in looking.' I walked inside and picked up a copy of the firm, flesh-coloured book. It felt cool to the touch and smooth. I leafed through it, savouring the clear dark type on the pure, white pages. Then I started reading the poems and in no time at all I was hopelessly, eternally captivated. It was like falling in love at first sight.

These were not the verses that we'd learnt at school; these were funny and witty and serious and some were even political. I found Vanzetti's last speech to the court; it was powerful, heart-rending, glowing with courage and innocence. I knew about Sacco and Vanzetti, the anarchists who were tried in America for a crime they did not commit; it was part of my political education, and now I felt as if I were meeting long-lost friends, reinforcing my hero-worship of them. Both were sentenced to die and here was his last speech to the court where Vanzetti spoke not of himself but about his comrade and fellow-accused, Sacco. Standing there in the shop I was moved almost to tears; here, I decided, in these broken words, lies the soul of poetry.

> Sacco is a heart, a faith, a character, a man;
> a man, lover of nature, and mankind;
> a man who gave all, who sacrifice all
> to the cause of liberty and to his love for mankind;
> money, rest, mundane ambition,
> his own wife, his children, himself
> and his own life.

I turned the pages and came across poets of whom I'd never heard before, A.E. Houseman, Ogden Nash, W.B. Yeats. Others, like Spender, C. Day Lewis and Auden I had long admired, not only for their poetry of which my knowledge was skimpy, but for their commitment to the Republican cause in the Spanish Civil War. I decided that this was a book I must have; but to spend so much! Such mad extravagance! I replaced the book on the shelf with a tender stroke, left the shop, hesitated, started to walk away, turned round and came back. My mind was made up. I handed over one of my crisp pound notes, collected the change and feeling that I had passed an important milestone, I walked out clasping my book to my chest.

When I reached home I discovered I'd lost my wage packet somewhere between the bookshop and home. I should have felt sad or sorry or cross, but I didn't; I felt elated and pleased with myself for having had the perspicacity to invest in my book. Now I had something tangible and lasting to show for my first month's wages, and I was right. That book has been with me in all my travels and I still turn to it again and again, though I now know most of the poems by heart.

D AD'S health showed no sign of improvement and he continued to spend days in bed. Mum worked tirelessly in the shop and in the house but still found time to wait on Dad and to humour him.

'Can't he get his own cup of tea?' I grumbled at her.

'You don't understand,' she told me. 'Berl has never really recovered from his terrible war years. He came back a wreck.'

In 1912 in Kurkl, Berl was the handsome young village schoolmaster. He sported a neat little dark moustache and had a proud and upright bearing. In the old photograph I have of him, Berl confronts the world with a clear, untroubled gaze, calm and confident. Young Hannah, with her thick blonde tresses, downy skin, grecian nose and sky-blue eyes was one of his pupils. She was not very interested in reading, writing or arithmetic but she was captivated by the stern young schoolmaster. By the time Berl was called up for military service, he and 15-year-old Hannah were already in love and they became engaged.

To serve the Tsar was no honour and there were ways and means of evading military service. One could try bribery, trickery or emigration, as many of his contemporaries did, but Berl, who hated the Tsar more than most, followed his own implacable sense of honour. If Russians and Litvaks had to do military service, so should Jews, Berl maintained, even though he knew well enough that Jews were subjected to far worse treatment than others in the army. He accepted his call-up papers, kissed his betrothed good-bye and was sent off to Russia for training. His letters to Hannah, when they reached her, were passionate declarations of love and he composed long poems in her praise. Mother blushed a little as she confided this to me. It was rare for my parents to speak of the past and rarer still to refer in any way to their feelings for each other.

When the 1914 war broke out, Berl, as a trained recruit, was among the first to be sent to the front. Of the grim years that followed Berl wouldn't speak, not even to Hannah. But there was one incident that he once described

'In the forest one night we found ourselves next to a Cossack cavalry brigade. The Germans opened fire and some of us were killed. Many were wounded, including a great big beautiful horse belonging to one of the Cossacks.' Father shook his head in wonder as he remembered. 'I think a Cossack loves his horse more than his woman. Anyway, this Cossack went wild when he saw his horse bleeding and neighing pitifully. Before we could restrain him, he'd climbed out of the trench and was running to the German lines, yelling at the top of his voice: "What's my horse ever done to you, cowards, mongrels, swine. Shoot me you bastards, leave my horse alone." He was still running, cursing and shouting when they shot him dead.'

From Mother I learnt that Father was taken prisoner of war in 1917 and were it not for the food parcels which his English cousin sent through the Red Cross, he would have starved to death. Many of his fellow-prisoners did. The German guards were sadistic and the officers, with their refined cruelties, were worse. A prisoner would be called in to be told that a parcel had arrived for him and he'd be ordered to open it in front of the officers, ostensibly for checking. Then the starving prisoner would have to stand by and watch as tins of beans were pierced, bars of chocolate crumbled and biscuits scattered on the floor on the pretence of searching for weapons. Once a German woman, taking pity on his skeletal appearance, threw Berl a piece of bread over the wire fence. She was seen by the guards and beaten while Berl had to look on from the inside of the camp, impotent to help his would-be benefactress.

Two years after the war ended, Berl was still in the camp, awaiting repatriation. By 1920 he had had enough. He made his escape from the camp and tramped across Germany, begging and stealing food on the way. It took him six weeks to reach Kurkl and that was no mean feat for a foreigner who spoke little German, was hungry, shabby and penniless. When Hannah and Berl confronted each other after a separation of eight years, she saw a gaunt stranger with hollow eyes on the point of nervous and physical collapse. She nursed him back to health and married him.

'Were you still in love with him after eight years?' I asked her. 'Of course,' she answered. 'We were engaged,' as though that answered the question. Then she smiled wanly. 'Mind you, it wasn't long before I realised I'd made a mistake but by then I was pregnant with you.'

One day I walked in unexpectedly on a row between them. As I opened the door I saw Dad raise his hand and slap Mother on the face. I'd never witnessed such a thing before. They both looked embarrassed when they saw me and he stomped out. 'How can you stay married to him when he hits you?' I demanded angrily. Mother looked surprised. 'How would I leave him? He's ill.' Then she added 'Besides, do you think I don't love him?'

M OTHER'S war was no picnic either though it didn't start off too badly. In the *shtetl* of Kurkl where Hannah lived with her parents, two brothers and two sisters, Grandfather Yosse was the burgomaster, admired and respected by Jew and Gentile alike. Their house was big and comfortable and their shop served the whole district. I wish I'd known my grandparents Pesse and Yosse after whom my brother and I were named. Grandfather Yosse stares out at me from the only photograph I have of him with a wide-eyed innocence. His is a trusting face, that of a man who likes his fellow-human beings and expects them to like him. And why should they not? He was a man of character, brave, honest, compassionate and humorous.

As a boy of 16 Yosse decided to leave home to seek the excitement and opportunities that he craved and which Kurkl could not provide. His young, widowed mother had married again, a widower with many children of his own, and Yosse decided that it would serve everyone better if he were out of the way. He tramped across Lithuania and reached the port of Gdansk where he persuaded the Polish sea captain to let him work his way across to Liverpool as a cabin boy. Although he knew no one in England and could not speak the language, Yosse found a master cabinet maker who apprenticed him for four years and taught him to carve beautiful objects in wood.

One of these was an oval full-length mirror framed in lustrous black wood on which he'd carved exotic birds, fantastical flowers and leaves in shapes that never grew in Lithuania. Did I imagine it or were there trees and rivers and deep, dark forests hidden in the hollows of its carving? It was the most beautiful object we owned and my mother's sole inheritance. I would gaze at it for hours, lost in dreams of unattainable beauty and marvelling at the skill and imagination of the craftsman who made it − my grandfather. During our years in Lithuania, as we moved from town to village and back again, this mirror was lovingly packed and carefully transported. Mother guarded its passage from place to place with concentrated passion which impressed me greatly; it mattered more to her than all the rest of our furniture put together. When we left Lithuania Mother decided that a mirror was too fragile to ship across the world and she gave this heirloom to her younger sister Leah with many admonitions about its care and protection.

Poor Leah! She could no more save the mirror than she could save the lives of herself, her husband and their six children. All of them were murdered by the Nazis. I've often wondered which Nazi killer stole our beautiful mirror and where it hangs now. Does it decorate the living room of a smug, self-satisfied, comfortable assassin? Does it enrich the lives of the children or grandchildren of Leah's murderer? Does it add lustre to their existence, enhance their vision, add depth to their imagination?

In the 1880s, when young men gave their all to emigrate to America, England, Latin America, Yosse decided to return to his native village. As a fully qualified craftsman, speaking English as well as German, Polish, Lithuanian and of course, Yiddish, he was soon accepted as a leading citizen of his community. Throughout the 1914−1918 war the battles raged around them, pointless, stupid, meaningless carnage in which young men who had forgotten why they were there, died horribly in their thousands. The invading armies came and went, replacing each other with relentless repetition. There were White Russians, Reds, Poles, Lithuanians and also Germans who, in that war, behaved no worse than any other army.

As befitted the Burgomaster of Kurkl, Yosse Garber had the unenviable honour of playing host to the officers while their men camped out wherever they could. Hannah, the burgomaster's eldest daughter, helped her mother prepare food for the ravenous hordes. Hannah's unexpected blonde beauty caught their unwelcome visitors by surprise and seemed to exert a civilizing influence. She smiled fondly as she recalled how the officers would swagger into the house, shouting, cursing and demanding food. Then she would enter the room and greet them demurely. 'Good day, Gentlemen!' Instantly the noise died down, the officers shuffled their feet and then stepped forward. 'Good day, pretty lady,' they saluted her, clicking their heels and kissing her hand. 'But if you think that stopped them from looting,' Mother added, 'you'd be wrong. As soon as they filled their bellies they'd start searching the house, lifting whatever took their fancy, always pretending they were searching for deserters.'

At 16 Hannah decided to become independent. There was only one way to do it: she'd set up in business on her own. Her father, always encouraging, agreed to back her. She opened her own shop, the first in Kurkl to sell pins and ribbons and combs and socks and her friend Luba was her assistant. To get supplies from Wilkomir, the nearest town, they often had to cross two or three opposing army patrol posts. Mother laughed when she recalled the tricks she and Luba played on the dopey guards, pulling their sledge with their contraband load through the dark winter nights. 'Where do you come from?' the guard would bark at Hannah as she rolled down the hill, landing in the snow at his feet. 'From the snow, can't you see?' Hannah stood up and shook herself, fluttering her eyelashes. By the time she'd explained, slowly, carefully, with many a gesture, that she came from Wilkomir and was going to Kurkl without any arms or contraband on her, Luba had taken the sledge in a wide arc round the post and was waiting for her friend further down the road. 'But weren't you scared?' I asked Mother. 'They might have caught you!' 'Oh yes,' she answered, 'the risks were great but you have to take them if you want to survive. And anyway,' she added, 'we enjoyed outsmarting them.'

As the war dragged on and the carnage mounted the mood became grimmer and even the girls' natural high spirits could not be sustained. The Germans set up a prisoner-of-war camp on the outskirts of Kurkl. On the Eve of Yom Kippur the Burgomaster and two Jewish elders went to the camp to see the commandant. They asked if the Herr Commandant would be kind enough to let the Jewish prisoners spend the Holy Day of Atonement with Jewish families in the *shtetl*. The commandant greeted them courteously and agreed readily. As they waited for their guests they watched the prisoners gathering for their evening meal in the courtyard. This consisted of a watery soup in a big cauldron cooked over an open fire. The ravenous prisoners hopped from one foot to another, trying to keep warm while waiting for their rations, tin mugs at the ready. The German guards stood watching and then, as the cook was about to ladle out the soup to the first man in the queue, two guards ambled up and with a kick, overturned the cauldron's contents into the earth. Grandfather Yosse described to his family how the starving prisoners fell on their knees, licking the earth, trying to scoop up what they could from the mess on the ground, while the guards fell about laughing, slapping their thighs with their whips.

'How can human beings do such things to each other?' he wondered. He had raised his children to believe in kindness and generosity and good humour and he'd often tease his wife, to coax her out of her dark moods and what he considered to be her irrational suspicions.

On the second Seder night in 1918 the Garber family seated themselves as usual to celebrate Pesach. Food was getting short but there was *matzo* on the white tablecloth and all were dressed in their festive best. They were into the second verse of '*Chad Gadya*,' when a loud knocking interrupted their singing. Grandma Pesse looked up startled. 'Don't open the door,' she pleaded, frightened. 'Nonsense, my dear,' Grandpa Yosse answered reassuringly. He smiled at his wife and patted her shoulder. 'For all you know it might be Elijah himself at the door and you would keep him out?' He motioned to Lazar, his elder son. 'Open the door and welcome our guest.' Lazar drew back the bolt and four masked men rushed in, each brandishing a weapon. The first shot was aimed at Lazar and as he fell with a bullet in his hip, Grandpa Yosse ran towards his son. Before he could reach him the killers fired a bullet through Yosse's heart. It killed him instantly and he fell to the ground, his arms outstretched in a vain attempt to embrace his wounded son. Grandma Pesse was killed as she reached her husband's side. She threw herself on top of him, desperately trying to protect him with her own body, unaware that he was already dead.

When the shooting started, Hannah ran into the street, shouting for help. She screamed and screamed but no one answered; the neighbours' windows remained dark and shuttered. In despair Hannah turned and ran back into the house. As she reached the front door the killers burst out waving their pistols. Roughly they swept her aside and sent her sprawling in the mud. Hannah picked herself up and entered the house. As she did so she tripped, and looking down, found herself staring at the dead bodies of her father and mother lying in a pool of their own blood. Pesse's eyes were still wide open as she lay across her husband's lifeless body. At her side little Chava was tugging at her arm. 'Mummy, Mummy, get up,' she was wailing. 'Please Mummy, talk to me.' Nine-year-old Leah crouched in a corner of the room. She was staring wide-eyed at the carnage around her, frozen dumb with horror. Shlomo, the younger son, lay dead beneath the window; he'd been shot through the head.

The only time that Mother spoke of this terrible night she paused at this point and we waited in silence. When she continued talking her voice had hardened and her eyes had glazed. She spoke with a cold matter-of-fact tone. 'Then the neighbours came running but by then it was too late. What could they do? My Mother and Father were dead and so was Shlomo. Lazar was wounded and I had to take him to the hospital in Wilkomir. It wasn't easy finding a horse and cart; they'd been requisitioned by the army. When I eventually managed to get Lazar to the hospital I waited until they'd removed the bullets from his hip – I helped to hold him down, there were no anaesthetics – and then I had to leave him. I had to return to arrange for the three funerals and to look after the children. Chavale wouldn't stop crying and Leah wouldn't speak; it was months before we could get a word out of her. I was seventeen at the time,' Mother added.

I was seventeen when I first heard this story, told so baldly, without a trace of self-pity. As if to explain the bleakness of her tale, Mother added: 'There was no time to think or mourn properly or feel sorry for myself. They all depended on me – who else was there? – and I had to get on with it.' I tried to put myself in her place but my mind shied away, my brain switched off. 'Did they ever catch the murderers?' I asked. 'Who knows,' she brushed it aside. 'They had a trial of some deserters and then they hanged them. They thought they were the ones who killed my family, but no one knew for sure.'

Hannah became the head of the family and took over the running of the family business. As soon as Lazar recovered from his wounds, she packed him off to America. He, at least, she decided, would be spared military service in this interminable war. She would look after her two little sisters and wait for her fiancé to come back from the wars.

Years later, in Israel, Chava recalled how she had saved my father's life when she was five or six. He had just returned from Germany and Mother bought him a pair of shiny new boots. These proved irresistible to the soldiers loitering outside the house while their officers ate the food that Mother was cooking inside. This was 1920 but marauding armies still came and went, and the officers continued to billet themselves in Mother's house. 'The war was officially over but the fighting was still going on between the Whites and the Reds, the Polacks and the Litvaks, and who knows what else.'

While mother was working in the kitchen Father came out to look for Chavale who was playing on the front step. A group of soldiers eyed Father's boots and decided they liked them. They gripped his arms and started dragging him to the back of the house. Chavale flung herself at his feet and threw her arms round his ankles, holding fast and screaming at the top of her voice. Mother came running and when she saw what was happening she called the captain, demanding help. He came out cursing his men for disturbing his meal, laying about him with his whip. 'These are dogs, *liebe fraulein*, they must be treated like dogs. If they'd got him to the back of the house, out of sight, they'd surely have killed him for his boots,' he assured Mother cheerfully.

BERL and Hannah married and decided to leave Kurkl. They packed what they could of the family possessions, wrapped the big carved mirror in layers of sacking, and with the two little sisters set out for the capital, Kovno. Here began a pattern of life together which was to continue until the end. Mother opened a shop and worked tirelessly to please the customers and make a living. Father grumbled at the indignity of having to work behind the counter and through his condescension, sarcasm and downright rudeness managed to antagonise and drive away one customer after another. He was far more interested in the Bundists whom he joined at this time than in the paltry, undignified demands of the miserable little shop, as he described it, choosing to ignore the fact that it paid for our bread and soup and potatoes.

When the shop finally closed, Mother opened a private meal service at home. She shopped, cooked and served dinners to the single men of the neighbourhood. There were usually ten or twelve of them sitting down to a meal in our one-roomed flat and that's how we, too, managed to eat.

By this time her two uncles, who had returned from Russia with their families after the Revolution and settled in Wilkomir, offered to look after the two little sisters. Then Father found a full-time, relatively well-paid job with a national forestry company. As the company's financial overseer his job took him to one town after another, wherever the company had branches. He seemed to be away most of the time but Mother received a regular weekly allowance for the first time in her life.

She was alone in the flat when the River Neman burst its banks and flooded Kovno. As they ran past our house the neighbours shouted out the warning. Mother wasted no time, she packed Yossele and me off to the neighbours who lived on the upper storey and left us there, with a muttered apology, then she turned and ran back to our flat below. She was convinced that she had to be there to discourage looters. Before long the thought must have crossed her mind: were the risks she was running justified for the poor objects around her? In our overcrowded room there was little of value: there were the table and chairs, the iron beds and the pots and pans in the kitchen. Two items only could be considered non-essential and so, by definition, luxuries. These were the thick, fringed tablecloth which decorated the dining table between meals and our beautiful oval mirror, carved by Mother's father. The rest, the essentials, were of little value, cheap and shoddy but to Mother they represented her home. She watched despairingly as the waters rose; soon they were surging into the courtyard and climbing up the three steps leading to our door. When they reached the top step and roared into the living room, Mother climbed on to the table which soon began to float. She then leaped onto the windowsill and shouted and waved to attract the attention of the one and only boat which was picking up trapped tenants, all of them vying with each other for help. Below our house was the coal cellar and the trapdoor leading down to it was heavy and solid, standing up well to the heavy weight of water above it. The water was inches beneath the window-sill to which Mother was clinging when the trapdoor below her suddenly burst open and with a roar like thunder the flood cascaded downwards into the dark and windowless cellar below. Mother realised that if she wasn't rescued within minutes, she, too, would be swept into the cellar once the waters reached the windowsill. If that happened, nothing could save her. She clutched at the window and shouted in growing desperation for the boatman. He reached her with seconds to spare.

Upstairs, Yossele and I found ourselves wedged in among other kids of the neighbourhood and their mothers. The kindly elderly couple who were our hosts could hardly move around their flat for the crush of bodies. Yossele and I squeezed our way through to the top of the stairs where we could watch for Mother's return. 'Is she coming back?' Yossele demanded anxiously. 'Of course she is,' I assured him but I wasn't feeling as confident as I sounded. When Mother finally appeared at the foot of the stairs we screamed with relief.

Mother was not only brave, she was also beautiful and had many admirers, one of whom I well remember. Mr Kravitz was a big burly man who seemed to dissolve into a kind of jelly whenever Mother entered the room; he'd gaze at her adoringly and his eyes never left her. He came often to our one-room flat bearing gifts for Yossele and me and he gave me the one and only shop-bought doll I ever possessed. One day he took the three of us to the big park by the lake and ordered the first and best ice cream I ever tasted. Nothing since has quite matched it.

IN DURBAN, in 1935, I often envied my friends Helen, Jane or Melanie for their carefree ability to enjoy life without the sack of guilt that I seemed to trundle around with me everywhere. I resented the weight of responsibility for other people's crimes. Must I suffer the pain on my back when someone, somewhere, was lashed? I burned with indignation at stories of cruelty or injustice, wishing I was there to stop it yet longing to direct my mind to easier, pleasanter dreams. I saw myself rushing in to save a child from abuse, warding off a horde of maddened whites from burning down a homestead, confronting a mob of would-be lynchers. My fantasies always began and ended with me leaping in to save, protect, succour. What was I doing when So-and-so was tortured, I blamed myself.

Of course it was silly, pointless, even arrogant, I told myself, to concentrate on white-tipped waves and blue skies, on the smell of grenadillas and the taste of pawpaws, on pretty clothes, parties, boys. I didn't want to change places with my friends, to become like them, indifferent to the world around them, silly, shallow, smug. I was different, I had an aim in life, I would be a revolutionary, a Communist. My friends were selfish, superficial and lacking in compassion, I consoled myself. Yet these friends of mine were not hard or insensitive. Helen cried when her cat was run over; Jane turned green with nausea and distress when she witnessed a man knocked down by a tram; Melanie talked of becoming a nurse because she wanted to help people. So why were they so blind to the life around them? How was it that race and colour could distort their perceptions?

One day Jane and I watched as two white policemen chased a black youth and then beat him with their batons when they caught him. Jane was dismissive. 'He's probably stolen something,' she shrugged. 'Wouldn't you, if you were hungry?' I searched her face for fellow-feeling but all I could see was impatience with me and my concerns. It was the same with Helen. 'I do wish you'd leave it alone,' she told me when I commented on the beach one day how unfair it was that black nannies could sit there with their white charges but weren't allowed to swim.

Even Herman, who was sympathetic, tried to divert my interests into safer, less contentious areas. 'The world is full of marvellous things,' he told me. 'Don't rush to commit yourself to causes.' He took me to the Durban Jewish Club and introduced me to the man who was producing *The Belle of New York*. 'Would you like to come for an audition?' he asked me. I'd never been on a stage before but I went and was given a part in the chorus of the musical comedy. When they picked me to appear in a bathing costume for a solo rendering of 'The Lady from France' I hung back at first shyly until I noticed the other girls giggling. That's when I assured the director that I would do it and what at first started as an act of defiance turned out to be great fun. It was tempting to join the girls in the Club, to become one of the crowd – giddy, flirtatious, having a good time. But there was no escaping the differences between us and the gulf that separated them and me. These were daughters of the well-to-do; kind or cruel, clever or dumb, their aim was to enjoy life and to catch a good husband. If they went to university it was not to seek independence but to be better placed in the matrimonial stakes. They didn't give a hoot about the people outside the Club or, if some of them did sometimes stop and ask themselves why there was hunger in a land of plenty, they took good care to hide the fact. I knew that I'd sealed my future long ago and their life was not for me. I was just marking time until I could take up my pre-ordained tasks.

Just as school had been, so now work was a nuisance that interrupted my real pursuits: for pleasure, literature and for duty the study of Marxism/Leninism. I tried to read the few booklets that Father owned and then I would test my new-found knowledge by engaging him in discussions. 'If workers are satisfied with their lot is it right for Communists to make them discontented?' I would challenge him. Father was his usual, admirable, uncompromising self. 'Yes,' he said. 'It is the duty of Communists to open their eyes to the unjust society which exploits them and to show them how it can be changed.' He was right of course and I relished his clarity of thought and refusal to equivocate.

W HEN I heard that Martha was going to work in Johannesburg I felt that here was an opportunity to make my get-away and find the place where there was bound to be a Communist Party. Safe, slow, dependable Martha peered at the world through thick glasses and weighed the pros and cons of every action she undertook. She was good-humoured, kindly and stolid. Mother agreed reluctantly to let me go provided Martha shared a room with me. Martha agreed.

Mr and Mrs Jones were a childless, well-to-do couple whose smart flat was situated in the centre of Johannesburg, right in the middle of a big apartment block in Rissik Street. Our room in their flat was small but comfortable and Mrs Jones enjoyed her role *in loco parentis*. In no time at all she'd introduced Martha to 'a nice Jewish boy' and presided over their growing friendship with open satisfaction. The boys who came to take me out would be scrutinised critically and those who brought flowers and chocolates earned her approval. 'I must find you also a nice young businessman,' Mrs Jones told me. 'But I don't want to marry a businessman,' I answered. 'I want to marry a working man.' Mrs Jones looked at me in amazement. 'Why ever would you want to do that? Businessmen are much better providers. Look at Mr Jones.' It was no use explaining to my incredulous, uncomplicated landlady that I wished to be identified with the working class, with men who made things in workshops and factories, not with wheelers and dealers who lived like parasites, by manipulating the wealth that others made without producing anything themselves. I'd seen pictures of the working-class hero that I thought I could one day marry. He was lithe and strong and dedicated to our Cause but he could also laugh and dance and enjoy himself. In the Spanish Civil War he'd stood on a hillside, his rifle held aloft, shouting 'Non Pasaran.' In French films he always dangled a cigarette from the corner of his mouth and when he flung open the door of the bar and stood outlined against the light, the villains quailed and the girls' eyes lit up. And anyway, I didn't want a 'provider'. I wanted a partner, a lover, a friend. Explain that to Mrs Jones!

Our landlady had two passions in her life. One was for china dogs which occupied every available space in the apartment. The shelves, window-sills, side tables all supported china dogs of every shape, size and species so that not only Martha and I, but also Mr Jones and every visitor who entered the flat, was kept constantly aware of the need to circumnavigate the spaces between the furniture slowly and with great caution; one dare not risk knocking a dog off its pedestal. On her birthday we asked Mrs Jones what she would like. 'A nice little doggy,' she said, unabashed, and was delighted with the pink pug that Martha found after much searching. I marvelled at the devotion she lavished on inanimate objects. Martha took a charitable view. 'It's because she has no children,' she explained to me. 'But china dogs,' I protested. 'Have you tried cuddling one of those?' Mrs Jones's other source of never-ending enthusiasm was the stage duo of Bebe Daniels and Ben Lyon. She had not missed a performance during their season in Johannesburg and one night after the show Mr and Mrs Jones plucked up courage and walked backstage to meet their idols.

The two stars received them graciously and the programme which they both signed shared pride of place on the side table with the china dogs. As other people produce pictures of their grandchildren so Mrs Jones regaled her visitors with photos, press cuttings and memorabilia of her stars.

I FOUND work in the office of the Johannesburg Ice Rink. It was a glamorous and exciting place at night but cold and dreary in the daytime when I was there. One compensation was that Andrea, the blonde, baby-faced Czechoslovak skating star offered to give me free skating lessons during my lunch hour. But much as I enjoyed ice skating, I reminded myself that I had come to Jo'burg for other, sterner reasons. Before long, and quite by chance, I came upon the noisy, violent public meetings on the City Hall steps on Sunday nights. I watched in growing excitement and then I approached the Communist Party organisers and volunteered my services. They didn't know what an important event this was in my life; hurriedly and without much ceremony they stuck a bundle of leaflets in my arms and told me to go around the crowd distributing them. The next week someone showed me how to link arms with the other comrades and encircle the platform to protect it from the attacks of the Greyshirts, South Africa's own brand of Nazis. Our speakers had to make themselves heard above the continuous taunts and abuse of Hitler's supporters.

'Would you let your sister marry a kaffir?' became a standard, predictable interruption, no matter whether the talk was of African trade union rights, a united front against fascism, the pass laws or the Soviet Union. Issy Diamond earned himself a niche in our Party mythology when he retorted one night, amid a howl of laughter, 'Only if I had something against the kaffir.'

The attacks were not confined to verbal abuse. The Greyshirts came in gangs with sticks, whips and knuckledusters which they didn't bother to hide. They were big, muscle-bound, ugly brutes. There were no girls in their ranks, nor any of the weedy little guys, brave but ineffectual, who formed a good part of our defence force. At a signal from their leader they would link arms and rush the platform, inflicting serious injuries on those of us who tried to bar their way. They were well drilled and we stood little chance against them. The police were always in attendance; they'd watch the attacks on us with unconcealed satisfaction and then they'd barge in to arrest some of our comrades, never our attackers. Invariably some of us had to be taken off to hospital for treatment after the Sunday night meeting. It wasn't until we succeeded in recruiting a tough group on our side that our fortunes changed.

Like the cavalry riding in to relieve the siege of Mafeking there appeared one Sunday night the three brothers Natie, Joe and Jack Marcus leading a group of other tough young men from Doornfontein, the suburb where the poorer Jews lived. These were fighters who had experience in defending themselves against

Greyshirts in the schools and on the streets and they had learnt to do so with courage and vigour. Without discussion or debate they formed a circle round the platform, arms linked, jaws set. Clearly, anyone hoping to knock down the speaker would have to get past them. No one tried. The meeting proceeded almost peacefully except for the insults from the outer edges of the crowd which we could afford to ignore. To me it was another demonstration of the efficacy of self-defence or how to deal with bully-boys.

M Y AUNT Zivia also lived in Doornfontein. Since my Uncle Reuben's death Aunt Zivia had struggled to bring up her two daughters, Becky and Dora, by toiling away in her little shop, selling fruit and vegetables and salt herrings from a large tub. She was forever on the go, her large expansive body in perpetual motion, serving, chatting, running back and forth. Aunt Zivia had no time to spare for buying new shoes, visiting a hairdresser or even to see a doctor when pains began to wrack her insides. She shuffled about in slippers, her wispy grey hair barely combed, wearing a long apron of indeterminate colour. But Aunt Zivia had a capacity for laughter that bubbled up against all the odds. In the middle of a frantic Friday morning, when the little shop was crowded with irritable housewives impatiently jostling to stock up for Shabbat, there would suddenly ring out Aunt Zivia's high, girlish laughter, usually at her own joke, and a smile would appear on the face of even the grimmest customer.

When I came for a meal on Saturday or Sunday Aunt Zivia would ply me with roast chicken, potatoes, cabbage, cauliflower, peas, followed by jellies, trifles and slices of cakes oozing with cream. My two cousins would join her in urging me to stay a little longer. 'What's the rush?' Aunt Zivia would demand. 'But Aunty, I've got a meeting to attend.' 'Meeting, shmeeting,' Aunt Zivia would answer. 'It won't run away, tomorrow or the next day, it'll still be there.' The Sunday I announced on my arrival that I would definitely have to leave at three o'clock as that day's meeting was really important, Aunt Zivia, surprisingly, didn't argue. She smiled enigmatically and it was later that day when I discovered why: she had moved the clock hand back an hour. My distress when I realized what she had done sent her into peals of merriment. She had no sympathy for my predicament. What could be more important than spending time with the family over a meal?

Another lady who had scant respect for meetings was Benny Sichy's grandmother. Benny was an active comrade, involved in numerous activities connected with the Party. He was also involved in amateur theatricals and was constantly borrowing household items as props. One day someone turned up at the Sichys and left a message for Benny. 'Would you tell him please,' he asked Mrs Sichy 'that we'd like him to take the chair on Sunday.' Mrs Sichy shook her head. 'Not another shtick furniture leaves this house,' she announced firmly.

I GUESSED there was an inner sanctum in Johannesburg where real Communists met – there must be. But I also knew that you didn't apply to join; you waited until you were asked. The day when Beila Page invited me to go with her to a meeting of the Young Communist League was a proud day in my life. I was beginning to earn their trust. We climbed the steps leading to Dr Max Joffe's waiting room and found there nine or ten young men and women, all white. They met every Friday night to study Marxism/Leninism and to undertake tasks like selling *The Guardian*, the Communist Party's unofficial paper, and distributing leaflets in various parts of the city. Max was a busy general practitioner in the daytime and a stern teacher of Communist theory when the surgery closed. His wife Socky shared his serious approach to politics and smiled rarely. All in the group regarded them with awe and I, as the newest recruit, more than most. I listened entranced as Max expounded on Communism, its theory and practice, and everything I heard only went to confirm my convictions and my faith. Here was a theory, a philosophy of sanity, compassion, logic. It appealed to the head as well as to the heart.

The following Sunday night, on the City Hall steps, °Jackie Gordon told me that he attended another study group on Wednesday nights, and asked if I wanted to come. This was the Labour League of Youth run by Comrade Hilda Watts, newly arrived from England. She too, taught Marxism/Leninism in a serious, dedicated manner. It soon emerged that each of my teachers was critical of the other's ability to provide us with the correct Marxist interpretations of the past and the present. But the occasional sour note that crept in to mar the comradely criticism of each other's line did not dim the marvel of discovering the wisdom, beauty and good sense of Marx and Lenin. I listened entranced to what I found to be so patently obvious; it seemed as if my instructors were merely laying bare the secrets of the world that had always been there, just waiting to be uncovered. I admired both Hilda and Max, never missing a class.

After meetings we students would traipse down to the Golden Ray Restaurant at the corner of Kotze and Claim Streets in Hillbrow and here, over coffees, milk-shakes or lemon sodas we'd continue the discussions begun at the meetings, but in an easier, more relaxed manner, away from the supervision of our mentors.

SATURDAY nights were spent in another milieu altogether. At nine o'clock sharp my new acquaintance °Ulli Peiser would present himself at the Jones's flat with a bunch of flowers and a box of chocolates. After formally greeting Mrs Jones he would perch himself bolt upright on the edge of a chair and wait for me to get ready. Ulli was always meticulously kitted out in his black bow-tie, boiled shirt, dinner jacket and shiny patent leather shoes. I emerged in my long, white, evening dress sparkling with silver spangles around the bouffant net skirt. The well-fitting bodice and the short puffed sleeves enhanced my self-image of glamour and romance. This was my first evening gown; Mother had designed and made it, stitching away for many hours to have it ready for my departure. High-heeled white sandals and silver evening bag completed my ensemble. I would have loved to add a necklace or bracelet but I accepted Father's dictum that if you can't have the real thing – meaning gold or silver or diamonds – it is better to do without. Imitations would be vulgar.

The Saturday night programme never varied. Ulli led me down to his Ford and handed me into the seat with punctilious courtesy. Five minutes later we'd arrive at the Moonlight Night Club around the corner where Ulli would order for us steak and chips and brandy and ginger ale, the most expensive, and therefore the most desirable items on the menu. Like all the other couples we danced between courses. Ulli danced as he did everything else, correctly and stiffly, the waltz, the foxtrot, the tango, the conga, the two-step. He knew all the steps but his body never yielded. At one o'clock we stood up to leave, Ulli adjusted the scarf round my shoulders, and handed me my silver evening bag. On the way back he'd pull up at the corner to buy the Sunday papers, one for him and one for me. At our block of flats Ulli would stop, walk round to open my door and escort me to our flat. There he would peck me on the cheek and depart.

After some weeks of following this immutable programme, the Saturday nights began to pall. The outings which had started as new and exciting were now becoming boring and predictable. Even Ulli's bronzed good looks began to seem wooden. When I first met him I thought him beautiful; I'd never seen such sculptured features, the image of a young Greek god. But it soon dawned on me that for all his conversation, or lack of it, he might as well have been one. The night when I told Ulli that no, I would not be seeing him next Saturday as usual, I saw unsuspected lines of emotion cross his hitherto carved features. It almost made me change my mind but by then I had met °Mike Stanley and promised to go out with him.

Mike was craggy, volatile and quick-witted. When he entered a room people's spirits rose. He told tall stories and made us laugh. He was always with us on Sunday nights on the Town Hall steps, and at Labour League of Youth classes his contributions to the discussions made up in entertainment what they lacked in profundity. When we danced together I felt airborne. Never before had I partnered someone who fused with me in the joy of motion and who made my head spin with the sheer pleasure of it. He made me feel light and supple and full of grace. I was beginning to find him very fascinating.

O NE night, in the Golden Ray Restaurant, at our usual after-meeting drinks, I found myself next to comrade Colin, he of the blotchy skin and hair full of dandruff. Colin leant towards me and whispered conspiratorially, 'You see that floozie in the corner?' pointing to a peroxide blonde with a deep *décolletage*. 'She's a pro.' As intended, the whisper reached everyone round the table and the fellows all perked up. The pupils of their eyes dilated as they swivelled round to look. 'How do you know?' Mina challenged him. 'A fellow can always tell,' Colin said, winking at the boys and making sure that the girls saw him doing so. 'I can tell if a girl is a virgin,' Ricky asserted, looking smug. 'Does it make a difference to you whether she is or not?' Beila demanded. The fellows laughed uncomfortably and the girls bristled. Then Mike spoke. 'I would never marry a girl who is not a virgin.' He leaned back smugly as if to say, 'Wouldn't everyone?' The boys obviously endorsed his opinion but what pained me was that none of the girls challenged this male arrogance. They looked cross and uncomfortable but said nothing; neither did I.

The talk veered into lighter channels but Mike's comment niggled away at me. The more I thought about it the more insulting I decided it was. So that was the most important attribute a girl could have for the great institution of marriage – an unbroken hymen! How little girls mattered as people if their virginity or lack of it determined their value as wives. A girl could be clever and kind and beautiful but all that paled into insignificance if she was not a virgin. And when the fellows did their damnedest to persuade a girl to say yes it was only to despise her afterwards if she was foolish enough to comply. Perhaps not immediately, for a 'fast' girl could count on lots of dates – but not on marriage. And what if a girl said yes because she too enjoyed sex? That would put her well beyond the pale. She would be used and then abused, not only by conservative, reactionary, ignorant white males but also by these 'liberated' comrades, these people who should know better. And if 'purity' was so desirable a quality why did it not apply equally to men? Well, I was a virgin but that was something I had to change, get rid of. No one would ever marry me for such an irrelevancy: it was a veil that had to be brushed aside if true love and real worth were to be revealed. And if marriage depended on virginity then phooey to marriage!

THE week before war was declared on 3 September 1939 I received a letter from Mother asking me to come home. She explained that she had bought a new shop and needed my assistance to get started. 'Just for the first few months,' she urged. 'Then, if you want to, you can return to Jo'burg.'

Mother had changed many shops before and had never depended on my help. But never before had she appealed for my assistance so directly. I suspected that this was a subterfuge to get me back home but I knew I had to go. I could not turn my back on such a direct call for help.

The following Friday night, before I could announce my sad news, I received a message that Comrade Max wished to see me in his office after the meeting. Seated round his desk were Max, Socky and two other senior comrades. 'We have been watching you for some months now, Comrade Pauline,' Max announced pompously and my heart missed a beat. What had I done? But he went on: 'You appear to be a conscientious worker and keen to learn. We have decided to recommend you for probation membership of the Party.' This was something I'd been waiting and striving for, the fulfilment of a life's ambition. At last it had come true. I could join the Communist Party, become one of the band of dedicated, zealous fighters for freedom. What happiness! I could have danced for joy.

'There's just one difficulty,' I stammered in embarrassment. 'My mother needs me and has asked me to return to Durban for a few months. Could you please give me a letter of recommendation to the Party in Durban?' 'Out of the question,' Max proclaimed. 'You will have to go and prove yourself to them.' To be so close to one's goal and then see it slip away! I was bitterly disappointed but I accepted the unyielding justice of it. It merely confirmed how disciplined the Party was.

The night war was declared my friends and I went out into the streets and joined the crowds milling about, seeking an outlet for their pent-up emotions. Outside the German Embassy we shouted slogans with the rest of them and then the crowd broke up, some wandering off and others forming gangs looking for excitement. We watched in growing discomfiture as these erstwhile allies began to overturn and set fire to all the German cars they came across. It soon became clear to us that as an expression of patriotic fervour it lacked dignity or conviction; this was just an outlet for simple thuggery. What were we doing getting mixed up in it? We left the mob and made our way to our usual table at the Golden Ray Coffee Bar. I bade my comrades a sad goodbye. Mike said he was sorry to see me go and promised to write.

D URBAN at the end of 1939 and beginning of 1940 was a place quite different from the sleepy town I had left a bare six months previously. The English-speaking whites of Natal had always clung to their ties with 'home', meaning Britain. They were contemptuous of Afrikaners and disdainful of Afrikaans. The teaching of Afrikaans was compulsory but I was not alone in leaving school with the barest smattering of what I came afterwards to appreciate as a crisp, rhythmic language which rolled sonorously off the tongue when spoken properly. At the outbreak of war the country divided sharply between the supporters of Britain, mainly the English-speaking South Africans and the Afrikaners who opposed the war, either from historic hostility to Britain or from ideological identification with the Nazis. The bulk of the population, the non-whites, were mainly indifferent to what they saw as primarily a quarrel between whites. After Japan entered the war they tended to sympathise with the enemy in the mistaken belief that the Japanese would naturally be on the side of the black races and, anyway, my enemy's enemy must be my friend.

General Jan Smuts won the pro-war motion in Parliament by a very narrow majority and became Prime Minister. He was staunch in his commitment to the Allied cause but was never sure enough of popular white support at home to introduce compulsory military service. Only whites could bear arms; African, Indian and coloured (mixed race) volunteers were accepted only as stretcher bearers, cooks, latrine diggers – they must never be allowed to suspect that there could ever be circumstances in which they could be poised against white men, even Nazis. English-speaking Natalians embraced the war effort with much enthusiasm and patriotic fervour but they shied away from the implications of what such a commitment involved; they had no doubt that the war had to be won but did it necessarily follow that blacks should be included in the struggle? Who knows what they might demand in return?

It was on the bus one night, on my way home to Umgeni where we then lived, that a young black man found himself downstairs, in the area reserved for 'Whites Only'. It was easy to see that he was a stranger in town; he looked about him helplessly, clearly frightened to find himself in the midst of so many angry white faces as he tried to make himself as unobtrusive as possible. The conductor strode up to him, grabbed him by the back of his neck and pulled him unprotesting to the entrance. Two brave young whites, hefty and red-faced, rushed to the conductor's assistance and I watched in horror as these three grabbed the black youth by his arms and legs and hurled him out of the moving bus. 'That'll teach the kaffir a lesson,' the conductor smirked. By the time I'd lunged forward the black youth was already on the road, spreadeagled as though dead. The bus continued on its journey.

I was beside myself with helpless fury. 'You evil, stupid bastards,' I stormed at them. 'How dare you treat a man like that? You're nothing but cold-blooded murderers.' The three whites looked at me in amazement, they'd expected congratulations, not this torrent of abuse. I turned my back on them and addressed the rest of the passengers who had witnessed this atrocity without saying a word. These were ordinary whites, young and not-so-young, men and women, returning home after a day's work, ready for their evening meal, a cuddle from their children, a hug from their parents.

'One of these days you'll live to regret your behaviour,' I cried. 'If the Japanese ever land here the blacks will welcome them as saviours. Then they'll avenge themselves on all of us whites, and who can blame them.' My fellow-passengers shifted uneasily in their seats, then one of them spoke, 'She's right, you know.' A few of the others nodded agreement. We'd reached my stop; I jumped off and ran home. I went into the living room where Dad was reading the evening paper. Without a word I rushed past him and threw myself on my bed where I started sobbing uncontrollably. 'What's the matter?' Mum asked anxiously, 'Are you hurt?' I waved her away, too full emotionally to be able to talk about it. 'I'm all right,' I muttered. 'Leave me alone.' She went back to the living room and I heard Dad say, 'Better leave her, it's her age.'

Rumours of impending Japanese landings multiplied; air raid precautions (ARP), were organised and a black-out was imposed in Durban. I joined ARP expecting to be given roof-top duty, watching for air attacks and incendiary bombs, but as I was the only girl in the section I was instructed to operate the switchboard, 'An important job,' my superior, Mr Shepstone, assured me, 'in case of an enemy attack.' While waiting for the enemy to announce himself I had to listen to Mr Shepstone's daily bulletins on the state of his considerable stomach and how he kept it in order. 'Twelve glasses of hot water every morning before breakfast,' he'd intone. 'Nothing like it for keeping the inner works in good running order.'

The days were spent working in Mother's shop which proved to be not as irksome as I'd feared it would be. I took quite a pride in sorting the cartons of cigarettes, tinned peaches, apricot jam, tomato soup, and stacking them neatly on the shelves, the newer articles at the back and the older products in front. Customers came in a constant stream for matches, candles, milk, custard powder, lettuce and white bread. Commercial travellers arrived and I soon learnt to place orders with those offering better value at lower prices, earning Mother's approbation.

THE Left Book Club re-emerged and took on a new lease of life, and on Sunday nights I'd accompany Father to listen to lectures and debates. 'This war is a struggle between two imperialist powers,' was the proposition moved with great vehemence one Sunday night. It followed, the speaker maintained, that the working class should keep out of it and not ally itself with one or other of the capitalist countries to fight against their class brothers. Not so, retorted another, speaking against the motion. 'This is a war of the democracies for survival. Haven't we all been demanding a stand against Nazism and Fascism ever since Hitler came to power?'

The debate hotted up with would-be participants all trying to attract the chairman's eye. Father succeeded and stood up to speak, almost losing his nervous stammer in his determination to make his point. 'Can't you see that this is not 1914?' he asked with passion. 'Then it was right to refuse to fight for either side; both sides were just after grabbing land and power. But this is a war against Fascism. If we lose there's no hope for any of us.' It was the first time I'd heard my father speak in public and I glowed with pride.

L ANGUAGE in our family did not normally flow easily. Father was usually sparing of words to the point of meanness and Mother was no gossip. Things were said that had to be said but conversation as an art form was foreign to our household. Meal times were silent events, except for 'Have some more' or 'Finish your soup.' In other families fathers told anecdotes and mothers exchanged news with the children, but not in ours. It never occurred to me to entertain the family with reports of the silly, unimportant things that had happened that day in the office, to exchange views and opinions, to laugh together. Nor, it seemed, did it occur to my parents or brothers.

At other people's houses, where relations or friends invited me for lunch or dinner, talk flowed around the table. I always found it strange that amusement could be gained from small, insignificant events. Why should it be interesting to hear what she said to me and I said to her or what she wore or where he was seen? What difference did it make? What a bore to listen to the non-events at their boring old office. I felt superior to their small-time, insignificant, chatter. It seemed to me that if people couldn't discuss important matters then it would be better if they kept quiet.

In our house, as well as our natural taciturnity there was also the great divide of language between English and Yiddish. By now my brothers and I found it difficult to express ourselves in Yiddish, but we understood our parents, who addressed each other and us in their native tongue while we spoke in English. This served well enough for everyday bits of information but it failed us when important issues had to be discussed or when passions ran high. To intimate the exact nuance of a feeling was impossible when one had constantly to search for the simplest synonym of a word. To choose an unfamiliar expression carried risks. More and more Mother came to impose her own interpretations on words and phrases which, in her opinion, gave cause for offence. It didn't help to try to explain that we didn't mean this, we meant that. It became easier not to talk. When we had to say something it was no use getting bogged down in subtleties. Our meanings had to be unequivocal: yes or no; good or bad; today or tomorrow; there was no room for maybe, perhaps, sometimes. Our limited choice of language compelled us to opt for the clear, the certain, the unambiguous.

My life has, in the main, followed the same pattern. It has always been a choice of either/or, black or white, brave or cowardly, true or false. It took me many years to acknowledge that the choice was not always clear-cut and that the colours in between black and white were just as valid. I had to learn that it was sometimes wiser to dip a foot in the water rather than dive straight in and that it didn't matter if I wasn't always first in the sea.

But that came later. At this stage of my life I felt compelled to respond to every challenge, even if it meant doing things I didn't feel like doing, like kissing a boy I didn't care for, just because I was dared to do it. A promise to myself was as binding, if not more so, than one made to others. My childish resolve never to tell a lie still weighed heavily with me, even though I came to understand that it was not always the wisest or the kindest thing to do. My decisions had to be clear-cut and my judgments brooked no shilly-shallying or smudged borders. It occurred to me in later years to wonder whether my early years of limited language were instrumental in determining my later years of uncompromising choice. Do we think what we can express or do we express what we think?

On rare occasions – I can only recall three though it must have occurred more often – Father sang for us. He had a pleasant tenor voice and many folk songs, in Yiddish and Russian, stored in his memory. 'Sing for us, Berl,' Mother would plead and Yossele and I would add our entreaties, 'Yes, Dad, please do.' Then, when he finally agreed we would listen entranced. How I wished he would sing more often! I enjoyed listening to my Father sing as much as he seemed to do when listening to his favourites, Chaliapin and Caruso.

It was Sam Melamed who brought a gramophone to our house when he moved in as our lodger. Mum and Dad had argued about letting the room in our flat which was already cramped, she maintaining that we needed the money and Dad protesting that we couldn't possibly fit another person in. They compromised and Sam moved in. When Dad saw the gramophone which Sam carried in and placed on our dining-room table with excessive care, his objections fell away and he was reconciled to having another body in our crowded flat. Sam loved opera; he'd wind up the gramophone, lean back in his chair, close his eyes and melt into the sounds of Chaliapin, Caruso and Melba singing arias from Borodin's *Prince Igor*, Moussorgsky's *Boris Godunov*, Verdi and Puccini.

Sam was a mild and gentle person with a half-smile forever hovering on his kindly features. He was unassuming and ever ready to offer whatever help was needed. He paid his rent on time and if he did spend more time in the bathroom in the mornings than I considered fair, it was not a grievous fault. In fact it was his very virtues and unblemished character that added to my intense dislike of him; for I did indeed develop such hostility to him that I could not bear to be in the same room. If I sat in a chair which still retained the warmth of his body I'd jump up with loathing and when he greeted me with a sweet 'Good morning', I'd shrink away in disgust. My loathing of him was irrational and undeserved yet it was total. 'Can't you tell him to go?' I'd demand of my Mother and she, surprised, would protest that Sam was the best lodger we ever had, as indeed he was. Only I couldn't stand the sight of him and I never discovered why. Years later, when I met him again and realised what a thoroughly good person he was, I hoped he'd never noticed my girlish malice and that, if he had, he'd forgiven me, as he gave every indication of doing.

MR AND Mrs Alper were a short, middle-class, elderly Jewish couple who were fiercely Trotskyist. Mr and Mrs Rubin were a short, middle-class, elderly Jewish couple who were implacably Stalinist. All four were unfailingly present at the Left Book Club meetings where debates invariably ended with a verbal flare-up between the two women, their men participating as loyal back-ups. At first it added zest to the proceedings but very soon it became predictable. The white audience did not much care for the Alpers' criticisms of Stalin, certainly not at a time like this when the Soviet Union was defending itself against the Nazi onslaught and fighting for its life. Stalin was the great leader, the great defender of everything we all held dear and it ill behoved us to denigrate him. Now that Soviet Russia was in the war all doubt about supporting it evaporated.

The Rubin's daughter, Sarah – small, dark, intense – often came to meetings and participated with a fluency that I admired and wished I could emulate. One Sunday evening, following another predictable debate, she called me aside.

'This is just a talking shop. If you really want to do something, come with me to the Liberal Study Group.' I accepted eagerly and the following Tuesday Sarah and I met on the corner of Grey and West Streets. Walking down Grey Street we left behind us the familiar white area and entered another, stranger country. The scents and sounds were quite different from anything I was used to and it occurred to me that I'd never really walked in the Indian quarter before. We'd passed through it, Mother and I, going to and from the Indian market but we'd never shopped in the gaudy sari stores or dreamed of eating in the pungent curry restaurants. But there was no sense of danger, only the excitement of something new and adventurous.

We turned off Grey Street into a narrow, malodorous alley between two buildings until we reached an outside rickety staircase leading to the entrance of the Liberal Study Group. The Group occupied two intercommunicating rooms with bare floors and peeling walls. In the first room was a well-used manual duplicator, a typewriter, and a shaky small table on which stood a chipped kettle and a collection of discoloured tin mugs. In the inner room wooden benches were lined up haphazardly in front of the speaker's table and two chairs. It was not so much spartan as forlorn. The group of young men lounging casually on the benches were mostly Indians with a sprinkling of Africans and coloureds – not a single woman present except for Sarah and me. Sarah was greeted like an old friend and she introduced me: 'This is Comrade Pauline. Meet Comrades Reddy, M.D. Naidoo, Seedat, M.P. Naicker, Docrat, Ismail Meer, Peter Abrahams, Wilson Cele.' They regarded me curiously, as I did them. They made welcoming noises and tried to seem unconcerned but could not hide either their curiosity or their lack of ease. No more could I.

Peter Abrahams, small, intense with large, round eyes, lolled on a bench and

Maternal grandfather, Yossel Garber.   Paternal grandmother, Esther Podbrez.

Berl, a soldier in the Tsar's army.   Brother Joe, SAAF.

The Podbrez family in Lithuania.

Pauline in the Drakensberg, 1940.

Above Top (L to R)   Henry Woolfson, H.A., ——, Pauline, Ismail Meer.

Above   At Currie's Fountain before the mass meeting 27 September 1942. *(L to R)*   Pauline, Mick Harmel, Harry Snitcher, H.A.

At the wedding of Dorothy Naylor & Errol Shanley, Durban. 4 December 1941. *(L to R)* Jan Zoutendyk, two ladies in hats, Athol Thorne, Henry Woolfson, Frank Fokine & his daughter Mary, Adie Israel, Pauline Podbrey & Vera Ponnen. *(Behind)* Andrew Goldie, *(Standing)* Pauline Urry holding Zoutendyk baby. *(Front)* Lorna Zoutendyk & unknown lady.

H. A. Naidoo, Durban, 1940.

(L to R) Errol Shanley, Dhanum Naidoo (sister of H.A.), H.A., P.M. Harry, George Ponnen.

Some of the Naidoos, with Krishna centre left.

COMMUNIST PARTY OF SOUTH AFRICA
DURBAN DISTRICT COMMITTEE

PRESENTS

MASS RALLY and PAGEANT

ON

SUNDAY, SEPTEMBER 27th at 2 p.m.

AT

CURRIE'S FOUNTAIN, WINTERTON WALK, DURBAN

SPEAKERS :

Adv. HARRY SNITCHER (C.T.)
MICHAEL HARMEL * (Jhb.)
H. A. NAIDOO (Durban)
WILSON CELE   ,,
Miss P. PODBREY   ,,

Guest Speaker :
Dr. Y. M. DADOO   (Jhb.)

● Community Singing

● Songs

● Mass Recitations

● Banner Pageant

COMMUNIST RALLY — CURRIE'S FOUNTAIN — SUNDAY SEPT 27th AT 2 P.M. ★

FOR VICTORY IN 1942

Universal Pig. Wks., 9 Bond St., Durban. Phone 26296.

Outer pages of a Party leaflet.

simulated ennui: 'I'm a poet,' he announced as he waved a limp arm in my direction. It was a declaration he clung to on many occasions in the future, especially when called upon to help with the duplicating or collating, as though practising the art of poetry precluded his participation in all things manual. Years later, after leaving South Africa, he surprised us all by becoming a successful and respected author. Ismail Meer, with his finely drawn features and beautiful hands, his well modulated voice and air of good breeding, looked like a younger edition of Pandit Nehru whose picture decorated the wall.

Soon a third white woman arrived and she took the chair for the evening. Fay King Goldie, introduced as 'a writer,' was older than most of us, confident, mature. She greeted me kindly but with condescension.

THE speaker of the evening was H.A. Naidoo and his arrival galvanized the audience. Suddenly everyone was sitting up, fully awake and aware, ready to give this man full attention. I, too, felt myself responding to the aura of leadership about him and then I remembered. This was the man I had met three years previously, at my first Communist Party meeting in Old Dutch Road, where Bettie du Toit was the speaker and he was the chairman.

H.A. Naidoo spoke of the need for a new awakening among the Indian community. Too long, he said, had it been led by collaborators like A.I. Kajee of the Natal Indian Congress and Sorabjee Rustomjee of the Natal Indian Association. Instead of rejecting the iniquitous Indian Penetration Bill which aimed to deprive Indians of their homes and businesses, these so-called leaders were drawing up maps and charts to prove that the Indians had not 'penetrated' European areas. The Indians were herded into overcrowded ghettos and their leaders should demand more land for development, not apologise for occupying the space they had. Instead of demanding arms for Indian and other non-white soldiers, they were acting as recruiting agents for the demeaning posts of hod carriers and latrine cleaners. Indians were dying of poverty and malnutrition and TB was rife among them, but the discredited leadership could only think of currying favour with their white overlords.

H.A. Naidoo was no rabble-rouser. He didn't shout or declaim or wave his arms. He presented his facts dispassionately and trusted his audience to make up their own minds. In the years to come I attended many meetings at which he spoke and I never saw an audience that failed to live up to his expectations. At the end of that particular Tuesday night meeting it was resolved to set up the Nationalist Bloc whose aim it would be to wrest the leadership of the Natal Indian Congress from the old guard, and H.A. was elected chairman. From this modest beginning the Bloc grew rapidly among the Natal Indians. Local committees were soon established in Newcastle, Pietermaritzburg and many other towns and our speakers were in great demand.

It never ceased to bother me that among all these dedicated men the only active women participants were just a couple of white girls. 'You have a lot to say about liberation,' I'd accuse them. 'What about liberating your own women first? Why don't you bring your wives and your sisters to meetings?' H. A. always backed me up. 'We've got to set an example to the rest of the community; we've got to start somewhere.' The men agreed in principle but found many reasons why it couldn't be done. Their women were shy, they never left their homes and anyway, they had no English so what good would it do them to come to meetings? In that case, I told them, I'll go to them and teach them English in their homes. It was an offer they could hardly refuse and it was agreed that I start with Docrat's wife. I climbed the dark stairs to their airless flat and found a young, pretty woman, shy as a gazelle and as easily frightened. I'd never taught English before. Where should I start? I'd brought along some primary school readers and invited Mrs Docrat to repeat after me: 'The cat sat on the mat.' She regarded me fearfully and blankly. She was doing her best to humour me, as directed by her husband, but we weren't getting anywhere. I persevered for four or five lessons and then had to concede defeat. It was clear that Mrs Docrat was not thirsting for knowledge, she was acting out her role as an obedient Moslem wife and finding it very irksome. Maybe if I'd been a more skilful teacher I might have been more successful; as it was I decided to call it a day.

Apart from the emancipated, liberated Dr Goonam, we never did manage to enrol Indian women activists at our meetings — with the honourable exceptions of two, Dhanum, H. A.'s sister, and Kwela, the sister of M. D. Naidoo, no relation of H. A.'s. Dhanum and Kwela arrived one evening looking ill at ease in an environment that was foreign to any Indian woman. H. A.'s younger brother, Krishna, who had brought Dhanum to the meeting did his best to put the two young women at ease, introducing them to all of us and trying to include them in the banter which dried up as soon as they appeared and which anyway was in English, a language with which they were not at home. They sat with their hands in their laps, eyes downcast. The men, for their part, were equally uncomfortable. They were not used to socialising with Indian women and it was plain to see that their traditions and background were fighting their intellect and conscience. They realised that the least they could do now was to try to accept the strange visitors on an equal footing, but they didn't know how. I sat next to Dhanum and tried to reassure her but conversation was stilted. It was the same with Kwela.

I admired Krishna and M. D. for proving that it could be done. Indian women could, and should, be drawn into the movement, yet I could not help feeling sorry for Dhanum and Kwela who had, after all, been used as symbols. I thought that once having made the gesture they would not be seen again at meetings. To my delighted surprise both young women did return and took to accompanying us to trade union meetings and helping with the recruitment of Indian women workers. They spoke in a language the Indian factory workers could understand and with which they could identify. A few years later, during the big resistance campaigns, Indian women throughout the country emerged from their seclusion and proved every bit as courageous and determined as their men. All the pre-conceptions about the timorous little Indian woman, the housebound wife and mother, came up for serious re-appraisal when they went into battle against the bulwark of white domination.

Fervent Dawood Seedat rapidly found himself in trouble with the authorities. Protesting at the imprisonment of Pandit Nehru in India and of Yusuf Dadoo in Johannesburg, he waved his arms at a big public meeting and thundered, 'The British Empire is not an empire; it's a vampire.' What his pronouncement lacked in assonance it more than gained by its ringing political challenge. It soon became a popular slogan, chanted at many a subsequent meeting. Sedition charges followed – a serious crime in wartime – and it proved very difficult to find a lawyer to defend him.

Mr Goldberg was a Member of Parliament for the anglophile Dominion Party and a leading barrister in Pietermaritzburg where the case was to be heard. We called on him and asked him to defend Dawood. 'You expect me to defend a bunch of unpatriotic agitators?' he stormed at us. 'You insult me,' and he showed us the door. There were no non-white barristers in Natal and no white lawyer would take on the case. As a last resort we called on our Johannesburg comrades for help and they sent down Harry Bloom, a newly qualified barrister, dedicated to the cause and hungry for work. He brought with him his new bride, Beryl, vivacious, volatile, witty, somewhat overpowering but fun to have around. Harry won the case and H. A. persuaded the Blooms to settle in Durban. 'We'll have plenty of work for you,' he promised, and we did.

W HEN Mother announced that she could now manage on her own in the shop I did not rush back to Johannesburg as I'd been planning to do in the months before. Durban had become a good town to be in and it provided action, interest, excitement. So when I saw the advertisement for a 'Personal assistant/ model, able to work on her own initiative,' I applied and was given the job.

My new boss, °Mr Joel Brent, import/export agent in ladies' wear, required me to answer the telephone, write out invoices, make out price tags and type the occasional letter. Every now and then customers would visit the showrooms and I would be required to model the clothes, which I was quite happy to do, changing modestly behind a screen. Mr Brent was tall, bony, vulpine and he liked to pretend to pressing demands upon his time. He would rush in and out of the dingy showroom, mopping his brow and exclaiming at all the imaginary calls he had to deal with. Squeezing past my desk his hand would trail along the back of my chair and then, as if accidentally, linger on my arm, shoulder, neck. To complain would be to acknowledge that something sexual existed between us and that I found unpleasant and embarrassing. The mere touch of his fingers was repellent; if I pretended it did not exist, it would go away.

Then came the day when there were no customers and Mr Brent asked me to try on some new summer frocks, 'to see how they hang'. I changed and came out. 'Bend over a little,' he directed, 'I want to see how the length looks.' I obliged. 'No, no,' he called, 'turn your back to me. Now, bend over, more, more.' The horrible man was trying to look up my skirt! I cringed with shame. Straightening up, I rushed behind the screen and changed back into my own clothes. Grabbing my handbag, I ran out of the showroom, to the accompaniment of Mr Brent's whining complaint. 'What's the matter? You'd think I hurt her or something.' I felt angry and humiliated and couldn't bring myself to talk about it, certainly not to my parents.

I was reminded of the time, when, aged 12, I was sent to Pretoria to spend a holiday with our friends the °Mahlers. Mrs Mahler was Mother's good friend – they'd met on the *Watussi* coming over – and their son Dicky was my age. Dicky and I played chess, visited the bioscope and played together quite happily in the garden. One afternoon when the family had gone shopping and I was alone in the house, Dicky's father came home early from work and stretched out on the sofa, sighing noisily. 'Be a good girl and bring me a glass of cold water,' he asked. When I brought it to him he patted the sofa next to him and invited me to sit there. Reluctantly I obeyed but I jumped up and ran when I realised his hand was creeping up my skirt. It was a relief when my holiday ended and I could leave but I never spoke of this to anyone, feeling guilty and ashamed, as though I'd done something reprehensible.

THE only one I told of the humiliating incident with my boss was Gunther Rost, a man I'd met on the beach some weeks before. He offered to go and beat up Mr Brent but I dissuaded him. 'I just want to have nothing more to do with him,' I told Gunther. 'I'd like to forget about it.'

When I first met Gunther on the beach he'd made no pretence of interest in young Maurice who was with me that Sunday morning, slung, as usual, on my right hip. 'You're a girl I've been watching for a long time,' he announced coolly as he lowered himself beside me on the sand. 'I'd like to get to know you.' This was a challenge. His foreign accent and appearance intrigued me. He was old, at least ten years older than me, with balding high forehead, wispy blonde hair unfashionably long, jutting chin and cold, pale blue eyes; his straight, short nose seemed too small for a man. But it was his beautiful body which held the eye – tall, lean, tanned, with broad shoulders and narrow hips. I was not the only girl on the beach to find him attractive and that, of course, added to his charm. Soon he was telling me about his escape from Nazi Germany where his German mother and Jewish father still lived, his boring work as a house painter on a construction site, his interest in music and his contempt for this backward, uncultured, brash country. He it was who relieved me of my burdensome virginity and though he was considerate and kind and experienced, the process proved to be uncomfortably, unexpectedly painful. I was glad to have passed that milestone – I was now a more liberated woman. Virginity had typecast me in a role I resented and I felt that in shedding it I had asserted my rights not only as a woman but also as a human being. Later I was also very pleased to find that sexual intercourse, under Gunther's skilful guidance, improved with practice and could even be enjoyable.

A few weeks afterwards, when a letter arrived from Mike Stanley, enclosing a catalogue of diamond rings and inviting me to choose one as an engagement ring, it pleased me to inform him that as I was no longer a virgin I was presumably no longer eligible and no thank you, I would not marry him. Mother sighed with disappointment, 'He seems such a nice boy.' She meant particularly compared to Gunther whom she disliked and always referred to as '*that chazershe Daitch*'.

Gunther was lucky to have got out of Germany but his eyes grew misty with nostalgia when he remembered his childhood in Berlin. 'You South Africans are so crude,' he'd complain, 'you can't even peel an orange delicately.' And then he would demonstrate with what finesse his mother used to perform this simple task, slowly and with great deliberation, sectioning the skin into even parts, paring it, and then, while the patient family looked on, stripping it clean of every vestige of pith before dividing it evenly amongst them.

'But Gunther,' I'd protest, 'we have plenty of oranges here. There's no need to wait for mother to give you a bit; we can each have a whole one to ourselves.' I would then pick an orange from the sack, squeeze it and toss it and pummel it about and then, with great and noisy gusto, proceed to suck it through a hole in the skin which I'd made with my thumb. It pleased me to shock and annoy him, especially when I felt I was puncturing more than an orange; I was denting also his maudlin sentiments for Germany and all things German.

Gunther persisted in his efforts to 'educate' me and to raise my cultural level. When Richard Tauber arrived in Durban to give a concert, Gunther bought two tickets which were expensive, even though they were in the gallery. Himself swooning with delight, he demanded as we were leaving, 'Well, what did you think?' I was no music critic but I found the saccharine sentimentality of the Viennese catch in the throat as distasteful as too much sugar in a cup of tea. I knew about too much sweetness; had I not trained myself recently to do without any sugar in tea? It was part of my own personal war effort. 'I think he's passed his prime as a singer,' I pronounced loftily, thus managing with one blow to establish my cultural independence and to infuriate my escort.

Gunther disapproved of my political involvement. 'What have the non-Europeans got to do with you? Let them fight their own battles. Sure they have a case but it's their business, not yours.' This raised my hackles. 'It's a pity you Germans didn't concern yourselves a bit more when others were attacked by the Nazis, instead of turning a blind eye, pretending it wasn't your business.' 'I'll have you know,' Gunther answered, 'that my brother was a Social Democrat and he got his head bashed in at a demonstration in Berlin against the Nazis.'

We went camping in the Drakensberg and were ostracised by our fellow campers because we were the only unmarried couple to share a tent. This didn't prevent us from bathing naked under the waterfalls and exploring the breathtaking grandeur of the mountain range. Photography was Gunther's hobby and it absorbed more and more of his time. Naturally I became his model and we spent many hours in his makeshift studio, under the glaring arc lights, while he photographed me from all angles, standing up and lying down. One day Mother came across a batch of these nude studies in one of my drawers and she tore them into shreds. 'I've been married to your father for 20 years,' she stormed at me, 'and he's never seen me naked.' This was uncomfortably close to sex talk between my mother and me and it embarrassed both of us. We never referred to it again.

IT WAS Gunther who introduced me to Lesley de Villiers. 'She's a lovely girl,' he enthused. 'And she lives on her own in a flat in Broad Street. You two should get on well; she seems to share a lot of your ideas.' This was intriguing and made me impatient to meet her. When I did, she measured up to all my expectations. Here was a girl my age, living alone and independent, earning a living as a hairdresser but finding time to upholster her chairs, sew her curtains, create lampshades and paint pictures. No one in our home made things with their hands – one didn't count Mother's cooking and baking and sewing – that was just woman's work. Manual skill was despised and only intellect counted. Father couldn't change a fuse but he wrote poetry; Joe didn't know one end of a screwdriver from the other but he played an excellent game of chess. This was a legacy of the less attractive Jewish tradition, the Ghetto mentality which I despised, the Chasidic culture where women worked to support the men who spent their days and nights studying the holy scriptures.

I, who couldn't even cook, admired Lesley for all the qualities I lacked – her skills, her artistic ability, her independence, her good taste in decoration, make-up, clothes. It was in Lesley's flat that I first heard 'La ci darem la mano,' on her wind-up gramophone and it struck me as right and proper that this heavenly duet should always be associated in my mind with her. Lesley was not only skilful and beautiful and independent but it soon emerged that she did indeed have left-wing views.

'Where did you get them?' I demanded arrogantly, knowing how rare it was to find someone with my views among Natal whites. In this sphere at least I felt myself to be ahead of her. She didn't bridle at my assumptions of superiority but explained with great good humour how she had been influenced since childhood by her adored elder cousin, Jack Cope, whose handsome likeness decorated her dressing table. 'I'm going to marry him,' she assured me matter-of-factly, and a few years later she did.

Lesley soon became a popular member of our group, courted by quite a number of the fellows. We would gather in her flat, listen to music, drink wine and talk, talk, talk. Henry Woolfson was one of her many admirers. He would stand in the middle of the room, cigarette in outstretched hand, swaying on his heels and dropping ash on the carpet, his eyes half closed and an inane grin on his face. 'For goodness' sake, Henry,' Lesley would scold him irritably, 'can't you use an ashtray?' 'Oh, sorry,' Henry would mutter and reach for an ashtray but the next moment he was back on his heels, flicking ash on the floor.

D URBAN woke up one morning to find the sleepy streets alive with foreign men in uniform. They'd been disgorged by the troopships on their way to North Africa and India, re-fuelling and stocking up in Durban. The Australians hit town like a load of rockets, they were noisy, boisterous, and tough; short men with thick necks and big hats and a disconcerting readiness to pick a fight. They were as quick to smash up a bar as to empty a barrel of beer and suddenly girls weren't safe on the streets. We were warned not to go out alone with them; there were horror stories of girls who'd had their nipples bitten off on the beach at night by over-passionate Aussies. But all the same they were 'our boys' and white families vied with each other to entertain them at their homes and lavish good food and drink upon them.

As the ships came and went, we began to identify each national group by their appearance and behaviour. The New Zealanders were tall, lanky and courteous in a nice, old-fashioned way. The American sailors were somewhat overweight, rosy-cheeked and friendly, offering chewing gum and cigarettes to all who would take them. Among them were some Puerto Ricans, one of whom serenaded me on the beach one evening, accompanying himself with the plangent tones of his guitar. It was very romantic.

On every convoy there were one or more comrades, members of fraternal Communist Parties and all of them found their way to the Durban Party office to pay their respects. We made them welcome and entertained them. We loved this contact with the outside world and the feeling of universal brotherhood which it fostered.

When the British came, they took us by surprise. They were not one group but two, worlds apart. The officers were smartly uniformed, beautifully spoken with clear vowels and clipped consonants, and courtly manners to delight a girl's heart. In sad contrast the men were undersized, bandy-legged, had cheeks with pink spots denoting not health but the lack of it and wore spectacles with wire frames. They wandered around as if dazed by the sunshine and the abundance they saw around them. People told stories of how they'd refused butter at the homes of their hosts on the grounds that as they'd never tasted it before they did not wish to get used to something which they might never taste again. Their uniforms of baggy shorts and ill-fitting shirts hung limply on them, accentuating their poor build and sallow skins. These Brits produced the greatest number of Party members, including the Scots whose accents turned English into a foreign language. Among them were the most intelligent and stimulating comrades whose company we enjoyed enormously.

From these new arrivals a group of three friends presented themselves at the Party office. They attracted attention because they included an officer, an NCO and a private; it was most unusual to see officers and men mixing socially. We greeted them warmly and took them dancing, picnicking and sightseeing. All three were excellent company, regaling us with tales of the British class system as it operated in the army and of life in the British Isles. I liked them all but the sergeant won my total devotion. I soon imagined myself in love and agonised at the thought of him dying on some far-off battle-field without ever holding me in his arms. Had he asked me I would willingly have gone to bed with him, but he never did, maintaining always a fraternal, comradely attitude towards me.

After the convoy left Durban I began receiving affectionate, interesting letters from India where the troops now found themselves. The correspondence was stimulating and we kept it up for a long time but the letters came not from the sergeant but from the lieutenant.

In 1958, this story had a sequel. At a friend's house in London I met a comrade who'd been to Durban with the convoys during the war. Did he report to the Party office while in Durban? Naturally, he answered and then he went on to sing the praises of the wonderful comrades he'd met there and how good they were to him. Were you one of three, I asked, a private, a sergeant and a lieutenant who always went about together? Yes, he told me, he was the sergeant. And who did you meet in Durban? 'I can't remember all their names,' he said wistfully, 'but there was one girl I'll never forget. Her name was Pauline.' He looked at me without a trace of recognition. I was mortified. Had I aged so much? I didn't feel so changed! It didn't occur to me that despite his boast, his memory was possibly more impaired than my appearance.

M Y BROTHER Joe at 16 was undersized for his age, not robust or sporty but brainy and a quick learner. There is less than two years difference between us but I was always bigger, stronger and healthier. However, when it came to chess, Joe was the champion. It was a matter of family pride that Joe had played and almost beaten, the station-master at Hamburg during our stopover in that city – or so Mother claimed. Our train had just pulled in from Kovno and we were walking through the huge station on our way to the transit camp when nine-year-old Yossele saw two men playing chess, watched by a group of interested onlookers. He paused and joined them. One of the players, a large, jovial gentleman who later introduced himself as the station-master, inquired of Yossele whether he, too, played. Solemnly Yossele nodded that he did indeed play chess, whereupon the elderly gentleman invited him to a game. As the game progressed the kindly condescension of the onlookers for the little upstart from the East changed to grudging respect and when it ended the station-master congratulated Mother on having such a clever son, a real champion, he told her.

The little champion also had a lively imagination. When he disappeared one day from our flat in Kovno Mother searched for him frantically, and the neighbours joined in. One of them went down to the docks and was told that a child had indeed been seen, asking for his Dad. When Yossele was finally tracked down he was on board a river freighter, surrounded by puzzled sailors. He'd persuaded them that his Dad was also a sailor, dressed just like they were with pom-poms on their heads and they were trying to help him find the elusive father. The thought of a Jewish sailor became a source of great merriment in the neighbourhood; it was so bizarre that people wondered where the child had got the idea. 'Imagine that,' they chuckled. 'A Jewish *matroz.*'

Yossele was also a weak and sickly child. Before his fifth birthday he'd contracted rickets, measles, whooping cough, scarlet fever, diarrhoea, scabies, ringworm, tonsilitis . . . the list was endless. Mother always maintained that Yossele was the harbinger of all epidemics; he was the first to catch whatever disease appeared in the district and the last to rid himself of it. As if that were not enough, he was also prone to accidents. Hardly a day passed without Yossele falling, cutting himself on broken glass, tripping over stones. At four years old he had a serious accident, tumbling from a first-floor balcony on to a pile of builders' rubble. It happened when we'd been invited to the birthday party of our rich neighbour's son but by the time Mother had completed our toilettes – it was important to make a good impression – the party was over. The birthday boy opened the door, said 'You're too late,' and was about to bang it shut when his mother took pity on us, invited us in and gave each of us a glass of milk and a slice of cake. As soon as we'd finished they bundled us into our coats and led us outside. We were both subdued and a little sad as we made our way to the outside staircase for the party had not lived up to our great expectations. Yossele trailed his hand along the banister and then he stopped to gaze idly into the distance. I stood beside him and suddenly, to my great amazement, I saw my little brother hurtling through space, turning somersaults in the air as he made his downward descent. He'd found a gap between the uprights and managed with an effort to squeeze himself through them. 'If I jump after him,' I remember wondering, 'could I reach the bottom before he does and catch him?' Before I could decide, Yossele landed with a sickening thump on the stones and broken tiles below and he lay there as if dead. Then a big tumult arose. Neighbours came running, women were wailing and my mother pushed her way through the crowd. She snatched my little brother up in her arms and carried him inside. The doctor was summoned. He examined Yossele and then turned to Mother who was watching in grim silence: 'Frau Podbrez,' he said, 'you are an intelligent woman, I won't try to deceive you. I'm afraid this child is not going to recover. The best thing you can do is to go for a walk; when you return it will all be over.' He then took his fee and left.

Mother didn't answer. She looked round at the cluster of pitying neighbours crowding our living room and said, 'Please go away.' She shushed them out and closed the door. Then she drew the curtains, pulled up a chair beside the unconscious Yossele and took his limp little hand in hers.

As usual, Father was working out of town and in the age before the telephone, there was no way of reaching him; she and I were alone in the house. I crouched on the floor beside the bed, not knowing why I had to be silent but certain that I should be. We sat and waited in the darkening gloom, Mother and I. My limbs grew stiff and cramped but I remained immobile; I understood that no matter what happened I must not distract my mother from her vigil. She was holding Yossele's hand, gazing unblinkingly at his pallid face, pouring her own life force into his inert little body, forcing him to recover, willing him to live. And then the miracle happened. After what semed to me many hours Yossele fluttered his eyelids, sighed, opened his eyes and looked at Mother.

'I'm hungry,' he announced as he tried to raise himself. Mother sat up and took a long, deep breath. This was the Yossele she knew and loved, the child who was always hungry, who would try to snatch food from boiling pots if he weren't constantly watched. Together with his pot-belly and spindly arms and legs, this was another symptom of his disease. The neighbours streamed back into the house and marvelled. Those who believed in God praised Him and offered thanks. The doctor admitted that he could not explain how a body that seemed to be on the brink of death could suddenly return to life. Mother was utterly exhausted, drained of all emotion. Later it was established that Yossele had damaged his lungs in his fall but he would live.

When Yossele turned five Mother enrolled him in my school where I was already an old girl. On the first day of the new term she dressed him in his new sailor suit and put him in my charge. 'Be careful crossing the road,' she directed. 'When you get there take him to his class and leave him with the teacher.' I resented this extra responsibility, which impinged on my freedom and restricted my movement, but there was nothing for it; I had to take him. When we reached school I handed him over to his new teacher with great relief and made for my own classroom where I settled down to enjoy the lesson. My pleasure was shortlived. Soon there was a knock on our classroom door and a child came in and whispered in our teacher's ear. She beckoned me over. 'Yossele's teacher wants you; you'd better go over.' In Yossele's classroom I was confronted by my little brother looking miserable and smelling badly. 'There's been a slight accident,' his teacher told me. 'You'd better take him home.' In a fury I dragged him through the streets of Kovno wishing he would disappear. We reached home and I banged on our door. 'Mummy, Mummy, look what he's done,' I cried when she opened the door. Yossele continued to suck his thumb but managed to speak. 'Please, Mum,' he whimpered, 'it wasn't me.'

Yossele's fantasy world could be maddening but it could also entice me into realms which I, in my more practical frame of mind, might not have reached. When we changed clothes and emerged dressed in each other's garments our parents and their friends laughed at us in hearty encouragement. He became an engaging little girl and I was transformed into a boisterous young male. I enjoyed the chance to strut around in trousers, hands in pocket, jaunty cap on head. It seemed to confer a sense of freedom denied to skirt-wearers.

Once, when Yossele was four and we were living in a little *shtetl* whose name I've long forgotten, Mother developed a high fever – a most unusual occurrence. I remember our isolation for we seemed to have no neighbours, there was just Mother, Yossele and me. It was a primitive existence, the three of us in one room and in the middle a tub which Mother filled by drawing pails of water from the well outside. On Friday nights when it was bath time her journeys to and from the well seemed endless; then came the steamy wait for the water to heat. We had no way of guessing that this kind of life was hard on Mother not even when we both developed chicken pox or measles and Mother, alone and unaided, nursed us through it. We accepted without question that this was how people lived. But when, exhausted, she took to her bed and seemed unable to lift her head, we took fright. Yossele looked at her flushed face and turned to me, 'I think she's going to die,' he announced. 'Let's run away.' Long after Mother recovered she would relate this story with wry amusement. 'That's children for you!'

Now in Durban aged 16, still undersized but indomitable, Joe came home from school one day and announced that he was going to join up. 'You're crazy,' Mother screamed at him. 'You're a schoolboy, you've got to take your exams.' But Joe wouldn't budge. 'I'm not going back to school. I'm joining the air force.' Mother cried and pleaded. 'Berl gave up eight years of his life in the first war; must you risk your life in this one? Haven't I suffered enough in these wretched wars already?' She swore that she would never sign his permission form without which he would not be accepted, being under-age. Joe remained mute, stubborn, determined. Father withdrew from the argument. I could see his dilemma. This was a war to be supported, Fascism had to be defeated and this could only be done if men fought – hadn't he said so at the Left Book Club meeting? So how could he discourage his son from volunteering? Some 35 years earlier Father had gone for a soldier even when he didn't believe in the justice of the cause; how then could he tell Joe not to fight now when justice was so clearly on our side? Yet Joe was still so young, so vulnerable, so lacking in experience! Mom turned to me. 'Tell him,' she commanded, 'tell him what a silly young fool he is. Tell him he's got time, next year, perhaps, after his exams.'

'I know it's hard, Mom,' I told her. 'But you've got to let him go. You've got to sign his form; he's made up his mind.' After a great deal more anguish and tears Mother eventually gave her reluctant permission and Joe signed on for the S.A. Air Force where he became a radio operator.

Joe served in North Africa and flew regularly in the shuttle service from Cape to Cairo. He was lucky to escape the series of crashes over Central Africa which plagued this route. When his letters home were delayed Mother would turn on me. 'You sent him to his death,' she would accuse me dramatically and unjustly. But what if he did die? Could I live with that? 'Another Crash Over Jibouti,' the headlines screamed as I left the office. Glancing over the shoulder of the man in front of me in the bus queue I peered at the list of victims printed on the front page. I had to know but could not bring myself to get the newspaper – I could not bear the possibility of seeing Joe's name there. How sorry I felt for the sisters and mothers and wives of the men whose names were on that list. How thankful I was not to see my brother's name among them.

When the war ended and Joe returned, I could hardly recognise him. The sickly, scrawny youth of four years earlier had become transformed into a tall, broad-shouldered young man, good looking and self-confident, smartly turned out in his well pressed sergeant's uniform. He became a foundation member of the Springbok Legion, the militant ex-servicemen's organization, and played an active role in it. I hated to admit it but the air force had made a new man of him!

O N THE corner of West and Grey Streets stood a derelict building which used to be a shop a long time before but was now unused and seemingly unusable. We tracked down the Indian landlord who was quite happy to let us use the first floor for a moderate rent: he didn't mind to what use we put it. We all set to with pails and brushes, clearing out the cockroaches, sweeping and scrubbing the floors, washing whatever windows remained, and then erecting thin partitions to provide offices for the mushrooming number of trade unions. I was now working as secretary in the Durban office of the Trades and Labour Council where Errol Shanley was my boss. Our offices off Smith Street were not too far from the corner of West and Grey Streets and after I finished work at the TLC I would hurry over to the new offices to help in any way I could – and to be near H.A. Like everyone else I took a hand at clerical work, interviewing, typing, cyclostyling, dealing with telephone calls. It was busy, exciting, exhilarating.

At its centre, calm, reliable and ever courteous, was H.A. He was never too busy to listen to problems and he never complained of overwork or stress. My admiration for him grew by the day. We begged and borrowed desks, chairs and filing cabinets and as new unions were formed so the space was divided and sub-divided to accommodate each newcomer. Overnight, it seemed, were born trade unions for cigar and tobacco workers, bus drivers, workers in the chemical, tin, shoe and leather, and rubber industries, jewellers and many more. An endless stream of workers, mainly Indian, came knocking on our doors, pleading to be organized, wanting to be unionised. Their first choice for secretary or chairman was inevitably H.A. or, if not him, then Ponnen. If neither of these two was available then it had to be someone endorsed by them. They knew, they said, that these were men who could stand up to their bosses and who would not divert the union funds into their own pockets.

As the weeks went by every available comrade was drawn in: Mannie Pelz, Docrat, Seedat, Shanley, M.P. Naicker, P.M. Harry, Wilson Cele, R.R. Pillay, M.K. Moodley, Alec Wanless, Gladman Nxumalo. Not all were Communist Party members but they worked closely with us. H.A. was secretary of the biggest and most important Sugar Workers' Union, and he also became chairman or advisor to most of the new unions. His task in organising the Natal sugar workers, scattered as they were up and down the province, was formidable enough, but he broke new ground by including the field workers as well, and that in South Africa, was a milestone in trade unionism. I would often accompany him and his organiser/driver as we visited the branches on Sundays in the battered old jalopy belonging to the union. Word had been sent that H.A. would be coming and a crowd waited as we drove into Illovo, Rossburgh, Isipingo or any of the other sugar-growing areas of Natal. When addressing the agricultural workers H.A. needed an interpreter to translate his words into Tamil and his driver/organiser performed this task as well. The audience regarded him with awe and reverence, they drank in his words. He was the first man ever to concern himself about their miserable wages and appalling living conditions. Child labour was common on the estates and sick leave or annual holidays unknown. On one estate a woman invited us into her home for tea. We crouched down low to enter a cave where the family lived. A rag curtain served for a door and there were no windows. The only decoration on the wall was a picture of H.A. Naidoo, cut out of a newspaper.

One afternoon, running up the stairs, I passed a group of dejected-looking Africans. They had listened to H.A. explaining apologetically that he could not himself undertake to organize another union — both he and Ponnen had their hands full with their present commitments, but he promised that he would see what he could do to help. Their disappointment was plain to see. They'd come here full of hope that at last something could be done to improve their lives. These were men at the bottom rung of the urban ladder, workers in the distributive trade who were at the beck and call of every shop girl or office boy, no matter how junior, provided they were white. They were employed in carrying, fetching, packing, delivering, making tea — men without whose labour the shops and offices could not survive. But no matter how diligent and responsible they were, their hopes of advancement were nil and they earned whatever it pleased the boss to pay them. They were subject to instant dismissal at the boss's whim and they lacked any legal entitlement to paid holidays or sick leave. These men had never belonged to any trade union before but now they too had caught a whiff of the exciting new militancy, the fresh wind sweeping through Natal, and they wished to become part of this liberating force.

The Africans left, arranging to return the following day, and H.A. turned to me. 'You know, Pauline, there's no reason why you shouldn't undertake the job.' I accepted the fact that he'd turned to me by default — no one else was available — but I didn't mind. At eighteen, to be entrusted with such an important task by no less a man than H.A. filled me with pride. 'Do you really think I could do it?' 'You've been with us long enough to see how we work,' he said, 'and you did pretty well when you spoke to the milliners.' The week previously I'd been asked to join H.A. in addressing the inaugural meeting of these women workers and we'd succeeded in enrolling nearly everyone present. 'But not so well with the dock workers,' I replied and we both laughed at the memory of my unsuccessful attempt to win over the African dock workers.

A month earlier a message reached us in the office of the Trades and Labour Council that the African dockers had come out on strike. We knew they were not union members and we felt we should offer them assistance. Both Errol Shanley and H.A. were fully occupied so they suggested I go down with an interpreter. 'Just find out what's happening and offer them help,' H.A. told me. 'We could assist with negotiations or collect money. I'm sure they're short of funds.'

When my interpreter and I reached the dock area we found a group of Zulus sprawled on the grass verges. We motioned them to gather round. 'Tell them,' I said, 'that I have a message for them from the trade unions in Durban.' The dockers remained where they were; they did not choose to gather round. Not discouraged, I climbed to the top of a hillock and proceeded to address them. One of the older Africans stood up. 'Tell the white woman,' he instructed the interpreter, 'that if she has anything to say she should tell it to our leaders.'

'Where are your leaders?' I asked and was told that they were in the administrative office, negotiating with the port authorities. 'That's all right,' I said, confident that they could not help but be interested in what I had to say. 'We'll wait for them and while we're waiting I'll tell you how we'd like to help.' To my dismay a number of the men shifted their positions to face the other way and turned their backs to me. 'I'm not trying to tell you what to do,' I pleaded. 'I want to offer to collect funds for you. All strikers are short of money.' If only I can get it across to them, I thought; I was sure it was just a question of making myself understood. Why should anyone refuse such a disinterested offer as I was bringing?

One of the men stood up. He didn't look at me, he spoke to the interpreter. 'Tell the white woman to go away,' he said. 'We know that the government has sent its men to the war so now they are using women spies.' I became desperate. 'But I'm not a government spy, I'm a trade unionist,' I pleaded. My interpreter tugged at my sleeve. 'I think we'd better go,' he muttered, 'their mood is turning ugly.'

I looked around for help and suddenly saw, in the road above me, Comrade Philemon Tsele, secretary of the African Railway Workers. Here was a friend who could vouch for me; we'd been to many meetings together; he knew I was no spy. Philemon sat high in his railway cart, driving a pair of dray horses and puffing away at a clay pipe.

'Philemon, Philemon,' I called to him and waved, 'tell these people that you know me. Tell them who I am.' Philemon looked at me, then turned his gaze on the men on the grass and without a word leaned forward in his seat, whipped up his horses and disappeared down the road.

'If you don't leave immediately,' my interpreter said, 'I'll go on my own, but I warn you, there's going to be trouble.' Reluctantly I joined him in our ignominious retreat. What, I wondered, had I done wrong? Why was I so inept? It didn't occur to me that no matter what I'd said or done, the dockers would not have trusted me or any other white. I returned to the office and reported on my failure.

Soon afterwards the strike was broken and the men were forced back to work. They did gain a shilling a day extra, but that only brought their daily rate to five shillings, still a starvation wage. Then we read in the papers that Zulu Pungula, their leader, had been arrested. He was kept in gaol for a month, found guilty of contravening the Riotous Assemblies Act, and deported from Durban for the duration of the war. It emerged that Pungula had been warned before. The Native Commissioner had called him in during the strike and threatened: 'If you don't send the workers back, we'll sack the lot of you.' Pungula had replied: 'It is funny the way you white men think. If your wife tells you that her children are cold and hungry because she has no money, do you kick your wife out and take a new wife?'

I WAS both pleased and frightened by H.A.'s suggestion that I organise the African distributive workers. I was thrilled by his confidence in me but also nervous of failure. 'Of course I'll help whenever you need me,' he said, 'but the responsibility must be yours.' I didn't have to think long. This was a challenge which I could not ignore. 'I'll try,' I told him. When the workers returned the next day H.A. introduced me as the prospective secretary. They looked uncomfortable but were too polite to express their disquiet. It was easy to read their thoughts. To have a woman secretary! And not even a woman – a mere girl! It could be interpreted as a slight on their manhood, a denigration of their self-esteem, a complete break with tradition and custom. They sought some reassurance, some saving grace. 'Will you be our chairman, Comrade Naidoo?' H.A. guessed at their dilemma and agreed to stretch himself just that extra bit more. 'I'll be your acting chairman until you have your elections and appoint one of yourselves,' he told them. They went into a huddle and exchanged some rapid words in undertones. Then their spokesman turned to H.A. and addressed him gravely, with hardly a glance in my direction. 'So be it. We will do our best to help the young woman.' And so the African Commercial and Distributive Workers' Union was born in Durban.

°Benson was a delivery 'boy' who had come with the deputation and acted as their interpreter. He agreed to give up his job and work for the union full-time. We undertook to make up his weekly wage from contributions amongst ourselves until the union was established on a sound financial basis. In the months that followed we worked with the dedicated energy that a good cause demands and gets. We composed leaflets in English and Zulu, cut stencils, cyclostyled them on the manual duplicator and then went out to distribute them to the African workers in shops and offices. We waylaid them as they left work in the evenings, and approached them when they walked out at lunch time to buy their bun and lemonade at the corner shops, taking care to keep out of sight of the boss and his henchmen. We learnt how to avoid being chased off company premises or having our leaflets snatched out of our hands and torn up. I became quite adept at standing on soap-boxes, gathering groups around me, explaining, haranguing, persuading workers to organize, organize, organize. I also learnt to ignore the taunts, jeers and occasional threats of white passers-by who couldn't or wouldn't believe that any good could come from a white girl talking to 'kaffirs' in the street. My African audiences would greet me first with incredulity and then, as the message got through, with enthusiasm and support.

When we called the inaugural meeting of the union the large hall we'd booked for the event was filled to overflowing. I sat on the dais and watched in relief as the hall began to fill up. I had hardly dared hope that our leaflets inviting workers to attend would receive such large-scale response. The hard wooden benches were soon fully occupied but still they kept coming – men in their overalls, worn and hungry after a long day's work but even more hungry for the possibility of change. And always the seated men would shuffle up a little more to make room for the newcomers. The acting chairman Comrade H. A. Naidoo, then stood up to address the meeting. He was greeted with a burst of applause. We'd come to expect this from the Indian workers but how gratifying that the Africans, too, were now accepting him as their own. Here at last was non-European unity between the Zulus and the Indians. For years we had urged united action between the two groups: don't let tribal, racial or religious differences divide you we had pleaded and now, at last, our slogans were springing into life! H. A. spoke clearly and with great deliberation, pausing every few minutes to have his words translated into Zulu. He explained that a trade union is only as strong as its members make it; he stressed the need for unity and for active participation by the members in all its affairs and decision-making. He urged them to prepare for struggles ahead and to stand firm in support of just demands. His remarks were heard with intense concentration and followed by enthusiastic clapping. Then came the elections. °Comrade Nathan Dhlomo, a grave and dignified man in his fifties whose grey hair and lined face added years to his appearance, was elected chairman. On the committee were representatives of most of the big stores. Then it was my turn and when I was elected secretary we were all conscious of breaking new ground. They, the workers, were demolishing old traditions by placing their trust in a woman who was young and white; I, for my part, was accepting responsibility in a post that was new and challenging; all of us were launching out on untried paths.

Our union consisted of members who were mostly illiterate and their experience of industry, commerce and indeed of city life, was brief and undoubtedly confusing. I anticipated many problems in explaining the mechanics of a union constitution which I myself was still swotting up. Like all our unions, this was based on the constitutions operating in the old, established craft unions and it was as democratic, rigid and formalised as theirs. But while theirs were subject to scrutiny by the officials of the Department of Labour and had by law to conform to the provisions of the Industrial Conciliation Act, we adopted these constitutions voluntarily. Although our union was not recognised as a legal union in terms of the Act because Africans were not considered to be 'employees', we nevertheless undertook to abide by all the provisions of the Act even though many of these rules were formal and foreign to the experience of our members. We struggled with the minutiae in the conviction that they embraced guarantees of democracy. The chairman regarded me quizzically as I explained that not only had resolutions to be proposed and seconded but so also must amendments. I expounded on the need to take amendments before the resolution, with the last amendment first. I pointed out that an amendment might change a motion but should not negate it: if it did the chairman must advise the proposer to vote against the main resolution. There was more. A financial report must be submitted to every meeting, showing itemised and proven receipts, payments, cash in hand and cash at the bank. There was a right way and a wrong way of drawing these up; certain lines had to be drawn, horizontally and vertically. All cheques had to be signed by the secretary and counter-signed by the treasurer; petty cash expenditure had to be accompanied by signed slips. What constitutes a point of order? Who appoints the tellers? These and other intricacies of constitutional procedure and financial management had to be mastered by my committee and myself. But whereas I, at least, had some apprenticeship in these arts, my committee members had none; to them the concepts were new and strange and so was the terminology. But, before long, the treasurer was presenting meticulously drawn-up statements of receipts and payments and dealing confidently with questions arising therefrom. The chairman was soon controlling meetings with easy mastery and found no problem in having his rulings accepted as fair and just. It seemed an effortless transition from the traditional Zulu *indaba* to the democracy of a union meeting.

What did surprise me was the injection into union business of traditional Zulu courtesy and good manners. It opened a window into the culture of my fellow-countrymen that I knew nothing about. I doubt that many of my white compatriots had any more inkling than I of this aspect of Zulu life. In accordance with Zulu tradition every contribution from the floor – which had to be translated of course – was preceded by words of praise and appreciation for the officials even when it went on to make firm proposals for a different course of action from those proposed by them. Meetings which elsewhere lasted two or three hours here continued far into the night. Precedence was always given to age and it was the oldest who spoke first and who were listened to with respect and attention. But everyone had to be heard with courtesy and patience no matter how long he spoke. How rude and crude and ugly the whites must have seemed to these people who were never addressed in offices, workshops, homes or in the street except as 'Hey you, boy' or 'Jim'.

The Industrial Conciliation Act regulated the functions, obligations and rights of registered trade unions. When a union was strong enough to negotiate with employers, the Act provided for the establishment of an Industrial Council for the industry. These Boards consisted of an equal number of representatives of workers and employers who could then become self-governing and employ their own inspectors to ensure that the wages and conditions laid down by the Board were adhered to. White, Indian and coloured workers could take advantage of these provisions because they were 'legal'; Africans could not. They were specifically excluded from the Act which stated that 'pass bearing natives' (and all African males had to carry passes) were not covered by the definition of 'employee' in the Act. This ensured that industrially, as well as politically, Africans were deprived of any say in their affairs. The powerful, white, established unions like the miners, printers, engineers, boilermakers, were among the staunchest in upholding and maintaining this status quo. That meant that black workers were excluded from union membership and were not represented on the industrial councils. A registered union might present demands for a reasonable rate for the Africans but when it came to the bargaining these were the groups who were the first to be sacrificed in return for higher rates for the whites. So the African Commercial and Distributive Workers' Union which was self-reliant and not subservient to any other union was an exciting, exhilarating venture. We were not 'legal' so we had to be strong. We could not rely on the provisions of the industrial legislation to force employers to the bargaining table; we had to wrest recognition from them through our own strength.

A few years later, in Cape Town, when I was National President of the Sweet Workers Union of South Africa, my union challenged the Minister of Labour in a court action over the definition of 'employee' in the Industrial Conciliation Act. Like most legal arguments, this action depended on a fine linguistic quibble. If only 'pass bearing natives' were excluded from the Industrial Conciliation Act, then, we argued, African women could not only join registered trade unions but could also form them because – at that time – African women did not have to carry passes. It was a great triumph when we won the case but it was short-lived. In 1956 the Minister of Native Affairs introduced a new law extending the pass laws to African women. The struggle against this detested law led to one of the biggest and most bitter anti-government campaigns in S.A.'s bloody history. Not for the first time African women proved what a force they could be. 'When you touch the women, you hit rock, you have dislodged a boulder; you will be crushed,' they said and sang and shouted as they turned out in their thousands to defy the government. The struggle continued until the pass laws were abolished in 1986.

The African Commercial and Distributive Workers' Union grew so rapidly that I had to give up my job in the TLC to become its full-time secretary. We moved into our own office on the first floor of a West Street building and every morning, as I arrived at 8.30 to open up, a line of men, stretching down to the pavement, would be waiting patiently to join or to report on unfair treatment of one kind or another.

'Mr D —, I have here your employee, Martin, and he tells me that you dismissed him without paying him a week's notice money'

'Who are you? What's it got to do with you?'

'This is the Union of African Commercial and Distributive Workers and . . .' Slam goes the receiver. I try again.

'Mr D —, if you don't listen to me and pay Martin his week's notice pay . . .'

'Oh yes, what will you do?'

'I'll call your staff out on strike, day after tomorrow. Do you think it's worth it?' A pause.

'Tell him to come here and collect his bloody pay.'

Not all complaints were so easy to settle. Many bosses called my bluff and we were in no position yet to flex our muscles. Our membership was growing rapidly but we had a long way to go before we could bargain with employers on anything like an equal footing. In the meantime I tried where possible to enrol the assistance of inspectors from the Department of Labour in cases where existing labour laws were being flagrantly flouted, in respect of safety, overcrowding, sanitation – and to establish some kind of contact with the Durban Chamber of Commerce.

The Secretary of the Chamber of Commerce spoke suavely: 'We don't have to talk to you, Miss Podbrey. Your union has no legal standing whatsoever.' 'That is true, but we have a lot of members and there's nothing to stop your employers from negotiating with us and maintaining peace in the industry. We're only asking for a reasonable standard of living and fair conditions.'

'But of course, Miss Podbrey, that's what we all want and what we have, by and large. There are always a few bad apples in every barrel, ha ha ha.'

Recruiting became more difficult. Employers would lock their workers in the yard at lunch-times, post their guards to intimidate our leaflet distributors, threaten their workers and sack men who were suspected of acting as shop stewards. Despite all this our membership continued to grow and workers would queue to enrol and to pay their subscriptions.

The line of workers outside our office was longer than usual one day in September 1942 and I was sitting with my head down, trying to deal as expeditiously as possible with one complaint after another. Then I became aware of a presence, of shuffles and murmurs among the waiting men and it became clear that someone important had arrived. I looked up to see an older man of less than medium height, carrying a knobkerrie, slowly enter the office. The men in the queue drew aside to let him pass and I stood up to greet him although I'd never set eyes on him before. There was no mistaking the aura of leadership which enveloped the newcomer, Zulu Pungula, the exiled leader of the dock workers who had been banished from Durban and who now came to visit me. Calmly and with great dignity he introduced himself and explained, through the interpreter, that although he was banned from Durban, he felt he had to come and see me, to apologise for the behaviour of the dockers during their recent strike.

'I too thought you were a Government agent,' he told me, 'I couldn't believe that any other kind of white woman would concern herself with our fate. Since then, in Zululand, word has reached me of the work you are doing and I see now that we were wrong.'

It was the first of many meetings I had with Zulu Pungula in my office; he would appear unannounced, question me closely, and talk for hours on end. 'Aren't you worried that you might be arrested if you're found in Durban?' I asked him. 'No Zulu would betray me,' he replied, 'and to the whites I'm invisible, just another native.'

When H. A. met Pungula he was inspired to revive his neglected artistic skill and to draw a fine portrait of the Zulu leader. This was later published in *The Guardian*. In July 1948 Zulu Pungula returned openly to Durban and announced that he was forming a trade union for African dockers. He was received with jubilation.

IT WAS a hot, steamy, late afternoon and I was sitting in H.A.'s office watching Ponnen next door as he bent over his desk, humming tunelessly and drawing lines in his ledger. 'Why are you wasting your time?' H. A. asked him, not for the first time. 'You can buy a ledger with the lines already printed in it.' In reply Ponnen smiled his usual sweet smile, dipped his pen in the inkstand, and carefully traced a neat line in the book. To see Ponnen absorbed in his pointless occupation and to hear H. A. tease him about it had become a regular office entertainment. That day an unusual event occurred. A strange white woman walked in unannounced and flopped unceremoniously into a chair.

'My name's Vera Albert,' she announced as she looked about her. Her black eyes regarded us without surprise, as though she had expected to find everything just so, or – which seemed more likely – as though she had trained herself never to betray curiosity. Her thin, sharp features and sallow skin were clearly not South African; they betrayed a lack of sunshine and air. But what stamped her even more a stranger was her extraordinary outfit. On this humid, Durban day when the rest of us wore our coolest, thinnest cottons, Vera appeared in a tailored tweed suit with a mannish hat to match, a satin long-sleeved blouse and a pair of thick, brown leather gloves. Even more extraordinary were her shoes. These were not – where one might expect to see them – on her feet, but in her hands, as casually carried as her handbag. On her feet were her silk stockings, tattered and shredded.

'Did you walk down West Street in your stockinged feet?' I blurted out. 'Oh yes,' she was nonchalant. 'My feet hurt so I took my shoes off.' We were embarrassed but Vera wasn't.

She told us that she had just stepped off the boat from England and come straight to us: someone in Cape Town had given her our address. No, she had nowhere to stay and she knew no one in Durban. 'I'm a comrade from London,' she announced and she was right in assuming that this entitled her to our friendship and concern. We took it for granted that visiting comrades had to be looked after; we'd hosted many such visitors from the foreign convoys. But whereas the British, American, Australian or New Zealand comrades came for short visits – while their boats anchored in the harbour – Vera looked set to stay.

She kept glancing at Ponnen as she spoke and he, shy, modest, kind, responded diffidently. 'I could put up an extra bed in my room,' he volunteered, 'but it's rather cramped and not very comfortable.' And so it was settled. Vera moved in with Ponnen and a few months later they married. They found a flat in an Indian block where their two daughters were later born. Vera didn't wear a sari and although she was the only white woman in this Indian area, she merged into its way of life. It turned out to be a stable and durable marriage – Vera volatile, mercurial, intense; Ponnen phlegmatic, solid, dependable, and kind. They made a good couple.

HARRY Rubens, rotund, beetle-browed and red faced, scowled at me whenever we met. He lost no opportunity of finding fault with my opinions, my minute-keeping, my general demeanour. It helped a lot that the comrades I liked and admired always rose to my defence but I failed to understand why this older, authoritative comrade should pursue this vendetta against me. It came to a head when at a full meeting of the Durban Party Harry stabbed a finger at me and accused me of endangering security by associating with 'that suspicious German character, Gunther'. Nor did he stop there. He elaborated on his dark innuendoes by pointing out that someone like me, privy to the inner Party secrets, had no right to associate with spies, pro-Nazis, dangerous characters. The comrades shifted uneasily in their seats and when the tirade ended someone proposed and another seconded that a sub-committee be set up to investigate and report on Comrade Pauline's association with Gunther. It was put to the vote and carried and Comrade H. A. Naidoo was appointed chairman of the sub-committee. What the comrades didn't know was that by now H. A. and I were drawn to each other in a more than comradely attraction. I was already seeking ways to end my liaison with Gunther but every time I tried to tell him so he'd either storm and rage or beg and plead and I found both responses hard to cope with. But I was not going to share this secret with the Party, not when confronted with such vile accusations. I considered Gunther to be cynical and over-critical but, heavens, certainly not a pro-Nazi spy!

I watched with growing admiration how H. A. conducted the enquiry, with what even-handed detachment he questioned and cross-examined Harry, me and every one else who wished to speak. After serious deliberation the sub-committee reported back that there was no basis for Harry's accusations and it recommended that the matter be dropped. Comrade Pauline was free to pursue her own affairs without interference. Soon after Harry dropped out of the Party and we saw him no more. Why had he attacked me so, I asked H. A. 'It's quite obvious,' he told me. 'The man was madly jealous.'

Gunther refused to accept that he and I were finished. He took a day off work and cycled to Clairwood where H.A. had his Sugar Workers' office. He embarrassed H.A. with his abject pleas, but he also evoked his pity. 'He begged me,' H.A. later told me, 'to give you up. "She's my girl," he claimed.' 'What did you tell him?' I asked. 'I explained to him,' H.A. answered, 'that it's not for us to bargain over you. The decision must be yours.' Soon afterwards Gunther finally accepted the break-up. He packed his bags and left Durban.

O N MONDAY 31 March, 1941 I walked into the Liberal Study Group to work on our weekly magazine and found an atmosphere of extraordinary excitement. 'Have you heard the news?' Seedat buttonholed me and without waiting for a reply announced triumphantly, 'Indira Nehru is in town.' The future prime minister of India, travelling with a group of students, was returning to India from England and, because the Suez Canal was closed, she had to travel round the Cape of Good Hope, stopping at Durban on the way. Her father, Jawaharlal Nehru, was imprisoned in India for opposing the war; so was our Johannesburg comrade and leader of the Transvaal Indians, Dr Yussuf Dadoo. But the Natal leadership of the Indian Congress was supporting the war effort and Sorabjee Rustomjee was actively recruiting for the segregated South African army. So when Rustomjee and A.I. Kajee tried to arrange a reception for Indira Nehru, she snubbed them. Instead she turned to H.A. and his comrades in the anti-war opposition. This was a great coup for the young guard of the Nationalist Bloc. They set about trying to arrange a mass meeting in the Gandhi Hall, the traditional meeting place of the Durban Indian community, but the old, discredited leaders refused to let the hall to them. 'In that case,' H.A. said, 'we'll go for an even bigger hall and book the Avalon Cinema.' It turned out to be one of the biggest public gatherings of Durban Indians ever held. By 5.45 p.m. on Wednesday 2 April, the Avalon was packed to capacity as H.A. took the chair and introduced the daughter of India's famous leader. Mahatma Gandhi's son, Manilal who was editor of the Natal paper *Indian Opinion* had until then been ambivalent about his attitude to the war. Indira's arrival and the warmth of her reception convinced him to join the young Turks. He made an impassioned anti-war speech as did Ismail Meer and D.A. Seedat who was then on bail.

Among the group accompanying Indira was Phiroz Gandhi who was to become her future husband, and also the brilliant Chandra Gupta who, it was rumoured, wrote Indira's speeches. The unexpected arrival of these people was like a gust of fresh air; it linked us to the liberation struggle of the world beyond our borders from which we had too long been isolated. Everyone was agog to see and hear our visitors, to rub shoulders with the famous, the sophisticated, the men and women from the world stage. But my heroine among the visitors was Parvathi Kamaramangulam. Like Indira, she too came of a high caste Indian family and both her parents also were in prison for resisting the British Raj. During her years at Oxford University and before that at her public school her English guardians were the banking family, the Montagu Normans, at whose country estate she and her brothers spent their holidays. It was here that she met our own General Smuts, another family friend of the Montagu Normans. She had us in gales of laughter as she mimicked General Smuts, trying to be nice to all the dark little faces around the breakfast table, doing his best to hide his discomfiture at such unusual proximity to young Indians. She may have been unfair to the General but she was certainly entertaining. She told us how, when their ship docked at Cape Town, General Smuts had sent his limousine and chauffeur to take her round the Peninsula, apologising for his inability to accompany her. 'And so I couldn't report at the Party office there as I'd planned to do,' she told us. Parvathi and Indira were the only two women in the party of students and the contrast between them could not have been more marked. Parvathi sparkled; Indira drooped. Parvathi was witty, sophisticated, beautiful; Indira was pale, listless and not a great conversationalist. Having just read Pandit Nehru's letters from prison to this his daughter, I was tempted to wonder whether she appreciated them as much as I did.

On the night before their departure Dr Monty Naicker threw a party for them at his house. As usual at Indian gatherings, the girls were greatly outnumbered by the men. Unlike most Indian parties, there was music and drink and dancing and I was swept into one dance after another. Trying to recover my breath between a foxtrot and a polka I overheard one young man telling another, 'Trust H. A. to win the lady. Did you see them? They've gone off together.' I sat up with a start. They must be talking about H. A. and Parvathi. Where was he? I looked round but could not see him or her. Are they off alone together, just by themselves? Has he got his arm round her? Are they kissing? A pang of jealousy such as I had never before experienced hit me like a blow. It was so painfully acute that it felt like a punch in the solar plexus. 'This is the end,' I decided there and then. 'He doesn't really care for me. He's fallen for her.' And how could I blame him? How could I compare with the scintillating Parvathi? I hadn't even finished high school and she'd been to Oxford. I was plain and she was beautiful; I was small-town, she was worldly wise. Monty looked across at me and saw my crumpled face. He hurried over and put his arm round my hunched shoulders. 'Whatever's the matter?' he asked. 'This is a party. You should be enjoying yourself. Why do you look so miserable?' I struggled not to weep. 'It's H. A . . . He's gone off with her.' Now I was crying and Monty was comforting me. 'Not that I blame him.' I sobbed. 'She's so beautiful and clever.' 'Don't take it so much to heart,' Monty tried to comfort me. 'Tomorrow they'll be gone and you'll still be here.' 'That's not the point,' I shook him off. How could I explain that even if tomorrow H. A. came back to me, having known and loved

Parvathi, he could not help comparing me unfavourably with her. I couldn't bear it. I would never be anything but second best. Better to finish it off now, never to see him again. Just then H. A. came in from the garden. At his side was not the fascinating Parvathi but the mousy Indira and they were easy, relaxed and obviously deep in a political discussion. I breathed again. What a fool I'd been ever to suspect him!

S UNDAY 27 September 1942 was a milestone in my life. That was the day on which the Communist Party of South Africa Durban District Committee, held a mass rally and pageant at Currie's Fountain to call for a second front in Europe and invited me to be one of the speakers. It meant sharing the platform not only with H. A. Naidoo and Wilson Cele, but also with national leaders like Advocate Harry Snitcher from Cape Town and, from the Central Committee of Johannesburg, Michael Harmel and Dr Yussuf Dadoo. I was awed by their presence and shaking at the prospect of standing up in front of all the thousands of people we expected to attend that day. It was one thing to address a small indoor meeting or to speak from a soap-box on a street corner. Those were challenges I had come to relish but this was different. This was a proper mass rally and I was an official Party representative. Should I prepare notes? Should I write the speech out in full? I'd never done this before, I'd always stood up and talked, saying what was on my mind. But this was different. I tried to put my thoughts on paper and to fill them out with rounded, resonant phrases but it soon became all too clear to me that that was not my style. I could only speak as I had always done – spontaneously, with conviction; I had to appeal to my audience directly, without any bits of paper coming between us.

There's a photograph of me talking to Ismail Meer before the meeting. I'm in a white knee-length pleated skirt with a red blazer, drawing nervously on a cigarette while he smiles at me reassuringly. A week earlier Dorothy Naylor had asked me why I'd started to smoke. 'It's easy to look intelligent,' I'd answered, 'without saying anything.' Puffing away at a fag denoted anything you wished it to do. It could indicate deep thought, superior judgment, commitment or withdrawal. But now I did have to say something and my throat went dry as I watched the huge grounds filling up with a sea of faces. In the front row sat Father, a pocket handkerchief covering his thinning hair to protect him from the hot afternoon sun, conspicuous among the black and brown faces surrounding him. Father had brought my young brother, Maurice, to hear his big sister speak – it was Maurice's first mass public meeting and he was looking round with unabashed curiosity. H. A. passed by, deep in conversation with our important visitors who gave me not a second glance. He broke away from them, walked over to me and patted me on the shoulder: 'Don't look so worried,' he said. 'You'll do all right.' I cannot remember now what I said and how I said it. All I recall was my relief when it was over. When I sat down to the usual applause I looked down at Father and he was smiling encouragingly. The thought crossed my mind: I think he's quite proud of me. It was one of the rare occasions when Father showed approval.

I GREW up believing that I was a disappointment to Father. Whatever my achievements, Father would invariably ask, 'Couldn't you have done better?' If I came second in a test, Father would want to know why I wasn't first. I cannot remember a single occasion when he offered praise. Some months later when I announced that I was going to leave home and it led to the inevitable argument I blurted out, 'You've always been ashamed of me; you've never approved of anything I've done; you've never even liked me!' Father looked at me in amazement. 'You don't know what you're saying! Me, ashamed of you? Why I'm proud of you, proud of everything you've done. I'm forever boasting about you, ask any of my friends. And you think I don't like you? Nobody could love a daughter more than I've loved you. How could you not know it?' 'Because you never once said so,' I muttered. All those wasted years when I might have basked in my father's approval, unhappy teenage years which would have been so much easier to bear if I knew that I had my father's uncritical love. Father looked at me as if he were seeing me for the first time. 'Naturally, I thought you knew,' he said. 'Wasn't it obvious?' He paused for a while. 'I can't help it if words don't come easily to me.'

I ASKED my parents if I could invite H.A. to dinner at our home. Father knew him by repute and Mother said 'Of course, if he's a friend of yours.' They welcomed him and Mother cooked a special Friday night meal with chicken soup and *kneidlach*. Eight-year old Maurice gazed in awe as Father and H.A. talked politics. Father was enjoying himself; here was a man with whom it was a pleasure to exchange ideas, one he could respect; informed, intelligent, dispassionate. 'Now there's a real Communist for you,' Father said approvingly after H.A. had gone, 'Probably the only one left in this country, I shouldn't wonder.'

H.A. and I were falling in love and with the passing of each day the bond between us strengthened. We tried to see each other whenever our hectic programme of activities provided an opportunity. Sometimes, after a meeting, we would slip up to his room and spend a blissful hour together. By now his landlady, Mrs Chetty, accepted me with better grace; she'd welcome me with a wave and a smile as we slipped through her kitchen to get to H.A.'s small back room. Afterwards H.A. would hail an Indian taxi and see me home to Umgeni Road. We were grateful for the blackout; we could sit close together holding hands as we drove through Durban's darkened streets. By now our love affair was common knowledge among our comrades. I no longer tried to dim the light in my eyes when he entered a room and he, for his part, whilst maintaining the strictest impartiality during meetings, made no secret of his preference for me above all other women. In the wider world outside our circle we continued to pretend that our association was purely political. Politics alone was enough to rouse the ire and hostility of most people without introducing the explosive subject of sex across the racial barrier.

Finding a place where we could be alone together was not easy. We couldn't always get to his room and sometimes we'd slip into empty offices after working hours. Once we thought we'd found a place – the office of the Jewellery Workers' Union. H. A. had borrowed the key of the office and when the staff went home we crept in, turned the key in the door and switched off the light. We were locked in each other's arms when we heard voices outside; someone was trying to turn the handle of the door and complaining that it hadn't been left open, as it should have been. 'Oh, damn,' H. A. muttered, 'They're having a committee meeting here tonight.' Frantically we began to straighten our clothes. 'They musn't find us like this,' I whispered. 'It's too humiliating; let's jump through the window.' I opened the window and leaned out. We were two floors up and there was no ledge. Outside, the early arrivals had been joined by others. Now there were ten or twelve of them and then their secretary arrived and he had a key. When he opened the door H. A. was standing on the table, pretending to fix the light bulb; I rushed past the surprised committee members, trying to hide my face in embarrassment; they gaped and giggled.

Travelling together by public transport was also difficult. He was restricted to the last three seats on the upper deck of the tram and I was not allowed to sit next to him. When I decided to defy this discriminatory by-law and settled down next to H. A. at the back of the tram, the conductor challenged me. 'These seats are for non-Europeans only,' he said, looking at me suspiciously. 'You must move.' He sometimes had to order blacks and Indians out of the white seats, not usually the other way round.

'How do you know I'm not an Indian?' I demanded. This brought him up sharply. How indeed could he prove my race merely by my appearance if I chose to declare otherwise? He stammered in confusion then marched away. In a country like South Africa the races had mixed ever since the arrival of the white man and appearance was in fact the only yardstick used by racists. All the same, I could see the conductor's dilemma: if she can pass as White, why travel as black?

'I can't stand this secrecy,' H. A. said one night. 'This hole-in-the-corner way of meeting is humiliating. I want everyone to know that I love you.' 'I too. I'd love to shout it from the rooftops,' I told him. 'But what can we do?' 'Let's get married.' I stared at him in amazement. This was something I had not considered. 'But I don't believe in marriage,' I blurted out. 'In a normal world we wouldn't need it,' he agreed, 'but here and now I think it would help. I can't keep on pretending that you're just my comrade.' I thought about what he'd said and had to agree that he needed the extra security which marriage would give him in this crazy society. There was a kind of finality about marriage which even bigots had to accept whereas a love affair between a white girl and an Indian could only be explained by them if the white girl were no good, if she were 'white trash.' Not only whites. Non-whites, too, looked askance at a white woman who walked with a black man.

THE previous Sunday afternoon, as H.A. and I were strolling down a quiet side street in the Indian quarter, fingers touching, a group of garish, over-painted coloured women loitering on the corner saw us approaching and, shouting something incomprehensible, made a rush towards me. Their threatening postures and violent abuse amazed and frightened me. 'What's the matter with them?' I turned to H.A. 'What are they saying?' Before he could answer they were upon us, aiming blows at my head, my shoulders, my back. Like a band of enraged furies they pelted me with their fists and swung their handbags at my head. The curses which poured out of their mouths and the hate which blazed in their eyes left me gasping. I couldn't understand why they were doing this; to the best of my knowledge I had done them no harm; I didn't even know them. H.A. did his best to protect me but we were greatly outnumbered; the blows kept coming with ever greater ferocity as our attackers became more frantic and their insults grew more foul. I tried to defend myself but they were tearing at my clothes and yelling obscenities, pushing their faces within inches of my face; I could smell their sour breaths and look into their broken, misshapen teeth. Then a car appeared at the end of the road, a man poked his head through the window and shouted at H.A. and me to get in. 'Jump in quickly,' the driver shouted. We did and he drove off at great speed, followed by a shower of stones and curses.

'That was lucky,' H.A. said as he turned to the driver to thank him. He didn't know him but the driver recognised H.A. 'Glad to help,' the man said. 'It looked like real trouble.'

'What's the matter with them?' I demanded of H.A. 'Why did they behave like that? Why do they hate me? I've never seen them before in my life.' 'They think you're encroaching on their patch; they reckon it's unfair competition.' H.A. tried to calm me. 'Oh my God,' I said as I burst into tears, 'they thought I was one of them, one of those dreadful harpies, a prostitute!'

The encounter left me feeling soiled and humiliated. I had never met a prostitute before but the very mention of the word made me shudder. I'd read about them in books but I couldn't imagine how any woman could defile herself to the extent of selling her body to any man who could pay. The very notion appalled and repelled me. In theory I could argue that it was the fault of the system: women were forced into prostitution by poverty, lack of opportunity, unemployment. Change the system and you'll abolish prostitution. That was my belief intellectually but it still left me with a chasm of the imagination, a failure to comprehend, a shying away from the flesh-and-blood woman who actually practised this trade. And here I found myself called a prostitute! Was not the difference between me and a prostitute clearly visible to the naked eye? The humiliation hurt more than the physical blows.

'THERE'S a flat we could have in Wills Court,' H.A. announced one day and my spirits sank. 'I can't live like Vera,' I told him. 'I can't sink into a ghetto existence.' All the same we went to look at the tiny two-room flat on the third floor and I realised that we had no choice. If we were to live together it would have to be in the overcrowded quarter to which the Indians were restricted. Rich Indians had a wider choice but we were not among them. The block of flats beyond the Indian market to which H.A. led me was shabby and unpainted; the entrance smelled of urine and a pall of dejection hung over it. I hated the thought of making it my home. And on top of all that was the thought that weighed me down: how was I going to break the news to my parents? How would they take it? I didn't expect an enthusiastic reception for my news but I tried to draw comfort from their respect for H.A. After all, I reasoned, they know and like him, they're not like other whites – they're not racists. They may not like my news but they'll accept it. I tried to introduce it to them gradually, talking about H.A. and telling Mother stories about him and his family.

'Do you know how H.A.'s grandmother came to this country?' I asked Mother rhetorically. She looked at me warily. 'She was kidnapped,' I announced dramatically. 'She was a girl of 17 and already a mother of two when she and some of her friends went bathing in a river one day, near their home in South India. A recruiting agent for the Natal sugar estates tricked them on to a ship lying nearby, pretending to show them round. When they were on board the ship pulled up anchor and set sail. The girls never saw their families again.' 'It is a terrible story,' Mother agreed. 'But why, out of the millions of girls in India, did they have to choose H.A.'s grandmother?' So, I thought, she does suspect and she doesn't like it but she's bound to accept it. I couldn't have been more wrong.

WHEN I was arrested on the picket line at the Rubber Workers strike outside Dunlop's factory and charged with kicking a policeman on his shin, both Mum and Dad surprised me with their loyalty and support when I told them that I would have to appear in court. I would have preferred to keep this from them but I guessed there would be press publicity and I decided it would be better to prepare them for it.

'They were trying to break the picket line to bring in the scabs,' I told them. 'We linked arms and they drove into us, lashing about with their truncheons. I was lucky not to get coshed on the head. Two of the pickets were badly hurt. I honestly don't remember kicking the policeman but I might have done, in the melée. I was so angry at the police always siding with the blacklegs. They're supposed to be impartial but they're just bosses' stooges.'

I anticipated much blame and wringing of hands but all Mother said was: 'You must wear your good navy suit in court and don't let them frighten you.' And Father added, 'Of course the police side with the bosses, didn't you know that?' Then he asked, 'Were you the only white girl on the picket line?' I had to admit that I was the only girl there. 'H'm,' Father said; 'I'm coming to court. I'll be there.'

The magistrate was odious. He fined me £15 – a not inconsiderable sum in those days – but it was his comment that was so offensive. 'Girls like you,' he glared down at me, 'are a disgrace to the white race. Getting mixed up with natives!' He snorted his disgust; 'You lower our prestige in front of them.' Father flushed with fury. He clenched his fists and made to follow the magistrate as he swept out of the court room. 'How dare you speak like that about my daughter?' he shouted after the departing figure. 'It's you who are a disgrace.' My lawyer, Rowly, restrained Dad from chasing after the magistrate and led him out of the court room, still fuming.

M Y PARENTS' staunch support in the face of slanted press publicity and snide remarks from friends and neighbours, gave me courage to confide my plans of marriage. I expected opposition and argument, but I was quite unprepared for the deluge that descended on my head. Mother cried out, as if in pain, and she burst into tears, a thing she rarely did. Father went ashen grey and had difficulty catching his breath. 'Heavens,' I thought, 'he's going to have a heart attack and it will be my fault.' He recovered sufficiently to shake his fist in my face. 'Never, never,' he panted. 'Over my dead body.' I couldn't believe my ears. This was my father – my Communist, liberated, anti-racist father. I was prepared to deal with opposition but not with this kind of desperation.

'But you like H. A.; you know him!' I pleaded. 'That's not the point,' Father shouted and became incoherent with distress. I could see this was no time to argue. The atmosphere was too charged and was liable to erupt. I left the house and found a room in a sad little boarding house near my office. I hoped the storm would blow over and they would come round sufficiently to talk it over calmly. In the meantime I'd keep out of their way. I was reminded of Sholem

Aleichem's Tevye der Milchiker who, when he discovered that his beloved daughter was going to marry a goy, 'sat *shiva*', mourning her as though she were dead. Tevye was a God-fearing *shtetl* dweller, ill versed in the scriptures but devoutly steeped in tradition. One could feel superior to him but there was no doubting his searing pain. He loved his daughter and longed to embrace her but would not, could not, allow himself to betray his God. Now Tevye was my father – wrong and irrational but desperately hurt.

The weeks that followed were miserably unhappy for all of us. Father was like a man demented; he shouted and pleaded, threatened and reasoned. He called on Comrade Rowly Arenstein, the District Party Secretary and begged him to prevent this marriage. 'It is not for me to tell them what to do, Mr Podbrey,' Rowly told him primly. I was angry with Rowly when he recounted this interview to us, smugly self-satisfied at having followed 'the correct line'. 'You might have shown a little compassion,' I told him. 'Couldn't you see how he suffers.' 'But your father then threatened to go to the press and accuse the Party of encouraging mixed marriages,' Rowly said. 'Do you think he'll do it?' he asked anxiously. This was something the Durban press would have scooped up with relish. What a stick to beat us with! And what damage a story like that would have done the Party. 'Of course he won't,' I snapped at Rowly indignantly. I knew my father and not for a moment did I believe that he would stoop to such a tactic. But the mere fact that he could demean himself to make such a threat proved how desperate he was.

'HOW does your mother feel about our marriage?' I asked H.A. 'She's not at all happy about it,' he said, 'but she wants to meet you. And so does my grandmother. You know,' he told me, 'I've always called my grandmother, Mother, and my mother, Sister.'

H.A.'s mother, Valliyama, was ten years old when she married and fourteen when he was born. His father used to visit them at weekends; the weekdays were spent with his first wife who was unable to bear him any children. H.A. remembered his father, but dimly. Kunjebihari Naidoo was a prosperous businessman and a higher caste Hindu who was considered to have honoured the young Valliyama by marrying her. He delighted in the three children that she bore him and was generous with his support. H.A. recalled how he longed for Fridays when his father brought him sweets and gave his mother money. Grandmother Pooranam built the family home in Tatham Crescent and felt satisfied that she had done well in arranging the marriage. Then the father disappeared and some days later his body was fished out of the harbour. The family were convinced that he was murdered by relatives of the first wife who feared that he was about to forsake her in favour of the second wife. Nobody went to the police with their suspicions; they were far too fearful of what the killers might do to them. The family were left destitute and once again Grandmother Pooranam took charge. She arranged a second marriage for Valliyama with a man old enough to be her father. But he turned out to be a feckless drunkard and he died after siring six more children on Valliyama, two of whom died in infancy.

One day her teen-age son surprised Valliyama, sister/mother, in bed with a man. H.A. recalled how furious he was, lashing out at both of them with his fists, abusing and upbraiding his mother. He related this incident with a sense of indignant justification, convinced that he could not have acted otherwise. One may excuse a child's jealousy, I told him but it seemed to me as if he still thought he was entitled to set himself up in judgement. Didn't he think his mother was entitled to have a lover? Wasn't his attitude a bit priggish? It was clear that it had never occurred to him before. My remarks caught him by surprise but he didn't reject them out of hand. He remained thoughtful. Most men, I guessed, would react indignantly when their diehard attitutes were challenged, especially where these related to sexual mores. H.A. was different: he was no bigot; his mind was not closed to new concepts.

The grandmother was old and frail when I met her, but her indomitable spirit still glowed in her rheumy eyes. Two fingers of her right hand were missing; she had lost them when, as a young woman, she'd tackled a man who was trying to kill his wife with a machete. She, alone on the sugar estate, went to the wife's rescue; she lost two fingers but she saved the young woman's life. Had she ever tried to find her first family in India? I asked H.A. 'She never did. She felt guilty and ashamed,' he told me. 'She was convinced her first husband would long ago have disowned her, as though she had sinned by being abducted, made herself unclean.' In Natal Pooranam became one of the indentured labourers on the sugar estates and for seven long years she was tied to the sugar barons as though she were their slave. When her indenture ended she left the sugar estate, married again and started another family.

To help support the younger brothers and sisters H.A. left school early and found a job in a clothing factory. It was there he met George Ponnen and the two became inseparable. Together they signed up for evening classes; both were eager to further their interrupted schooling. They were fascinated by the art of public speaking and on Sundays the two boys would go for long walks in the country where, away from mocking onlookers, they declaimed to the trees, trying to emulate the long words and convoluted phrases of the traditional Indian leaders in Durban. At work the two friends did well. They both gained promotion and their wages rose. At night school they passed their exams and they looked forward to gaining qualifications which would lift them up into the higher clerical grades. Their personal ambitions to make something of themselves by hard honest labour and diligent study did not prevent them from active participation in youth group activities. Here, too, their personal qualities marked them out and both Ponnen and H. A. were elected by their fellows to play leading parts. H. A., the chairman, and Ponnen, the secretary/treasurer, took their duties seriously.

Their lives might have continued on this sober, pre-determined path had not an unexpected event occurred at the factory. In November 1934 an Indian worker was caught stealing some material and was sacked. As an object lesson to the rest of the staff the employer then drilled five three-quarter-inch peep-holes in the black workers' lavatories and appointed a guard to keep constant surveillance. The women workers were incensed at such humiliation and walked out on strike, appointing H. A. and Ponnen to act as their spokesmen. For the first time white and black women workers stood solidly together; they forced the boss to plug up the holes and gained a few other concessions but their own trade union refused to back them. The Union Secretary, J. C. Bolton, went so far as to inveigle two white women workers to testify against H. A. and Ponnen when they were charged with leading an illegal strike. They were each fined £2, which their fellow workers paid for them, but both were fired from their jobs. Attempts to find work in other factories failed; they had been placed on a blacklist. H. A. and Ponnen might easily have drifted into street-corner impotence as so many other young Indians did, aimlessly resentful of the injustice meted out to them but unable to find a way out. But not long afterwards as H. A. and Ponnen were strolling down Berea Road they came across Eddie Roux selling *Umsebenzi* on the corner of Grey Street and from then on their futures were set on a predetermined course.

This was my first visit to H. A.'s family home, a place he'd left some years before and where he was now received with affectionate respect – not only as the eldest son but also as the leader. The old lady, the matriarch, sat in a corner of the small, sparsely furnished room, smiling benignly with toothless gums while her children and grandchildren vied for the honour of serving her. The mother, Valliyama, was now the effective head of the family, and of her six children, all except H. A. were still at home, some with their own children. All the grown-ups contributed to the joint income which Valliyama administered. By astute management she had succeeded in saving enough to buy a large house set in extensive grounds. Here she raised fruit and vegetables and bred chickens to help support her large brood. Thanks to her capable management the family was now enjoying a higher standard of living than they'd ever had before. H. A. was the maverick, the son who'd left home, the one who contributed nothing to the family income. But Valliyama felt no irritation or sense of grievance; she was proud of her first-born and beamed with pleasure when he arrived. She knew about the work he was doing and the reputation he enjoyed in the Indian community – her neighbours were always telling her what a fine son she had.

As in our household, the two generations spoke different languages. H. A.

had very little Tamil and neither his mother nor grandmother knew any English, so communication was difficult and stilted, even more than in our family. We spent the afternoon of my visit smiling and nodding and drinking tea. The family regaled us with an endless supply of syrupy, over-sweet pastries, made from semolina, honey and nuts, which they kept on pressing me to eat. It was difficult to explain without risking offence, that, delicious as they were, a few were more than sufficient. After we'd smiled our good-byes and shaken hands, I asked H. A., 'Well, what do you think? Did they like me?' 'Oh yes, they did.' he answered. 'But before I left they told me: "Think carefully about marriage. It's better to marry one of your own kind."'

ONE morning Benson came running to the boarding house where I was staying with an urgent message.

'Your father is standing outside the office and he's telling everyone to go away. He's shooing them off, saying that there's going to be no work today. He seems very upset. Perhaps you'd better stay away while he's there.' I did so and waited in my room while Benson brought me bulletins from time to time. 'There's a long queue outside the office and they're wondering what is happening.' And later, 'Your father is lying stretched out on the floor outside the office door, not speaking to anyone.' Eventually, at about 11 o'clock, Father rose and went away. What, I wondered, did he hope to gain from such an undignified gesture? Such extraordinary behaviour, so out of character!

Years later I found out just how miserable my whole family's life became when the news about my intended marriage leaked out, as it was bound to do. 'Your sister's going to marry a coolie,' the kids in the street shouted after Maurice, waylaying him every time he left the flat. One by one his old pals deserted him leaving him lonely and isolated. He was miserable and vulnerable but he never conceded defeat. 'My sister's a lot better than your stupid sister,' he would shout back and then he would take them on, in one lot of fisticuffs after another, arriving home bloody-nosed and bruised, but proud and unbeaten. He didn't tell Mother why he had to fight so much but my nine-year old brother remained stalwart in my defence. When Mother applied for her usual ticket to attend the synagogue on Yom Kippur, she was allocated a seat at the back of the pews. After the service, when friends and relations greeted each other, Mother was cold-shouldered. She was left in no doubt that the mother of a girl like me was not fit to rub shoulders with respectable, God-fearing folk.

'We have to speak to your parents, to make them understand,' H. A. said. We persevered and eventually, after many messages were left unanswered, Father agreed to meet us. Mother refused and left the flat before we arrived. Father had aged since we'd last met, barely six weeks earlier. His face was more wrinkled and the outside corners of his eyes drooped downwards, as did his mouth. His suffering was plain to see but there was no bitterness in what he said, only resignation.

'Do you think,' he told us, 'that I don't know how you feel?' He turned to me. 'I can understand why you fell in love with him?' Dad pointed to H. A. 'He's one of the finest, straightest men I know. And he's handsome.' He sighed. 'Oh, yes, I can see the day coming when white girls will vie for the favours of young Indians; they're much better looking than the whites.' He sighed again. 'But not now, not yet.' I tried to say something but he motioned me to be quiet. 'What sort of life do you think you'd lead in this town, shunned by the whites and even by a lot of the Indians? Would you be prepared to lose yourself in the Indian community like your friend Vera has done? And not only that, think what future your children would have in this ignorant, stupid, prejudiced society.' Then he added, almost as an afterthought, 'Not to mention the humiliation and pain of your mother, brother and me.'

'Daddy,' I pleaded. 'What can we do? We really and truly love each other.' 'I'll tell you what you can do,' Father said and it was clear he'd given the matter a lot of thought. 'You must leave the country. Go right away from here. Go to England, America, anywhere. For your sake and ours you must promise me that you'll not get married in Durban. Promise!'

'But Mr Podbrey,' H. A. said, 'our work is here. We're committed to the Party, the trade unions, the national movement.' Father spoke doggedly. 'That's for you to work out. All I ask is your promise that you'll leave the country if you decide to marry.' 'We've got to think about it,' H. A. answered. 'You've got to give us time. We'll let you know.' And so we were left with a choice which seemed to me insoluble, yet we had to decide.

In the days and nights that followed we argued for and against each course of action so often and so plausibly that I felt my head would split. I could not bear to think of leaving the African Commercial and Distributive Workers' Union just as it was beginning to gain stability and *de facto* recognition from employers. Membership was growing daily and it would not be long before we would get the bosses round a negotiating table and begin to show real gains for our members. As for H. A., to remove him from the Durban scene would be like pulling out the linchpin from the movement. What would the Sugar Workers' Union, the Nationalist Bloc of the Indian Congress, the Durban Communist Party, do without him? And what about the other trade unions, the Liberal Study Group, the Non-European United Front? But if we stayed, could we work together, see each other every day, yet have to live apart? We knew it would not be fair to our comrades to seek their help in making up our minds. No one could help us. This was something we had to work out for ourselves. But one friend felt called upon to intervene.

DOUGIE Sanderson was a student at Natal University College who, together with David Kitson, Athol Thorne, Sylvester Stein, Pauline Urry, and two or three others attended meetings and study groups. They joined the party and took turns at selling *The Guardian* at street corners and *Inkululeko* on Sunday mornings in the African locations. They could always be relied upon to turn out when needed and they participated eagerly in all the campaigns. They could also enjoy life with a refreshing exuberance and a zany sense of fun which delighted me but which often made H. A. frown in disapproval. He shook his head when Sylvester and Athol arrived at the Party office one evening pulling a ricksha. The ricksha 'boy' was sitting inside his own vehicle, looking embarrassed and anxious as Sylvester and Athol panted up West Street, flaunting the ricksha 'boy's' colourful headgear on their own heads. 'It's only right that he should know what it feels like to ride in a ricksha and we should know how it feels to pull it,' they laughed, enjoying the shock and disapproval on the faces of the white passers-by.

Until my love affair with H. A. I had often joined the students to go dancing at the Blue Lagoon, the Stardust, the Cosmo Club. I loved their irreverent humour, their easy camaraderie, their wit. But much as I enjoyed their company I never felt one of them. Whilst I envied them their carefree lives and their opportunities to study I also felt somewhat superior, as if I were operating on a slightly higher moral stage. After all, I was devoting my life fully to the Cause while they were primarily concerned with their own careers. There were no public places where H. A. and I could go together, no dance halls, clubs, restaurants – except for Peter's Lounge, a rather sordid eating place which always smelt of onions – and of course he could not join us at any of the Saturday night outings, so gradually, but inevitably, I ceased going out with the students. One place where we might have gone together was A. I. Kajee's luxurious house. His candle-lit dinner parties were posh affairs, with damask tablecloths, sparkling wine glasses, polished silver. One dressed up to go there and the men behaved with courtesy and charm. Of course the men far outnumbered the women; the only two females present apart from me were Dorothy Naylor and Dr Goonam. When I excused myself from one invitation as I was meeting H. A., Kajee said, 'Bring him along, he's very welcome.' But H. A. wouldn't hear of it. Kajee was his political adversary and he knew how it would look if he hob-nobbed with him socially. More than that, he didn't trust his intentions towards me and made it clear that he would prefer me not to attend the dinner parties in future. Reluctantly I agreed. This was not petty jealousy, I told myself. This was political judgement and integrity. It involved making sacrifices but these were of little consequence compared with the issues involved. H. A.'s distrust of Kajee expressed itself in other ways, too. In my clerical capacity I was employed by Kajee to help them prepare the evidence for the commission on Indian penetration. Muslim businessmen employed male staff only and among these efficient typists were scarce, so every afternoon, after my normal working day, I'd walk over to Kajee's office and type there for several hours. Afterwards Kajee would invite me for a drink or offer me a lift to wherever I wanted to go. H. A. wasn't happy with this arrangement. He couldn't prevent me from working for Kajee so, at around 6.30 each evening, he took to dropping in at Kajee's office and waiting for me to finish my work. With a great show of politeness Kajee would offer H. A. a chair in the ante-room from where he could watch, through the glass partitions, as Kajee dictated and I typed. Then the two of us would leave together.

It was an unusually solemn Dougie who presented himself at my office one day and invited me to tea. 'There is something I want to talk to you about.' In the tearoom, over tea and scones, Dougie said: 'Look here, Pauline, I know that H. A. is a great man and we all admire him awfully, but you musn't marry him.' I stared at him in amazement as he added, 'Marry me instead.' Dear, kind, considerate Dougie, prepared to sacrifice himself in order to save me. I thanked him kindly but assured him that it was not necessary to go that far. That was not the answer.

W HEN the answer did come it appeared to be heaven-sent or as good as. It came from the very top of the Party, from the Central Committee itself and the messenger was Jack Simons, a lecturer in Native Law and Administration at the University of Cape Town and a leading member of the Central Committee. In the years that followed I came to love and admire Jack for his sharp, clear mind, his ability to convey the complexities of Marxism/Leninism without resort to slogans or clichés, and for his kindliness, courage and sardonic sense of humour. Jack came to Durban to tell us that as the Central Committee was now established in Cape Town it had been decided to make it more representative by co-opting leading members from the different provinces. H. A. had been chosen by them and he'd be required to move to Cape Town.

We had all welcomed the move of the Central Committee from Johannesburg to Cape Town. Up in the Transvaal the Party centre was riven by petty squables and unseemly in-fighting. We had greater respect for the integrity and political judgement of comrades like Moses Kotane, the General Secretary, Ray Alexander, Jack's wife and a leading trade unionist, and, of course, Jack himself. The Durban comrades were proud to have H. A. represent them on the Central Committee but, 'What about his work here?' some of them objected.

'No one is indispensable,' Jack said. 'There are enough capable young men among you to take over his duties and we do believe that his role in the Central Committee, helping to shape national policy, is even more important.'

As for me and my job, Jack said, 'It is best that an African union should have African leadership. You did a good job to help get it started and to initiate Comrade Benson. He seems the obvious person to take over now.'

To H.A. and me privately Jack said: 'You'll find Cape Town a far more liberal, congenial place to live in, compared to Durban. The atmosphere is more tolerant and you'll be able to marry and settle down. Give it a try, anyway, and if later on you find that you must leave the country and go overseas, we won't stand in your way.'

When I told Father of our decision he accepted it with resignation. 'I'd have preferred you to go overseas,' he sighed, 'but I hope you'll be happy in Cape Town.' Mother still refused to see me.

Travelling separately, we reached Cape Town at the beginning of 1943. Jack was right. The air was freer, the atmosphere more relaxed. The city was beautiful and the comrades were warm and welcoming.

Cape Town

CAPE TOWN: lovely, enchanting gem of a city! I loved it at first sight. I'll always remember Cape Town and one day I mean to return. A city has a personality, a character, a certain aura, and it is always my first impressions of a city that I've learnt to trust. Rome and Venice are *simpatico* – Florence is not. Contrary to popular choice, I prefer Los Angeles to San Francisco. Thumbs up to Budapest, Barcelona, Amsterdam and Lisbon – down to Prague and Munich and Madrid. I feel good in Basel but not in Lausanne. I'd like to believe that it has nothing to do with architecture, history, shopping. It has, it concerns all these and much more. But mainly, of course, it's about people. The collective vibes that a city emits are as mute as a fog and as palpable. They can be warm and welcoming, or harsh and hostile. Some cities smile on the stranger, others turn their backs.

What strikes the new arrival first in Cape Town is, of course, the towering, brooding presence of Table Mountain. But it isn't menacing. On the contrary, the mountain cradles the city in a warm, protective embrace. We came to love our mountain and its profusion of proteas and other wild flowers, dassies and all the rest of its rich flora and fauna. Many times, when driving along De Waal Drive, we'd pull up and scramble from our car to race up the lower slopes and beat out the beginnings of a mountain fire. No one knew how these started: some blamed the bergies – the homeless coloured folk who lived on the slopes; some maintained that these fires ignited spontaneously from bits of broken glass, while others hinted darkly at deliberate sabotage.

Mountaineering, on the few occasions when I tried it, was challenging and stimulating. My friends, Shipley and Webbie, were real climbers and now and then they would let me come too, once even on an E climb. That was the day when I knew the taste of terror, clinging to an overhang with endless space all round me, deaf to the urgings of Ship and Webbie to go forward or go back, having lost all confidence in the rope that tied me to them. Eventually, of course, I did manage to shake off my frozen immobility and then I learnt that even terror can be overcome.

The white sands of Muizenberg on the warm Indian Ocean coast, the cold Atlantic breakers at Clifton and Camps Bay: how glorious to stretch one's limbs on either. Constantia meant grapes and wines and mushroom-picking; at Kirstenbosch Lady Anne Barnard had bathed in her rock pool – or so we were told – and written 'Auld Robin Grey', a haunting ballad that still has the power to move me. Adderley Street – if you walked down far enough you'd fall into the harbour; Skotsches Kloof, home of the Malay community, and the busy bustling ebullience of District Six, slummy and impoverished, but pulsating with life and humour and vivacity. I savoured every part of it but Cape Town was more than a visual delight. I found there a haven, a circle of friendship entwined by common aims, mutual loyalties, shared tasks and shared laughter.

WHEN H. A. arrived in Cape Town he was billeted by the Party with Jack and Rhoda Pepys in their sprawling, comfortable Claremont house. This white, professional, middle-class couple made him welcome because he was a comrade and they, like many others in this heady, pro-Soviet period, were enthusiastic, albeit short-lived, Party supporters. I was lodged with my old friend, Lesley, and her new husband, Jack Cope, in their tiny, picturesque bungalow on First Beach, Clifton. The divan in their pocket-sized living room became my bed and every night I fell asleep to the sound of harsh Atlantic breakers crashing on the beach not twenty feet away. At high tide the waves lapped the steps of the flimsy wooden porch outside.

Jack, a writer, was intellectual, tall and fair; he was also a skilled craftsman who could build furniture, bind books, and cook delicious meals with the fresh clams which he picked on the seashore. Lesley was becoming an accomplished artist and when she wasn't painting she was sewing, upholstering, decorating. She had grown up adoring her cousin Jack and her marriage to him appeared to be the fairy-tale ending to this lifelong devotion. They made such a handsome couple: she with her slender, willowy figure, her flaxen hair and her pert little upturned nose; he so dashing, erudite, worldly. They complemented each other in so many ways and had succeeded in creating in this corner of First Beach a home where all the essentials were beautiful and the things of beauty served a real need.

'Are you happy now?' I asked Lesley as we strolled barefoot on the seashore, confidently expecting her to say yes, of course. Her answer surprised me and shattered many preconceptions about love and romance. 'Oh, well,' she said, kicking the sand, 'if you don't marry one man, you marry another.' Oh no, I thought, not me. I could never imagine marrying anyone else but H. A.

On the evenings when I visited H. A. in Claremont I was given a bed on the other side of the house but Jack and Rhoda could not help but hear the floorboards creaking as I crept along the passage in the dark to H. A's room.

'My dear,' Rhoda admonished me as I was modelling for her in her studio one day, 'I hope you're not thinking of marrying H.A. Of course he's a fine chap and we all think the world of him but mixed marriages don't work.' She screwed up her eyes and applied a dab of purple to the canvas. 'Besides,' she added, turning to regard me in all seriousness, 'a girl like you could marry anyone. You could even marry a doctor!' Rhoda frowned when I burst out laughing; she saw nothing funny in every reasonable girl's ambition to marry a doctor. She had succeeded in doing so and wasn't she happy? I couldn't even try to explain why I laughed; she would never understand that although we seemed so close and friendly our values contrasted as day and night. Compared with Mrs Jones, my former landlady in Johannesburg, who thought I should marry a businessman, Rhoda was a progressive, liberated woman, yet she too regarded marriage as a means of advancement. Like so many women, Rhoda looked on marriage as an alternative to a career, a rung on a social and economic ladder. I wished I could explain that marriage had to be a partnership, a union of free souls in which material considerations played no part at all.

H.A. also was advised against marrying me. He had started work as a journalist on *The Guardian* and his editor, Betty Radford, had a high regard for him but not for me. 'These white middle-class girls,' Betty told him, referring to me whom she hardly knew, 'they're looking for adventure. Don't take them seriously, don't get involved.'

CISSY Gool was a woman whose name evoked anathema or adoration among the people of Cape Town, depending on whether you were white or coloured, left-wing or reactionary, permissive or die-hard. She came of a well-known Cape Malay family; her late father, Dr Abdurahman, had been one of the first coloured students to graduate in Edinburgh and he returned to Cape Town with a Scottish wife. He became a leading member of the Cape Coloured community and a respected city councillor who could shuffle and deal with the best of them in the unsung but well-known game of municipal politics – only in the Cape could coloureds still be councillors. His widow, Mrs Abdurahman, lived on in her rambling, District Six house amidst the remains of her decaying Victorian splendour. Waradea, their elder daughter, qualified as a doctor and carried on a sober general practice in Wynberg, devoting herself with dedicated single-mindedness to raising her son Jehan. Cissy, the volatile, beautiful, irrepressible maverick, followed in her father's political footsteps but, in keeping with the changing times, established her reputation as a radical leader. She became the only woman to win a seat on the Cape Town City Council and for a coloured woman this was a singular achievement. She worked with, but not in, the Communist Party and was regarded with tolerant scepticism by the comrades who recognized her opportunism but who acknowledged her ability to sway a crowd as nobody else could.

Her lover of many years had only just left Cissy when we arrived in Cape Town. Although he'd made it clear that their affair was at an end, Cissy did not give up hope. 'He'll come back to me,' she tried to reassure herself. 'But in the meantime you can have a room in my house until you find something permanent.' Hers was one of the few encouraging voices. 'It's women like you and my mother that I admire,' she told me: 'women who can stand up to white prejudice.' We moved in gratefully and six months later, in December 1943, it was Cissy who threw a party for us on our wedding day. She was unfailingly generous and usually high-spirited. I loved to listen to her high, clear soprano, accompanying herself at the piano to a joyous rendering of Maschler's 'Let me dream out my dream of delight'. Our room was large, airy and comfortable but there was a fly in the ointment in the shape of Annie, Cissy's maid. Annie had served Cissy for many years and her devotion to her mistress expressed itself in bitter jealousy of me. She lost no opportunity of showing me how unwelcome I was; she'd lock me out when I came home late from meetings, serve my food cold, scowl as I passed. It galled her to see Cissy and me chatting and laughing together; she'd stomp into the room, clatter inanimate objects with tight-lipped, suppressed fury, and sweep out, banging doors behind her. Sometimes Cissy would shout at her, 'Stop it, Annie, leave us alone,' but more often than not she'd wring her hands in pretended helplessness. I think she derived a certain pleasure from these displays of uncontrolled jealousy but every now and then, when Annie's behaviour became unbearable, Cissy would throw her out, bodily evicting her and locking the door. 'Out, out, get away,' Cissy would scream at her. 'I never want to see you again.' The next morning, Annie would be there, huddling on the doorstep, wrapped in her blanket, cowering like a beaten animal, grey with cold. She hadn't gone to her sister's as she might have done; she'd spent the night on the back stoep, waiting to be taken back, as she knew she would be. For the next few weeks her bitter hostility was replaced by a sullen indifference which I hoped would continue but then the tantrums would begin again, and the same drama would be re-enacted.

THE sweet-workers of Cape Town wanted to be organised and Ray Alexander suggested that I should undertake the job. Ray was secretary of the Cape Food and Canning Workers' but, as H. A. had been in Durban, she was also a source of inspiration to all the left-wing trade unions in the Cape. I admired her energy and respected her dedication. The sweet-workers of Cape Town were mainly coloured women with a minority of coloured men and an African male workforce of about 5 percent. The majority of sweet-workers were employed by °Cape Confectionery Ltd owned by Mr Evans, a slightly-built, courteous, Englishman who shuffled about his factory in overalls and whose gentle, diffident manner belied his absolute mastery of every aspect of production. He was respected as a fair employer by his workers and I found him a tough bargainer but a man I could trust and even like. His junior partner was big, bluff and loud voiced. He took longer to acknowledge the right of his workers to organise but in time he too came round to accepting its inevitability and we managed to establish a fair working relationship.

The first general meeting of our union was crowded and enthusiastic. °Lena Martin was elected chairman and °Tommy West treasurer. Like the rest of the Committee, Lena and Tommy were sweet-workers, but as full-time organiser the meeting elected a student called Arnold who never used a short word when half a dozen long ones would do, and I was elected secretary. We found offices on the first floor of Union House, the centre which housed most of the left-wing trade unions. The Food and Canning Workers occupied the ground floor and the NUDW, the National Union of Distributive Workers, with Joey Fourie as secretary, were on the floor above us. My good friend, Lily Abrahams, worked here as secretary to Joey. Nancy Dick, secretary of the Textile Workers Union had her office on the third floor. Nancy came of an old liberal Cape family and she'd inherited all the best qualities of the English intellectual middle-class. She never joined the Party because she valued her independence but she always worked side by side with us. Her devotion, integrity and quiet courage were never sufficiently appreciated, largely due to her excessive modesty and her refusal to project herself.

The NUDW was the only union under Party leadership in Cape Town which consisted mainly of white workers. With the help of Kootjie Viljoen, a fellow-Afrikaner, and Beila Page Joey was building a strong, militant, white women's union. They put up a good fight when they came out on strike the following December. Of course we all rallied round and joined in the picketing with banners held high. We lined the street outside Woolworths and the OK Bazaars and our spirits soared to the rousing tunes of 'There once was a Union maid,' 'Union train,' 'Harry was a Bolshie' and other English and American trade union songs which we adapted to target our own class enemies. The national secretary of the NUDW, Katie Kagan, flew down from Johannesburg to help direct strategy. She was a small fireball of a woman, filled with restless energy and acumen. In contrast the Cape chairman of the Union, Nessie Man, was placid, patient, soft spoken and well groomed.

The Sweet Workers Union expanded rapidly and soon we had to employ a secretary to assist me. Kathleen Daniels was shy, quiet, efficient. There were not many coloured girls who were qualified shorthand typists and there were not many openings for those who were, so we were lucky to find her and she was pleased to work for us. Arnold and I concentrated on recruiting in the factories and dealing with the day-to-day complaints which were piling up. In the smaller factories the employers often proved to be intractable and vindictive against those of their employees who joined the union. One young woman arrived one day to complain that her boss was continually molesting her sexually; he'd push her into a cupboard and tear at her knickers. She told me that she had to shove and kick to get away and then he threatened her with dismissal. I tried to control my anger as I presented myself at the factory and confronted him with my complaint. He began to bluster. 'You're talking rubbish,' he waved his arms at me, 'I'm not going to talk to you.' I tried to explain that I had witnesses who would be prepared to corroborate the accusation but he'd have none of it. 'What, me, with a coloured girl! You must be mad to think of it. She'll have to go.' He knew and I knew that it was a common enough occurrence for white men with power – including policemen – to rape, assault and generally take advantage of coloured and African women who could seldom retaliate. But this case was different. This worker had the union behind her and I was determined to show what a difference this made. 'Mr L—,' I warned him, 'You're to leave Rosie alone in future and you're not to think of sacking her.' 'And if I do?' He pushed his purple face almost into my mine. I could have threatened a strike, court action, exposure, but I chose the most effective though not, perhaps, the most creditable option. 'I'll go and tell your wife,' I told him. 'You wouldn't dare!' he spluttered. 'Oh yes, I would.' He turned and marched out of the room and that was the end of the complaint. Sexual harassment ceased in that factory and Rosie kept her job. It was a telling triumph, the first in the history of the factory – a coloured woman had dared to complain, was listened to and believed, and managed to retain both her dignity and her job. Within six months we had gained enough members in all the factories to succeed in establishing an Industrial Council for the Industry with Mr Evans as chairman and myself as secretary. We negotiated the first agreement for the industry, raising wages all round, defining the occupations, providing for holidays, sick pay and other benefits. The Council employed its own full-time inspector whose job it was to check that the terms and conditions of the agreement were carried out.

WHEN the Iron and Steel Workers called a strike we got together once again to show our solidarity by joining the picket line. The strike dragged on and there seemed no solution in sight. The boss was obstinate and unyielding. He was prolonging the dispute by using up his stocks from the warehouse so we decided that we had to prevent his lorries from entering the factory. The next afternoon I found myself in the centre of the picket line blocking the entrance to the open factory gates. Facing us in the driver's seat of the company van was the boss. 'Get out of my way, I'm driving in,' he shouted at us. 'We're not moving,' we yelled back, linking arms more firmly. The van edged forward and continued to move. He'd never dare to run us down, I thought, he couldn't possibly . . . The next second a great shout went up, the pickets on either side of me jumped clear and with a sickening thump the van drove into me, knocking me down to the ground. The van grated to a halt and the women pickets looked down at me in horror. 'He's trying to kill her,' they wailed as they bent over me, wondering what to do. Some said, 'Let's lift her', others said, 'Best not move her, she might have broken limbs.' Someone ran off to call the ambulance. The men pickets did not hesitate. With an angry roar they rushed at the van, tore the cab door open and proceeded to drag the boss from the driver's seat; their intention was clear, they meant to tear him to pieces. They might have done so, but now the police, who were onlookers before, decided to intervene and to extricate the boss from the furious crowd.

An ambulance arrived to take me to Groote Schuur Hospital Emergency Department and I left to the accompaniment of lamentation from the women pickets; they feared I had been injured for life or even killed. Soon after I reached the hospital H.A. arrived, breathless and distraught. He'd received a garbled telephone message from the strikers and he half expected to find me dead. Then Sam Kahn turned up and neither of them would believe me when I tried to tell them that I was not badly injured; I'd felt myself all over and I was sure nothing had been broken. This was later confirmed by X-rays and other tests but I was kept in the hospital overnight for observation. The next day when I was discharged the doctors told me that I was lucky to have escaped with only minor cuts and bruises. All the same, it was decided to teach the boss a lesson and we charged him with criminal assault.

'Your Worship,' Sam declared in court, 'the defendant deliberately drove into my client after she had made it perfectly clear that she was not moving.' 'Your Worship,' said counsel for the defence, 'my client didn't for a moment imagine that Miss Podbrey wouldn't get out of the way when she saw he was determined to enter the gate.' 'Your Worship,' Sam intervened, 'this is a classic case of the irresistible force meeting the immovable object.' That was the headline in that evening's *Cape Argus* and to our great delight the magistrate awarded costs and damages to us. But our victory was short-lived. The boss took the case to appeal and won. It took me a year to pay off the costs.

It also took me some time to get over a source of embarrassment that occurred during this particular strike when a strapping young Afrikaner policeman grabbed me round the waist but instead of hurtling me in a police van he swung me round so that my feet left the ground. '*Ag, jy lekker ding,*' he sang out so that all could hear; roughly translated, this meant 'Oh, you lovely thing.' My fellow pickets stared in amazement and burst out laughing. I shouted at him to put me down and wondered how I'd ever live down such an unwonted tribute, coming as it did from a policeman.

AT THE weekly meeting of the Trades and Labour Council those of us representing left-wing trade unions – Ray, Joey, Kootje, Beila, Nancy and I – found ourselves confronting a solid line-up of white male representatives from the craft unions such as the printers, boilermakers, engineers. They were not as die-hard reactionary as their counterparts in Durban and Johannesburg – an AEU man was preferable to a white mineworker when it came to discussing racial issues – but even so this phalanx of brave white manhood could not resist taunting and patronising us. It needed only for one of us to get up to speak for these trade union leaders to lean back in their chairs, stretch out their legs and assume what they imagined was a benign expression of tolerance for 'the girls'. Or else they would start telling smutty jokes and making sexual allusions, with many winks and nods and nudges. 'I'd like to stick a firework up their backsides,' Joey fumed. 'Just ignore them,' Ray advised. 'Don't let them rattle you.' It took time but gradually the atmosphere changed and eventually we were accepted as equals and listened to with respect. What was said became important, not who said it. We didn't believe that our fellow trade unionists had had a change of heart but it became clear to all of us that our unions had become a force to be reckoned with and we, as their representatives, were entitled to be heard. Early in 1948 I was nominated for the position of chairman of the Trades and Labour Council and I was elected with the support of a fair proportion of the white trade union leaders.

ON SATURDAY mornings a group of us would carry a soap-box down to the Grand Parade behind the Post Office, spread the banner of the Cape District Committee of the Communist Party, and set about trying to engage the attention of the busy passers-by. We were not above staging little subterfuges to get the meeting rolling, like having one of us act the part of the *agent provocateur*. 'Why don't you go back to Russia?' Pete would shout at the speaker, or 'Would you let your sister marry a native?' the other inevitable interjection at all Party meetings. Invariably these tactics worked and on good days we had hundreds of people listening to us as we expounded on Party policies and engaged in quick-fire sessions of questions, comments and repartee. We became adept at dealing with issues as diverse as the Second Front in Europe, the Pass Laws, the coloured vote in the Cape, the Broederbond, the government's agricultural policy, Stalin's pact with Hitler. Hecklers added zest to the proceedings and livened up the meetings. 'What about the Russian brides who're not allowed to join their British husbands?' a man from the crowd demanded of me one Saturday morning. We were there to defend and explain all things Soviet, but this was something I could not justify. 'I don't agree with it,' I answered bluntly. 'I think it's wrong and I hope the Russians change their minds soon and let the brides join their husbands.'

I'd heard the argument that the Russian brides had to be protected from the hostile capitalist world and that the Soviet authorities were merely defending their imprudent citizens. I couldn't believe that Russian women were such tender, fragile flowers that they had to be preserved from the harsh western winds and I wasn't going to pretend that I did. A report on my deviationism was carried to the District Committee by a zealous, anonymous comrade. District Secretary Fred Carneson took a serious view of my misdemeanour. To criticise the Soviet Union in public was a grave act of indiscipline and I was summoned to appear before him and Chairman Brian Bunting. 'We understand that the Soviet Union was slandered at the Grand Parade meeting and you, Comrade Pauline, did not defend it.' 'I'm sorry,' I said, 'I just don't agree with the Soviet attitude to these brides, it makes no sense. I'm sure the Russians can survive without my defence on this particular issue.' They referred my transgression to a full meeting of the District Committee where, after a discussion, I was solemnly reprimanded. I was extremely fond of both Fred and Brian and I could understand the need to defend the Soviet Fatherland, but – really – this was stretching loyalty beyond the call of duty! It distressed me to be accused of a lack of discipline in pitting my private opinions against Party policy. Almost in tears I walked downstairs and appealed to Comrade Moses Kotane, General Secretary of the Central Committee: 'Is it such a crime to give one's honest opinion?' I demanded of him. Moses was calm and philosophical. 'We can differ and argue as much as we like inside the Party,' he explained to me patiently, 'but once a decision is reached we must all abide by it. That is democratic centralism.' Having delivered the correct line, Moses put his arm round my shoulders and gave me a hug. 'OK, don't upset yourself,' he consoled me. 'Carry on the good work.' How lucky we were, I told myself, to have men and women of the stature of Moses, Jack Simons, Ray Alexander and H. A. on our Central Committee. There had been times in our history when our national leaders were smaller and meaner people.

Moses Kotane became one of my special friends, I came to rely on his calm wisdom and affectionate concern. I would turn to him not only with political problems but also with personal dilemmas. Once when I complained about H. A.'s growing jealousy Moses asked me, 'Is he also jealous of me?' The idea seemed preposterous. 'Oh no,' I assured him, 'H. A. wouldn't be jealous of you.' Moses surprised me by receiving this answer not as a compliment to his unquestioned integrity but as a reflection on his manhood. 'And why wouldn't he?' he demanded, almost petulantly.

Only once did I see Moses in respectful mood; he did not usually defer to others or suffer from any lack of self-confidence. This occurred when he invited H. A. and me to accompany him to a luncheon appointment with Chief Tshekedi Khama of the Bamangwato. The Chief was passing through Cape Town and he was in the public eye for his stubborn opposition to the marriage of his nephew, the designated future chief, Seretse Khama, to Ruth Williams, a white woman from England. I don't know if by bringing us Moses hoped to suggest to the Chief that mixed marriages could work, even in Cape Town, or whether he merely needed our company in what proved to be a rather stilted encounter. Neither H. A. nor I had ever seem Moses in such an acquiescent role, as though he were deferring to a traditional chief.

WHEN the Government threatened to remove the coloureds from the voters' roll, we organised a protest campaign and called a mass rally in the centre of Cape Town. The streets around the Grand Parade started filling up early in the evening and by seven o'clock when the meeting was due to begin the whole area was packed and all the approaching roads were crowded. Loudspeakers relayed the words of the speakers to the rapt audience who'd gathered in their thousands. Speaker after speaker mounted the platform and addressed the crowd which was cheering and applauding enthusiastically. By ten o'clock as the meeting closed down and people started to disperse, we were congratulating ourselves on the tremendous turn-out and how well it had gone when a new sound reached us. It sounded like screams of fear and fury and we ran in the direction from which it was coming. I found myself wedged in a narrow street and to my horror saw a posse of mounted police advancing on us at a trot, wielding whips and truncheons with which they were lashing out indiscriminately around them. We tried to flatten ourselves against the walls and in the doorways and I saw one woman who was shielding her two children with her body receive the full force of two lashes on her back and head. An old man who'd lost his walking stick had slipped on the road and only just managed to roll himself into the gutter as the horses' hooves missed him by inches. 'What are you doing, you bastards?' I screamed at the policemen. It was obvious what they were doing but then I saw their faces, and suddenly I discovered something I had not realised before; these men were enjoying themselves, they were gloating and grinning as they listened to the cries of pain and terror around them. It was impossible to grow up in South Africa without witnessing cruelty by man against man and I had seen it before; but always it seemed to me that it was done in anger or in fear. If only one could change the system fear would be abolished and people would no longer need to be cruel, or so I fondly believed. Now I was witnessing men inflicting pain with obvious gusto, for the pleasure it gave them. It was a frightening insight into the minds of torturers.

Cissy Gool was driving away from the meeting standing on the back of an open lorry next to her sister, Dr Waradea. They were surrounded by friends and supporters and all were in a jubilant mood at the success of the evening. Suddenly the mounted police bore down on them, lashing out to left and right, as they had done to us. A crack from a police baton caught a white bystander full in the face and he fell down, bleeding profusely. Waradea looked down and saw that his nose was nearly torn off; it was hanging on by a thread of skin. She jumped off the lorry and ran to the man. With one hand she clamped the man's nose in position and with the other hand she reached for her medical bag. At that moment the police reappeared in a return sortie. 'Look at that Hotnot pulling off a white man's nose,' one of them yelled as he grabbed Waradea from behind and dragged her away, her hand still clasping the poor man's nose.

*T*HE *Guardian* was the unofficial paper of the South African Communist Party. It was a bright, intelligent, well produced weekly whose editor, Betty Radford, was a large, handsome lady. Her clipped accent, twin-sets and pearls and her patrician ways all proclaimed her English county background. Betty also had a sense of fun. Before taking over the *Guardian* she was social editor of the *Cape Times* and her parting shot on leaving that paper was a bold headline, 'Many Big Balls in the Peninsula Last Night'. She was married to George Sachs, a leading Cape surgeon and they lived in great style in Orangezicht. It was at dinner in their house that I first encountered footmen and finger bowls, wondering what to do with the latter. H.A. enjoyed working with Betty; she was supportive and encouraging as were his other colleagues on the paper, Brian Bunting and Naomi Shapiro. Although H.A. was paid the same as the rest of the staff the Journalists' Union turned down his application for membership because of their colour-bar policy. His colleagues stood by him and refused to join unless he was accepted. We were then confronted by the situation of the most left-wing paper in South Africa being a non-union shop, an irony not uncommon on the South African scene. Ruth First was the *Guardian*'s Johannesburg correspondent. She was a gifted and courageous journalist who risked her life in uncovering some of the country's most squalid scandals. Her exposé of the treatment of farm labourers in the Bethal district where they subsisted under slave conditions would have earned her top awards in any other country.

H.A earned less than I did from my two jobs, as union secretary and secretary of the industrial council, but this didn't bother either of us. It was accepted that all full-time Party officials, and those working on the Party paper, were paid the same meagre wage. The only exception was the editor, Betty, who chose to work for no salary. I was proud of H.A. who was man enough not to let my higher earning power interfere with our relationship; I felt pretty sure that not many men could rise above such humdrum, petty bourgeois considerations. When he left Durban H.A. relinquished his public persona and the adulation of the crowd. I realised he was missing not only the activity but also the acclaim that had been his in Natal. His work on the *Guardian* and his place on the Central Committee enhanced his standing within the Party but he'd lost touch with the people, the masses. His new role demanded endless theoretical and tactical discussions and the drawing up of reports, analyses, statements. From being an outstanding local leader he became a desk man and the transformation didn't suit his temperament. He didn't complain or grumble but I noticed a gradual furrowing of his brow and a decline in his former equanimity.

One of the qualities that I'd always admired in him was his ability to perceive the meaning behind the words. If a political opponent got up to speak and conceded publicly that certain things were amiss and needed rectifying I, in my naïvety, would be happy to welcome a change of heart. I accepted people at face value and was always surprised when H. A. took the words apart and explained what lay behind them. In his analysis he extracted motives, hidden meanings, intentions and as often as not, he'd be proved right. This was an admirable skill when applied to opponents; it became a disturbing trait when he began to use it against friends. It distressed me to find that one could impugn the motives of one's comrades. He was becoming suspicious and it did not sit lightly on him, didn't suit his former sunny temperament. Even when he was proved to be right, I still hoped he would revert to his former cheerful personality. Nor were these suspicions confined to politics. He began to display bursts of jealousy that had been foreign to his nature. At a party one evening when I, as usual, was enjoying myself enormously, dancing and laughing with friends, H. A. suddenly grabbed my arm: 'We're leaving,' he said through clenched teeth. He clutched my elbow and led me away, protesting and indignant. It was an unpleasant exhibition, unworthy of him, and I hoped it was just a passing phase. 'Were we right to leave Durban?' I asked him the next day, when our tempers had cooled. We both understood that to mean were we right to fall in love? 'What choice did we have?' he answered. 'Of course we had to leave.'

THE first time we tried to get married, H. A. was sent off to a conference in Port Elizabeth, so we postponed the event. The second time we set a date, it coincided with an ugly outbreak of racial rioting in Durban. A minor incident of an Indian trader slapping an African boy sparked off a series of violent attacks on Indians by Africans. Gangs of infuriated, frustrated Zulus, unable to wreak vengeance on the powerful whites, vented their spleen on their immediate neighbours, the Indians. It didn't surprise us to hear that the white police and members of the white public took malicious delight in fomenting the assaults on the Indians and even pointing out hapless victims to their pursuers. The papers carried reports of gruesome, senseless atrocities.

H. A. sought permission from the Party to go to Durban. Would his presence and his reputation help to restore some sanity to the crazed mobs? The Party agreed to send him with Moses Kotane and together they set about trying firstly, to find the causes for this eruption and, secondly, to bring some sense to the bitterly hostile factions.

Moses and H.A. went round Durban visiting African locations to speak directly to the men who were involved in the riots, men who'd attacked and raped and killed. 'What made you do it?' they asked. The answers surprised them, they seemed so trivial and inappropriate to the crimes.

'An Indian shopkeeper overcharged me last week.'

'My Indian landlord charges too much rent.'

'The Indian overseer in our factory always calls me "Kaffir." '

And over and over again, the recurring theme of sexual jealousy: 'The Indian men are always after our women but we can never get near to the Indian women.'

Moses and H.A. succeeded in convening joint meetings of Indian and African leaders who, although reluctant at first, eventually agreed to work together. At the public meetings which were addressed by both Indians and Africans, members of the audience would get up and confess to having taken part in the riots, and then they would express contrition. 'It was heartwarming,' H.A. told me, 'to see men stand up and say how sorry they were to have attacked the Indians and undertaking never to do it again.' They certainly managed to defuse the tension and to extract promises of co-operation between the Natal Indian and African leaders. But the truce was not permanent. In subsequent years the riots recurred and marauding gangs of Zulus found it simpler to attack their Indian neighbours than to tackle the real perpetrators of their misery, their white overlords.

It was during one of his absences that I suddenly got cold feet. I loved H.A. and I wanted to be with him but was I certain that I was ready for marriage? Was I giving in to the prevailing orthodoxy which had it that two people in love had to get married. Marriage was so permanent, so final, so serious – I certainly subscribed to the view that marriage is for life – then what would I do if I discovered that it didn't really suit me? Was there an element of defiance in my decision to go along with it? Was I just too proud or too obstinate to admit that it couldn't really work? Suddenly I was scared at what I was letting myself in for – and ashamed of my fear. When H.A. returned I poured out all my doubts and worries to him. Shouldn't we perhaps wait a bit longer? With great patience and kindness H.A. explained that my fears were quite natural, no doubt most brides had them before launching into the state of matrimony. That we loved each other was not in question; we must go ahead with our plans.

THE third time we tried to get married, we almost succeeded. I'd been to the Wynberg Magistrates Court and booked a time for the ceremony. It was 11.30 in the morning and I'd dressed for the occasion in my best grey tweed suit and white frilly blouse. H.A. too looked smart in his navy suit with red tie and a carnation in his lapel. On our way to the Magistrates' Court we stopped to pick up the ante-nuptial contract at our lawyer's office. 'Come in and sit down,' Theo Snitcher, our lawyer, invited us as we arrived. 'My secretary is just finishing typing the document, so I'll phone the Courts and tell them you'll be a little late.' A few minutes later he returned, looking crestfallen. 'I'm afraid you can't get married,' he announced. 'When I telephoned they told me that there isn't a single marriage officer who's prepared to conduct the ceremony.' 'But don't they have to carry out this duty?' H.A. demanded. 'No,' Theo answered, 'it's within their discretion. The clerk told me that if one of you had been of mixed blood they'd have done it but no one was prepared to "start the rot" as they so delicately put it, between a pure white and a pure Indian.' Dejected, we returned home and continued to live 'in sin'. But we persisted in our attempts to get married – it seemed to weigh heavily with H.A. It also mattered to some of our friends, like the Closes, as I was surprised to discover.

Rex Close was tall and thin; a poet with a laconic sense of humour, he begrudged wasting words on pointless chatter so he'd often lock himself up in the lavatory of their tiny flat when some of his wife's friends or family came to call. Sylvia, his wife, was small and round and bossy. She was a dedicated, highly qualified nurse who was inflexible, dogmatic, kind and caring. Their hospitality to H.A. and me was warm-hearted and generous. On the occasions when we missed our last bus home, Sylvia would offer us a bed on her living room sofa. Later they confessed that in putting us up they'd contravened their own puritanical rule never to allow an unmarried couple to share a bed in their house. They didn't believe in pre-marital sex. 'In your case it was different,' Sylvia confided and Rex nodded agreement.

Mike Chames was a little ferrret of a man who had no visible means of support. He was always engaged on a hundred projects which were all about to materialize but somehow never did. As a Raymond Chandler fan he could quote at length from all the books, and if you wanted a good haircut, a spare tyre, a lift to Johannesburg, slogans printed on banners for tomorrow morning, Mike could arrange it. Leave it to Mike. Call in Mike. Before either H.A. or I could drive, Mike had persuaded us to buy a second-hand car which he would look after until he'd taught us to drive. It turned out that it was always inconvenient to have a lesson; whenever we were free, Mike was engaged on important Party business, or so he maintained, and by the end of a year, when we were no nearer getting a licence, Mike was still in sole charge of the car for which we were paying insurance, tax and maintenance as well as petrol. It was no good protesting or getting angry; Mike could talk his way out of any situation and in the end we were happy to offload the car on to him for a fraction of its price.

But Mike did have his uses. He appeared in my office one day, breathless as usual to prove how busy he was, and announced that he'd found a way for H. A. and me to marry. He'd heard of a coloured baptist minister, the Revd Hendrickse, who was also a marriage officer. This minister, Mike assured me, was sympathetic and would probably agree to marry us if we approached him. The next day we visited the Revd Hendrickse in his home in District Six and explained our predicament. Yes, he agreed, he would marry us in his house and, seeing that I was Jewish and H. A. was Hindu, he would pare the Christian part of the ceremony to a minimum. And so it was done. With Mike and Esther as our witnesses the Jew and the Hindu were married in the name of the Father, Son and Holy Ghost. The hasty ceremony diffused our embarrassment and I was thankful when it was over.

Two years later, when I visited Durban, my atheist father confronted me. 'Tell me,' he asked, 'is it true that you got married in a Christian ceremony? In the name of the Father, Son and Holy Ghost?' 'Oh Dad,' I pleaded, 'we were married by a marriage officer who happened to be a minister. He did it in his house, not in a church.'

I hoped my evasion satisfied Dad. I knew how he felt. To have your daughter marry an Indian was a crazy and possibly harmful thing to do, but it wasn't bad or immoral: to get married as a Christian was a betrayal of a faith that went beyond religion.

PREM Cottage – Love Cottage – our first home. Hidden at the end of an unmade road, it was unexceptionally plain but functional, with its two bedrooms, a living room, kitchen, bathroom, verandah and, of course, the ubiquitous servant's *kaya* outside, in the big, unkempt space of overgrown brambles and bush, enclosed by a tumble-down wire fence. Where the road petered out beyond our gate Table Mountain began its untamed, upward stretch to its glorious table top high above. The isolation suited us; no immediate neighbours to pry and disapprove and tongue-click over our unorthodox establishment. The coloured folk who lived nearby were neither hostile nor interfering; they left us alone. We moved in with a single bed, a kitchen table, two chairs, two plates, two forks and one knife. There was a cooker and we must have owned a pot and a pan but I can't remember these. To celebrate our good luck in finding a home of our own we invited all our friends to a party and they came with wine and cups and peanuts and samoosas as well as a wind-up gramophone. We danced to 'Jeepers, Creepers', 'I Can't Give You Anything but Love, Baby', 'Begin the Beguine', 'Blue Moon', 'Three Little Fishes', 'Ma, He's Making Eyes at Me', 'The Butcher Boy', 'Run Rabbit Run', 'Suiker Bos,

Ek Wil Jou Hê' and other silly, catchy tunes with nonsensical, forgettable lyrics which are still firmly lodged in my mind, while other, more weighty words, are forgotten.

Three months after our wedding I discovered that I was pregnant and the news shattered me. Oh yes, I wanted children, but not now, not yet – at 21 I felt I could wait for motherhood: for the present my life was full enough. 'Can I please have an abortion?' I pleaded with Jack, our doctor friend, knowing what a risk he ran in agreeing to perform an illegal operation. 'Have you had any abortions before?' he asked me. 'Yes,' I confessed, 'twice, in Durban.' These were pre-pill days and although I took what were considered responsible steps to prevent pregnancy, they didn't seem to work for me. 'A man just has to look at you and you fall,' my friend Dorothy laughed at me but to the women of my generation, unwanted pregnancy was an ever-present terror, so all we could do was joke about it and make believe it was funny.

'Listen,' Jack said sternly, 'I could give you an abortion, and if you insist, I will do it. But be warned: you stand the risk of becoming infertile and never having any children. Are you prepared for that?' I recoiled at such a possibility. That was no choice at all. 'Oh no,' I said, 'I'll have the baby.' H.A. had reluctantly agreed to an abortion and he was very relieved when I told him that I would go ahead with the pregnancy. Having decided I quickly settled down to enjoy my time of waiting and growing. I was young and strong and fit and I suffered no aches or pains or morning sickness. I felt vibrantly alive throughout the nine months and I glowed with rude health and cheerful expectancy. One thing only made me nauseous and that was smoking. Suddenly the smell of cigarettes became repellant and this lasted until the baby was born. Long before we knew that smoking could be dangerous to unborn babies nature decreed for me and it was a pattern repeated in all my subsequent pregnancies. It became for me an infallible signal – if I suddenly gagged at the taste or smell of cigarettes, then I knew I was pregnant. Unfortunately, as soon as the baby was born, I resumed the nasty habit.

Finding a place to have the baby proved to be a formidable task. Hospitals would have me – reluctantly – but my husband couldn't visit in a European ward and the beds in the non-European wards were meant for non-whites, as I was tartly informed by the white sister in charge. I did the round of private clinics and public hospitals and the answer was always the same; the only difference was that sometimes the rejection came with cool politeness – more often rudely, with contempt. With hopes fading I knocked on the Matron's door of the Salvation Army Maternity Home in the Gardens, a pleasant private hospital in a neat Cape Town suburb. Matron heard me out and pursed her lips. 'We certainly can't put you in the general ward with the other patients; there'd be panic when your husband came to visit. But I also can't turn you away.' She thought for a while. 'I know,' she smiled, 'I'll ask the nurses to vacate their sitting room on the ground floor and we'll turn it into a private room where your husband will be able to come and go unseen through the side door.' I was overwhelmed with gratitude. Such kindness, such understanding! I could have hugged the dear lady.

I continued working throughout my pregnancy, growing bigger and heavier by the day. It was about this time that medical science discovered the possible dangers to a pregnant woman with RH negative blood grouping – as I was – developing antibodies if her husband was RH positive. I was kept under constant supervision but fortunately no antibodies developed. Occasionally, at work, I would suddenly feel an overpowering need to sleep and then, with Kathleen's connivance, I would close the inner door to my office, put my head on the desk and have a nap. If anyone called, Kathleen would raise her voice in the outer office to warn me to wake up. Sometimes I would slip out during my lunch hour and walk down to the Gardens. Here I'd find a secluded bench and close my eyes for forty winks. It was spring and I felt wonderfully, gloriously in tune with nature, with the nest-building birds and the burgeoning blossoms.

We were dining with Jean and Hymie Bernadt on 3 December 1944 when my labour pains started. But they weren't extreme and I was hungry so I continued eating. One by one H.A. and the other guests laid down their knives and forks and watched me with rising concern as I tucked into platefuls of chopped liver, pickled herring, salad, potatoes. 'Wouldn't you like to go in now?' Jean inquired anxiously at a quarter to ten. 'As soon as I've finished the pudding,' I replied, scooping up the trifle. By then the pains were coming at four-minute intervals and my fellow-diners were visibly relieved when I finally consented to let H.A. drive me off to the nursing home. Jean came with us and stayed to rub my back. Matron received us and shooed H.A. away. 'We don't need fathers now,' she told him. 'Off you go and we'll let you know when it's all over.'

After an enema and a bath I started pushing seriously, concentrating on the contractions, breathing deeply and purposefully as I'd been taught to do in my pre-natal 'natural childbirth' classes. It pleased me to reject all forms of painkiller and anaesthetics – this was an experience too important to sleep through – and whilst it would be an exaggeration to say that I enjoyed my labour, it is also true that I would not have missed it for all the world. Four hours later when I thought my body would be riven apart, I gave a final, searing push and the miracle happened. My baby was born! I leaned forward on my elbows and there she was, held upside down by her tiny feet, her little round wrinkled face covered in blood and gore. A mass of black hair hid any forehead she might have and her mouth was wide open in a scream of protest at such an unceremonious arrival. I stared at this little replica of H.A., this miniature edition of her Dad, and I was overcome with delighted wonder. 'She is so beautiful,' I breathed. Then I leaned back gratefully and burst out laughing for the sheer, miraculous joy of it. I continued laughing until my strength gave out and I sank into a deep, contented sleep.

Before the birth H. A. and I had bought a book of a thousand girls' and boys' names and we worked our way through all of them. In the end we settled on 'Sandra', the name we had favoured in the first place because that was what Rhoda and Jack's little girl was called and she had captivated H. A. What's more, our book defined the name as meaning 'helper of mankind' and what could be more fitting for a child of ours? I had always known it would be a girl, the daughter that H. A. longed for, and we hadn't even bothered to find a boy's name.

My time in the nursing home went by all too swiftly. Surrounded by masses of flowers I entertained a never-ending stream of friends. Nor did I neglect my work. Kathleen called daily with letters, documents and messages from the office and I dictated the replies, keeping abreast with Union business. At four-hourly intervals throughout the day a nurse would bring me my baby and keep watch to make sure that I fed her for four minutes precisely on each breast. The baby would then be weighed, changed and removed to the nursery until the next feed. Did she cry in the night? Did she sleep between feeds? I was too far from the nursery to hear and I accepted the nurses' assurances that she was 'a good baby'. Certainly the routine so strictly ordained by Truby King and religiously adhered to by all who worked with babies left mothers with little choice, even had we demanded one, which it did not occur to me to do.

My good friend, Frans Bongers, was a fully trained nurse and midwife and she moved into Prem Cottage for the first few days after my return from the nursing home. She was there to start me off on the right path and to initiate me into the mysteries of child care. It was under her guidance that I learned to bathe Sandra, gaining enough confidence to support her with one hand while I soaped her with the other. It was a strict rule that between feeds the baby was left in her cot in her room and must not be picked up, no matter how piteously she might cry. 'It is not good for the baby to be spoilt,' Frans would admonish me if I made as if to go to her. Frans would sit there, watch in hand, waiting for the hand to reach the magic fourth hour before I was permitted to go into the baby's room. Listening to her hungry cries, my breasts bursting with milk, I felt like a well-trained hound under starter's orders. Not a conformist by nature, I nevertheless accepted with docility the unnatural theories of that horrid Dr King, who was regarded as final arbiter and lawmaker on all questions pertaining to babyhood. I've often wondered how a generation of intelligent mothers subjected themselves to such an unnatural method of child rearing. Once a day, before her twelve o'clock feed, it was permitted to spend twenty minutes holding the baby and cuddling her. Then I would spread a blanket under the apple tree and put my naked little one on a towel so that I could oil her golden limbs all over. H. A. had told me how his mother used to massage her babies' limbs in olive oil and it seemed a wise and eminently satisfying thing to do. I held her close and marvelled at her perfect little nails, toes, eyes and at the beauty of her mouth, nose, hands.

But all too often my peace of mind would be invaded by sinister fantasies. I tried to suppress them but deep-seated fears would arise and force themselves on my consciousness. A gang of white thugs are attacking the house, brandishing knives and pistols; they've come to snatch my child away from me; they're out to destroy the baby of a mixed marriage; they're vicious. Their hate-filled eyes and distorted mouths blot out the sunshine, they've climbed the fence, they're getting nearer . . . It took a great effort of will to rid myself of these recurring daily nightmares, but all too often they'd sneak back unbidden from the dark corners of my mind.

AFTER four weeks of full-time mothering it was time to get back to work and now a nanny had to be found. Susanna was big, slow, shy and hesitant. She answered 'Yes madam' to all questions although I suspected she did not always understand what was asked. The first evening she arrived we invited her to sit with us at dinner table. She demurred. Looking floorwards she muttered, for the first time, 'Ag no, madam.' We insisted, explaining that in our household she was to consider herself part of the family. She was to address us by our given names, H.A. and Pauline, not 'Master' and 'Madam.' We sympathised with her obvious embarrassment but assured ourselves that given time she'd get used to what was clearly a new and unsettling experience. The next morning Susanna did not show up and when I went to call her in the *kaya* I saw that she had fled in the night, not bothering even to pick up her day's pay. It was obvious that not only did we discomfit her but she'd found our unorthodoxy positively threatening.

Our next incumbent was Doris who came from Langa where she lived with her mother, brothers and sisters. As the eldest child in the large fatherless family she was used to raising children. She handled Sandra with confidence and the baby took to her instantly. After the initial shock of surprise at finding a black husband and white wife Doris shrugged off what must have seemed to her a crazy mixed-up scene. I explained to her the rigid rules laid down by Truby King – the bottle to be given on the stroke of twelve and no lifting of the baby between meals. She nodded agreement and didn't argue. Another nonsense I could almost hear her thinking and I must have depended on it; for when I returned an hour later and found Sandra strapped on Doris's back, contentedly dozing as Doris went about her work, humming a soothing tune, I was grateful to her for doing what I realised was right and natural and what I had lacked the courage to do, defying the mighty King.

A fortnight later another member was unexpectedly dropped into our household and from being just two, suddenly we were five. Pedro was a conscript in the Portuguese army who was on his way to Mozambique with his regiment when his ship docked at Cape Town to pick up supplies. He seized the opportunity to seek out Mr and Mrs Lapuente, the former Consular representatives of Republican Spain, and confided in them his intention to jump ship. Pedro's mother was Portuguese but his father was Spanish and he was brought up in Spain. Both he and his father had fought for the Republican government during the civil war and when it was clear that Franco had won – with the help of Hitler and Mussolini – Pedro was persuaded by his mother to escape from Spain and to join her relatives in Portugal, so hoping to save him from the Fascist vengeance already wreaked on her husband. That was how Pedro came to be conscripted into fighting a war on the wrong side, with the Portuguese imperialists against the colonial fighters for freedom in Mozambique. Could the Lapuentes help him? They could and they did, explaining that they'd chosen our house as a temporary haven because it was isolated and because they knew they could trust us. The Lapuentes were a popular and respected couple in our midst. He was courtly, considerate and a man of unquestioned integrity; Mrs Lapuente looked and dressed like everyone's image of a gracious Spanish senora, with her gleaming black hair pulled tautly back to support her high, gilded combs, her fringed mantillas and her balletic hands brought into constant play to help her better express herself in a language forever foreign. They were worthy representatives of an inspiring cause and we were honoured to be asked to help.

'He sits in that chair all day,' Doris would say when we returned home from work, 'and he doesn't understand a word I say.' Poor Pedro, mute and bored, with no one to talk to and nothing to do, waiting for news that might come within a week, a month, three months. Then one day, shyly and diffidently, Pedro gave us to understand that he knew about cars and could he tinker with ours? 'Help yourself,' H. A. laughed. Pedro set to and our battered old jalopy had never enjoyed such loving care and attention. Pedro sang as he worked, taking the car apart and putting it together again. He must have done it a dozen times before the Lapuentes managed to find a passage for him on a ship sailing to South America where I hope he succeeded in building a new and better life for himself.

E AST London was the venue for that year's Trades and Labour Council National Conference and when I arrived with Sandra I found myself billeted with my old friend and ex-lover, Gunther, now a successful society photographer and part-time farmer. But his commercial success was not matched by personal happiness. Since leaving Durban Gunther had married and fathered a son but his wife had run off with a passing sailor, leaving him holding the baby. He was helped by his mother and father whom he'd brought out of Germany and who were now living with him. My stay was marred by tension and disharmony between Gunther and me. Boasting of his triumphs as a farmer,

Gunther adopted the terminology of his white neighbours, referring to 'lazy kaffirs', 'thieving hotnots', and 'good-for-nothing labourers'. 'And where do you think your farming profits would be if it weren't for these people slogging their guts out for the pittances you pay them?' I demanded. 'You Communists,' he sneered. 'You should hear what my father has to say about them. He was in Berlin when they marched in. He knows them.'

Gunther's Jewish father had survived the Hitler era in Berlin, hidden and protected by his Gentile wife. He had little to say about the Nazis but was full of self-righteous indignation about the iniquities of the Reds. 'Do you know what those people did as soon as they marched into Berlin?' he demanded rhetorically of me. 'They confiscated my radio, that's what those swine did,' he burned with wrath, inviting my sympathy. 'I should have thought that a Jew who survived the war in Berlin would have welcomed with open arms the liberators of his city. I'd have given them the clothes off my back, never mind your miserable radio.' My reasonable argument, delivered admittedly with some heat, was not too well received and it was with great relief that I left for home, smarting under Gunther's final insult when I refused to let him photograph me breast-feeding the baby. 'Hm,' he snorted, 'not only a Communist but a puritan as well now.'

THE next time I had to travel was as delegate to the Communist Party conference in Johannesburg. Again Sandra came with me; I believed that a baby should not be separated from her mother during the first year of her life. This time Sandra and I were accommodated by Tilly and Julius First in the luxurious white suburb where they lived. Their daughter, Ruth, had her own flat in the centre of the city. Tilly was a forbidding person, not given to easy displays of warm affection, so I appreciated all the more her attempts to make us welcome and comfortable. It occurred to me that part of Tilly's concern was to see for herself how a mixed marriage worked and especially what the baby of such a marriage looked like. There was a chance that such an eventuality might arise in her family. Ruth was deeply in love with an Indian comrade from Durban, and whilst the Firsts were good Party members and loyal Communists, I suspected that Tilly, like my parents, would have preferred her daughter not to marry an Indian.

Ruth was considered by many comrades to be cold and withdrawn. She had an aura of crisp efficiency and she didn't suffer fools gladly. I was drawn to Ruth and admired her enormously. She had already made a mark for herself with her outstanding investigative journalism, proving her courage and dedication. Years later, in Mozambique, Ruth was to die tragically, murdered by a letter bomb. The film about her, good as it is, does not do her sufficient justice. *A World Apart* tells the truth but not the whole truth about a complex, sensitive, outstanding woman.

'You know of course about Ismail and me,' Ruth broached the subject diffidently, unused to soul-baring, her hands on the wheel of her sleek Citroën, her eyes straight ahead. We were driving to Cape Town through the hot, dusty landscape of the Karoo, marvelling how this semi-desert could enthral and captivate so many people, including our favourite South African author, Olive Schreiner. Superficially the Karoo appears to be a big, open space, devoid of animal and plant life. But its emptiness is deceptive; it is filled with luminous sights and primeval voices; it imprints itself on the deep recesses of the mind and it is able to make one yearn for it a lifetime later. 'Yes,' I said, I knew about her and Ismail. One did not expect intimate revelations from Ruth so her next remark was all the more startling. 'Would you advise me to marry him?' she asked bluntly, her eyes as ever concealed behind the dark sunglasses which never left her face exposed, day or night. Was it merely the glare of the sun or the electric light that she could not tolerate or did she balk at revealing her emotions through the windows to the soul?

I believe she expected me to say, 'Yes, of course,' and when I answered, 'No, I would not,' she turned to me in amazement. Why?' she demanded, 'are you not happy with H. A.?' 'Oh yes,' I answered, 'I'm very happy with H. A. and I'd marry him again if I had to, but Ismail is not H. A.' 'What do you mean?' she bristled. 'Please understand, Ruth,' I tried to explain; 'I think Ismail is one of the most attractive men I know. I could have easily fallen for him myself if it weren't for H. A. but . . .' 'But what?' Ruth snapped. 'When it comes to the crunch,' I told her, 'I believe that Ismail is a Muslim first and a Communist second whereas H. A. is first and always a Communist.' A long silence followed, no 'girl talk', no cosy chatter. We travelled on in silence and I had no way of knowing whether my comment had offended her. Later, when I heard that their love affair had ended I wondered whether my remarks had played any vestigial part in her decision.

The second and only other time when Ruth confided in me was many years later in her London flat. 'Do you know,' she said, 'my mother was never able to show me any affection, to touch or caress or pet me, and I'm unable to show my girls how I feel about them. I regret it very much but there's nothing I can do about it. Do we all become like our mothers?'

WHEN the Trades and Labour Council National conference was held in Durban, I wrote to Mum and Dad, asking if Sandra and I could stay with them. They replied immediately, 'Of course.' This was our first reunion since I had left Durban and I entered the flat in Umgeni with Sandra in my arms, weighed down by the fear that our reception might be cool and distant. I will walk out immediately, I told myself, if they do not dote on my baby.

When H. A. had sent them a telegram announcing Sandra's birth it had at last elicited a reply – the first since our parting – in which they'd sent congratulations and good wishes but the letter was couched in moderate, measured terms; it lacked the exuberant Jewish delight that one was entitled to expect on the arrival of a grandchild. True, we had always been an undemonstrative family, a custom of which I approved, especially when I compared it with the suffocating bear hugs and smacking kisses to which uncles and aunts subjected us at times of arrival and departure. But anything short of ecstasy would not do when it came to their meeting my daughter, their first grandchild, even allowing for Dad's awkwardness and Mum's well-known tolerance rather than adoration of babies in general.

'So this is Sandra,' Mother turned her sky-blue eyes on my baby's clear, dark gaze and looked unsmilingly at her. 'I've made up a cot for her next to your bed in the spare room,' she informed me briskly and then, as an afterthought, added, 'She's dark but she's lovely.' 'There she goes again,' I raged inside. 'What do you mean, 'dark, but . . .'?' I wanted to shout at her. With an effort I restrained my outburst, reminding myself that to Mother blonde had always been synonymous with beauty and we had gone over these familiar exchanges a hundred times already in the years gone by. Mother would muse aloud that Malke, or Chana or Yentl was *tunkl, ober shain*, 'dark, but attractive'. Without fail I would retort, 'What do you mean, "*tunkl, ober* . . ."' Why the *ober*? Do you think that dark eyes and dark hair can't be *shain*?' She'd look at me in surprise. 'Of course they can be,' she'd answer but she never explained why, in that case, her admiration always had to be qualified when referring to those who were not blonde as she was. My protests never did make the slightest dent in her convictions or change the pattern of our pointless exchanges and now, at last, I was able to rein in my irritation.

'Do you think she's hungry?' Mother asked, quite oblivious of the effort I was making in exercising such unwonted self-control. 'Should I heat up a bottle?' 'No, Mum,' I told her with what I considered to be admirable composure, 'I still breast-feed her morning and evening.' 'Even though she's eight months old?' Dad was hovering uncertainly in the background. 'Would you like a cup of tea, or something?' he turned to Mother. 'Henneh, why don't you get her something to eat? She's been travelling a long time.' 'It's all right, Dad,' I assured him, 'I'm not hungry, just a bit tired.' I put the baby in his arms and burst out laughing at the consternation on his face. If he'd ever known how to hold a baby, he'd certainly forgotten it now but he was trying, terrified that he might drop her or that she might take it into her mind to jump out of his arms. That evening, when Sandra was asleep in her cot, I walked into my bedroom and found Father bending over her. Embarrassed at being caught in such an act of unwonted tenderness, he explained, 'I just wanted to make sure she's covered.'

In the days that followed I was even more surprised to find, on returning home from conference sessions, my dad on his hands and knees, playing peek-a-boo and piggy-back with Sandra. I never remembered Dad playing any such games with me or Joe or Maurice or any other child. As for Mother, she hadn't changed – she was cool, sceptical, suspicious, unsentimental, her thin lips set in an uncompromising line. She worked harder than anyone else I knew, except perhaps Aunt Zivia. Both women were the cornerstones of their families; on them depended the survival of their children and their sickly, obstinate, uncompromising husbands. They were the breadwinners and decision-makers as well as the pack-horses of the family.

'I must have a lie-down,' Mother would announce every afternoon at about four o'clock. She would then disappear into the bedroom. Ten minutes later Mother would re-appear, refreshed and full of energy. She never owned an alarm clock and would probably not have known how to set one if she had. But she didn't need an alarm. If Mother decided to rise at five a.m. she did; if she wanted to sleep for ten minutes, she would wake exactly ten minutes later. Her in-built clock never let her down. But Mother wasn't just a work-horse; she loved outings and parties and company and would respond instantly to any chance of a bit of fun. The phone would ring and on the line would be Malke or Esther or Golda.

'Henneh, what about a game of rummy?' Mother's tiredness would melt away and her eyes would brighten. 'Sure, what time shall I come?' Off she'd dash for her catnap and a warm bath and an hour later she'd emerge, smelling deliciously of Houbigant powder, elegant, fragrant, her prized fur cape draped caressingly over her shoulders, her soft flesh firmly corseted.

Among her friends Mother was considered a wit and a humorist. 'Nobody tells a joke like Henneh,' fat Aunt Malke would nod approvingly, her three chins wobbling at the recollection of the anecdote. 'She had us all in stitches the other night.' Like Mother Aunt Zivia also loved parties. The ungainly woman in overalls and slippers would become transformed when an outing beckoned. In her slinky black dress with the artificial red rose on the shoulder Zivia suddenly became a curvaceous matron, cheerfully suffering the constricting discomforts of her boned corset and voluminous brassière; she shed the years and her eyes shone.

W HEN I returned to Cape Town from Durban I found that we'd been served with notice to quit our house. Our landlord said that he needed the house for his own occupation and he gave us a month to find alternative accommodation. It had been difficult enough to find a house before but now, with a baby, the problem had multiplied. I was resolved not to settle for a slum but I also knew that the more salubrious suburbs were beyond our reach. Only in the richest areas where houses were set far apart in extensive grounds could a racially mixed family possibly survive, but that was only open to a financial group from which we were excluded here as we had been in Durban. What we longed for was a house in a racially mixed area that was neither dirty nor decrepit where we could raise our child in safety. We wanted a street where she could play with other children, free from abuse or attack. It proved to be a tall order, even in the days before the Group Areas Act was extended to Cape Town. Then Norman, a wealthy Party supporter, told me of a plot of land for sale in the undeveloped part of Newlands, almost opposite his own grand new house. H. A. and I went to look at the plot and could hardly believe our good fortune. This was just the place where we wanted to live, in this semi-rural part of Cape Town, with its magnificent vista of the back of Table Mountain, its mixed community of coloureds and whites who seemed to be living in neighbourly amity, its verdant greenery and the stream on the other side of the road. Kirstenbosch, the beautiful botanical gardens, was nearby and so was Constantia.

There were four plots for sale on Noreen Avenue and the owner wanted £800 for the lot. That was not an unreasonable price but we hadn't even £80. We had been looking to rent a place and had not seen ourselves as property owners. But this was an opportunity that would not occur again; I was determined not to miss it. Then I thought of a solution; I telephoned Sam Kahn and brought him to see the land. 'If you will lend me £800,' I told him, 'you can have two of the plots for £400 and I will owe you £400 which I'll pay off in instalments. We can each build a lovely house on two building plots and we'll be neighbours. Sam brought Pauline to see it and they agreed right away. I bought the plots and then, with the land as security I was able to raise a bank loan to build a house. We engaged our good friend Ernst Mittag to design for us the house of our dreams. They were modest dreams, two bedrooms, a study, a big living room with large windows, a porch, kitchen and bathroom. We pored over Ernst's plans, delighted at his ingenuity in managing to incorporate such extra features as a small dressing room and a big fireplace.

In the midst of this euphoria I received a call from Norman offering to buy the land back from me. It became clear that he regretted his good deed and decided that he could use this highly desirable bit of real estate himself. 'If you want to change your mind,' he told me, 'I'll give you back the £800 you paid.' 'I don't want to change my mind,' I told him, surprised that he should think I would. But Norman apparently belonged to those who believe that everyone has his or her price and he began to bombard me with daily calls, raising the price by £100 each time, convinced that I was merely holding out for a better deal. 'I'll give you 100% profit if you sell,' he finally urged. 'Believe me, Norman,' I told him, 'the land is not for sale, no matter how high you're prepared to go, so you can stop ringing me. I'm sorry to sound rude because I appreciate your help in finding this place but you've got to accept the fact that not everything has got a price.'

Ernst engaged a group of builders and they started digging the foundations. While waiting for the house to be built we moved in with Waradea, Cissy Gool's sister, who lived in Wynberg and every day on our way home from work we'd stop off at Noreen Avenue to see how the work was progressing. As we watched our home grow we could barely contain our joy at the prospect of living in what we became convinced was going to be the most beautiful house in the world. Every aspect, inside and out, delighted us: the satin-smooth parquet floors, the handsome fireplace, the brilliant white kitchen cupboards with space for plates and glasses and vegetables, the dressing room with mirrors and make-up table and plenty of hanging space for dresses, coats and suits to hang without crushing, leaving our bedroom neat and uncluttered.

After seven months' happy anticipation, we finally moved in and immediately H. A. began to build a garden, digging, clearing rocks and stones, erecting fences, planting the lawn, tuft by tuft. Our friend John Morley presented us with a peach tree on which he'd grafted apricots and plums. It took and grew and blossomed. Doris's *kaya* was a proper flat, with its own bathroom and lavatory, wardrobe and drawers, a great improvement on anything she'd lived in before and she set about making curtains and bedspreads and table cloths. Here at last, we told ourselves, was a place to live in and to raise our child, for years and years to come.

Our friend and colleague Nancy Dick decided to buy the land next to Sam's and to build her house there. Like us, she too loved her house which she named 'Pelindaba' (end of the discussion). Naomi, H.A.'s colleague from the *Guardian*, came to stay with Nancy. We were creating a community of like-minded people; we felt settled and secure.

IN 1946 the newly formed United Nations, at its first session in New York, placed on the agenda India's complaint against South Africa for its treatment of Indians. Mrs Pandit, Nehru's sister, led the Indian delegation and the South African Indian Congress asked H. A. if he would go to New York and act as her advisor and expert on South African Indian politics. He was delighted to accept and because he was travelling on United Nations business, the South African authorities could not refuse to issue him a passport for his travels. In New York H.A. worked closely with the Indian delegation, drafting Mrs Pandit's speeches, preparing documents and memoranda, carrying out research. The Indian Indians appreciated his work and commended him for it, but on the personal level he found a lack of warmth and camaraderie that he was used to expecting from those around him and which we in South Africa took for granted. 'I feel much closer to the Americans, black and white,' he wrote to me. He was amused to note that the Indians, many of whom came from the upper echelons of their caste-ridden society, continued to behave in egalitarian

FAMOUS AMERICAN NEGROES

Pauline Podbrey

THE SIXPENNY LIBRARY—No. 9

43 Noreen Avenue, Newlands.   Cover of Pauline's booklet.

H.A. in New York with Paul Robeson and Senator Basner, 1946.

Woolworth's shop-workers strike, early 1940s. (Pauline fifth from left).

Right   Pauline *(R)* with Naomi Shapiro and Yusuf Dadoo.

Below   Pauline & H.A., Sandra and Karen with Nancy Dick *(L)* and Walter and Vera Saxton.

Pauline in 1944.

Photo: Ann Fisher.

Right   Sandra in fancy dress.
Below   Sandra, Karen and Pauline.

Communist Party Empire Conference, London, 1946.
H. A. is on the left, Danie du Plessis in front of him (with pipe)
and Gerald Peel, third in back row (also with pipe).

Trades and Labour Council Conference, East London.
(Pauline in the centre in white blouse.)

America as though they were still surrounded by an army of servants, there to do their bidding. An Indian delegate would press the button on his desk to summon the attendant from down the passage. Then he would order, without raising his eyes, 'A glass of water.' The atttendant would have to walk round the desk, pick up the jug of water from the windowsill and pour a glass which he would then hand to the delegate who could easily have reached for it himself if he'd cared to stretch out his arm. In contrast H.A. found the Americans easygoing, friendly and helpful. He became acquainted with many black Americans and was invited to address numerous public meetings. At one of these he shared a platform with Paul Robeson. 'Now there's a big man,' he wrote to me, 'big in every sense. He has great inner reserves, is kindly, humorous and courteous.' Some of the other Negro leaders surprised him by their diffidence and lack of confidence. 'They wouldn't come into my hotel for a drink,' he marvelled, 'although there was no law against it as there is in South Africa.' They felt uncomfortable, out of place. They'd been humiliated for so many generations that now, when they were entitled to enter a place, they still preferred not to risk another insult. This feeling of inadequacy was something from which H.A. never suffered despite the rigid discriminatory laws of our country.

H.A.'s weekly cable to the *Guardian* highlighted the excellent case which Mrs Pandit and her delegation were presenting to the United Nations, forbearing to mention the vital role which his own contribution made to their presentation. His reports were lively, informative, well written and analytical in the best tradition of political journalism. It pleased me greatly to hear the compliments lavished upon him.

IN LONDON the British Communist Party convened an Empire Conference and invited South Africa to send delegates – we had not yet become a republic and were still part of the British Empire. The South African Central Committee appointed H.A. and Dannie du Plessis, an Afrikaner comrade from Johannesburg, as our delegates. The response of the British Party to this news was less than welcoming. The King Street comrades wrote to our General Secretary, Moses Kotane, himself an African, and complained about our choice of delegates. 'It would have been better if you'd chosen Africans,' they said. They'd met H.A. before, on his way to the United States, and they didn't much care for his independent, outspoken views. Moses was furious. 'Oh yes,' he said, 'they'd have preferred to deal with an African who was overawed and illiterate; then they could patronise him and show him off as "our little black colonial brother", and if he couldn't speak a word of English, so much the better. Then he couldn't argue with them.'

Our Central Committee discussed the letter from the brother party in Britain and Moses was directed to send a frosty reply, telling them bluntly that it was up to us, not them, to decide who should represent us. The South African Communist Party did not take kindly to the 'big brother' posturing from the British Party and the British comrades, the ones in top positions, were none too pleased. They expressed their displeasure in petty ways. When they arrived in London Dannie and H.A. found that no arrangements had been made for their accommodation and requests for assistance in finding a hotel were ignored. 'Naidoo's been here before, he knows his way around,' came the message from King Street. We in South Africa had always taken great pride in welcoming our comrades from abroad, including Britain, so it came as an unpleasant surprise to find that not all party members cherished brotherly feelings towards each other. Had it not been for Gerald Peel from Australia and Jack Henry from Canada, H.A. and Dannie would have been quite isolated among all the black, brown and yellow delegates whose deference towards the leaders and teachers of the 'home country' would not have been out of place in any other British colonial gathering. Gerald and Jack, Danny and H.A. established a quick and easy friendship and in the case of Gerald Peel this has survived the years.

The four representatives from Australia, Canada and South Africa distinguished themselves as irreverent, humorous, independent, and they earned the disapproval of the staid British Party leaders who made no secret of their feelings. H.A. argued stoutly against the anti-Jewish, pro-Arab attitudes that he found at this conference; he was shocked to hear the Syrian delegate declare in the Palestine Committee, 'The only good Jew is a dead Jew.' 'Is this supposed to be a Communist talking?' H.A. demanded. He described as equivocal the attitude of the British party towards the struggle for independence in the colonies. They conceded that self-government might be all right in the East but they demurred when it came to Africa. 'The Africans are not ready yet for independence,' they argued, echoing the British Colonial Office attitude.

Afterwards, when he visited France, H.A. discovered that the French Party attitude to the colonies was even more paternalistic. They were for 'French Union' and against the right of any colony to break away. But Paris, the city and its people, was a revelation. 'I saw a French girl and a black man wheeling their baby in a pram down the boulevard and they were greeted with smiles,' he wrote to me enthusiastically. In the immediate aftermath of the war all babies were precious – they were an affirmation that life would go on – and in Paris in 1946 this included black and brown babies. Paris was the first place he'd ever encountered which seemed free of race prejudice and he found the experience quite intoxicating.

AT THE Port Elizabeth conference of the Sweet Workers' Union I was elected National President and Haydee le Roux from Johannesburg was elected National Secretary. By now we had branches in most of the main South African towns and in our ranks were Indians in Durban, whites in Johannesburg and Port Elizabeth, coloureds and African women in Cape Town. African men were excluded from membership by law so we were compelled to establish parallel branches for them – a policy embraced with more enthusiasm in some branches than others.

The following year, when Haydee and I met again, it was in Johannesburg, at the Party conference. She was leading a campaign against the 'New Look' the post-war exuberance of full, ankle-length skirt, with well-fitting, well-defined top. 'This is just a trick of the capitalists to make us buy more cloth,' she proclaimed and she urged that a resolution to that effect be placed on the conference agenda, calling for a boycott of the New Look.' But I like the New Look,' I protested as I swirled round in my new New Look dress, on my high, chunky heels with bright red ribbons for straps. 'Surely there are more weighty political issues to debate,' I argued. Someone suggested we refer the matter to Comrade Buirsky, our Marxist guru who enjoyed great respect as a theoretician but who was also well-known as a boastful womaniser. Comrade Buirsky heard us out and in his foggy, guttural accent pronounced, 'Ag, long skirt, short skirt – it's as easy to lift one as the other.' Thus ended the debate on the New Look.

IN 1946 the African gold-miners on the Rand came out on a historic strike. They demanded a living wage and union recognition. This threw the country into near-panic. Gold was not to be trifled with; gold was king. As always when serious disturbances threatened the state, 'outside agitators' had to be found. It would never do to admit that conditions on the mines were less than perfect – much better to blame the Communists. The entire Central Committee were charged with sedition and placed on trial. H. A. was still overseas when the trial opened but as soon as he returned he was also included among the accused.

It was during this Sedition Trial in 1946 that the Special Branch raided many offices including mine. They turned up with wooden crates which they crammed full with letters, documents, books, papers; there seemed to be no method in their indiscriminate trawl. They grabbed armfuls of papers and stuffed them into their containers. After several hours when the boxes were full they demanded that I accompany them to my house where they proceeded to ransack the shelves and drawers for more material. Many months later after the trial detectives again turned up at my office and began off-loading files, books, documents. 'We're returning your papers,' the man in charge told me. 'You must sign this receipt.' He held out a form and I signed on the dotted line. As soon as I'd done so, I wished I hadn't. Who knows what rights I'd signed away?

How can one trust the Special Branch! I picked up the telephone and called our lawyer, Sam Kahn; he confirmed my fears. How can you sign a receipt when you haven't had a chance to check the contents?' he upbraided me. I turned to the detective. 'Can I have my receipt back?' I asked. 'Certainly not,' he answered smugly. 'Can I at least see what I've signed?' He held the form at one end and showed it to me. Before he could stop me I tore off the bottom part with my signature and stuffed it into my mouth. With an effort, I swallowed it.

'You, you, you . . .' he spluttered, making as if to strike me. With an effort he restrained himself and he and his men stomped out of the office. I winked triumphantly at Kathleen.

It was decided that Dr Jack Simons should give evidence on behalf of all the accused and during his cross-examination by the state prosecutor, Dr Percy Yutar, he managed to demolish the prosecution case. With his superior learning, his calm, lucid manner, his refusal to be provoked and by weighing each word carefully, Jack Simons succeeded in making nonsense of Dr Yutar and his 'expert' witnesses. Jack Simons never lost his composure but we who crowded the public benches every day found it harder to remain cool in face of the prosecutor's outrageous assertions. One of their 'experts' professed to know how one could recognise Communism and Communists. It was their use of certain words he claimed, the turn of phrase, the demeanour, almost the smell. More and more the testimony of these so-called 'experts' began to resemble the 'evidence' of witch-hunters; it became bizarre, outrageous, ridiculous. We couldn't accept that Percy Yutar believed the nonsense he was eliciting from his witnesses yet he solemnly led them from one preposterous allegation to another.

ILSE Dadoo, whose husband Dr Yussuf Dadoo was one of the accused, sat next to me in court. One day she could contain herself no longer and as Dr Yutar passed by on his way out of court, she hissed at him, 'Dirty Jewish prostitute.' Yutar span round. 'What did you say?' he demanded. Ilse's courage deserted her, 'Nothing, nothing,' she muttered as she turned tail and ran. The prosecutor was Jewish but, as far as I knew, Ilse was not, so was it irrational of me to resent her comment, much as I sympathised with the sentiment expressed? Is it permissible for a non-Jew, I wondered, to imply that certain unacceptable behaviour is linked to Jewishness, that the two are related? Did she mean, I wondered, that a Jew should behave better than others, and if so, by what right? Or was she implying that of a Jew one may expect such despicable behaviour? I preferred not to believe the latter. After all, Ilse was a friend and a comrade but either way I resented her comment. Then, and not for the first time, the question followed, should Jews demand of themselves a loftier conscience, a purer ethic, by virtue of their Jewishness? Isn't that merely arrogant, indicating a sense of superiority? Why should we be 'holier than thou'? And yet, and yet . . . I do expect of Jews a greater sympathy for the oppressed, a sharper sensitivity to pain, a fellow-feeling for the outsider, the persecuted, the vulnerable.

Years before, when I was 13, I spent a holiday with °Uncle Jacob and his family in Johannesburg. Uncle Jacob made his living from a concession store on the mines, selling clothing to African miners. He laughed as he recounted how his customers were bamboozled into buying jackets that were too short in the sleeve and trousers that were too long in the leg. One day he told us how a young, bewildered African had wandered by mistake into the white compartment of the train. It was full of white miners on their way to work. 'They rushed at this black boy,' Uncle said, 'grabbed him by his arms and legs, and threw him out of the moving train.'

'And what did you do?' I demanded.

'Me?' he shrugged. 'What's it got to do with me? I kept well out of it. I wasn't going to tangle with those *chataysim*.'

'Quite right too,' my Aunt nodded as she placed his plate of soup and *kneidlach* before him. 'We Jews have got enough troubles of our own without getting mixed up in things that don't concern us.' My cousins carried on eating as if nothing untoward had happened but I wanted to cry with shame and humiliation.

IT WAS in Port Elizabeth, while attending the Trades and Labour Council Conference, as I stood one lunch time watching a group of toddlers playing in a pool, that I was suddenly overwhelmed by the longing for another baby. I flew back to Cape Town as soon as I could and fell pregnant almost immediately. Before the year was out our second daughter, Karen Jade, was born. Unlike Sandra, who was beautiful from birth, Karen appeared crinkled, wide-mouthed, beady-eyed with a head that seemed to be too large for her body. Fortunately Truby King was now discredited and Dr Spock reigned in the nursery. With a clear conscience, I could feed Karen on demand, which was just as well because she was forever hungry. Whereas Sandra had slept through every night, Karen often woke and hollered, and nothing that either H.A. or I could do would pacify her. Once, in desperation, I woke Doris in the middle of the night and begged for help. Doris picked the baby up, rocked her in her arms, told her to 'sleep, baby, sleep,' and, to my great chagrin, Karen did. I used to look at this funny-faced baby and wonder, how is it possible to love a child as much as I love this one? Had I adored my lovely Sandra as much when she was this age? Was it Karen's very plainness that magnified all my maternal instincts? It took three months for my little ugly duckling to turn into a beautiful swan but it made no difference. It only proved the old Russian adage: we do not love people because they are beautiful – they are beautiful because we love them.

Sandra's birth was followed by a sunny period when I basked in attention and admiration. Immediately after Karen's birth both of us were thrown out of the nursing home. This was not due to any misbehaviour on her part or mine. It happened because Krishna, H.A.'s younger brother, came to visit me. Poor Krishna, always trailing havoc whenever he appeared and always doing so with the best intentions. Krishna was almost too handsome; his tall, slim body and finely carved features won him instant recognition wherever he appeared. Women, young and old, were completely captivated by the appealing innocence of his big, brown eyes and the diffidence expressed in the slight stoop of the shoulders as he leaned forward to offer his undivided attention to whoever he was addressing at the time. He had an air of childlike vulnerability which made all women want to mother him. Krishna was convinced that one day he would conquer La Scala in Milan and he had come to Cape Town from Durban to study music at the University. Knowing what legal obstacles Indians had to face when crossing provincial borders, H.A. asked his brother, 'Did you get a permit to settle here?' Krishna waved the question aside airily, 'I'll go down to the police and see to it,' he assured H.A. 'Do it right away,' H.A. instructed him. 'As a student you will qualify for a permit but if you're caught without it you'll be deported back to Durban.' 'Have you got a permit?' Krishna asked H.A. 'No,' H.A. confessed, 'but I've been here for nearly seven years and the authorities know about me. If I were to apply, they'd have to refuse but they probably think I'm less trouble to them here than in Durban so they're closing their eyes to my presence. I certainly have a less public persona here than I had in Natal. I've become a sort of back-room boy,' H.A. laughed ruefully.

'If ever you need a baby-minder,' Krishna volunteered, 'just call on me.' The night that we asked him to baby-sit for Sandra while we went out for dinner, Krishna assured us that we could trust him. When we returned a couple of hours later, Krishna was practising his scales in the living room and Sandra was not in her bed. A frantic search found her wandering in the garden, looking for her Mummy and Daddy. If I hadn't intervened to stop him, H.A. would have attacked his brother. Krishna was contrite; 'Honestly, it won't happen again,' he promised. 'You bet it won't,' H.A. assured him. 'We'll never ask you again.'

Two months before Karen's birth I went back to the Gardens Nursing Home where Sandra was born, expecting to be welcomed as I had been before. I found a new matron and she regarded me with unconcealed hostility.

'You don't think I'm going to make special arrangements for you?' she said, puckering her thin pink nose in disdain. 'This is a white nursing home. We don't provide beds for coloureds and Indians.'

Bitterly disappointed, I embarked on a renewed search for a maternity bed, repeating the frustrations and humiliations of four years earlier, only this time it seemed as if I wouldn't be lucky. Then my friend Pauline Kahn who was expecting her first child a few months after me, said, 'Why don't we try my nursing home? I've just heard that they've appointed a new matron from England; she might be more sympathetic.'

We were shown into Matron's sunny office and she listened to my story.

'My dear, that's what private nursing homes are for,' she beamed at me. 'Of course you must come and have your baby here. We'll give you the best attention possible.'

Pauline and I left the nursing home floating on air. Here, we told ourselves, is a woman of principle. It just goes to show, we said, how much more civilised the British are, how much more advanced than we South Africans. It didn't occur to us that what in South Africa was regarded as a big, bold step, was ordinary courtesy and good business practice in England. A fortnight later I went into labour and H. A. drove me to the nursing home. Pauline came with us and stayed to rub my back during labour, not as a doctor but as a friend. Matron waved H. A. away.

'Husbands only get in the way,' she explained, repeating what appeared to be the prevailing philosophy. 'Come back when it's all over.'

After an easy, normal labour my infant was born and the nurses declared her to be perfectly formed. They allowed me a quick look at her funny little face and wheeled me off to my room. By the time H. A. arrived I was washed and combed and thoroughly at peace with the world around me. The late afternoon sun cast golden handshakes at me and I fancied I could smell wild herbs on my sheets. My cup of tea tasted like nectar as H. A. held my hand and we gazed happily at each other. Our tranquility didn't last. There was a knock on the door and before I could answer it was pushed ajar. Through an armful of flowers peeked the puckish face of my brother-in-law. 'There you are,' Krishna sang out. 'I've been looking for you everywhere.' So he had, he'd waltzed down the length of the corridor, peering into each room, startling out of their white skins the occupants of rooms 27, 28, 29 and 30. 'Another girl I hear. Congratulations!' Krishna's voice pealed out cheerfully.

Outside my room a rumbling had started: alarm bells, running footsteps, raised voices. H. A. and I looked at each other in dismay. 'Oh Krishna,' I wailed, 'what have you done?' 'Who, me?' he asked brightly. 'I didn't know which room was yours so I went into some of the others by mistake.' He smiled engagingly. 'I suppose they thought the flowers were for them.' Outside the rumpus grew in volume and shrillness. 'What's that coolie doing here?' came from the room next door and another person shouted, 'Is there a black woman in this place?' 'Do you mean to tell me,' a harsh voice bellowed, 'that my baby is lying next to a black baby in the nursery?' My kind, foolish brother-in-law could not have wreaked more havoc if he'd been Old Nick himself, and all because he wanted to be the first to congratulate me. 'How stupid can you be!' H.A. was furious, clenching and unclenching his fists.

All three of us turned to the door as it was flung open and Matron stormed in. Behind her a flock of nurses and orderlies pushed and shoved to get a better view. I looked at Matron but could hardly recognise the gentle, calm woman that I had met. This person was rigid with suppressed fury and her peaches and cream complexion which I had so admired was now blotchy and discoloured, with purple spots. 'How dare you!' she spluttered. 'You misled me. You didn't tell me.' 'But Matron,' I said: 'I did tell you. I told you everything.' H.A. tried to speak but she wouldn't let him. 'I had no idea, no idea at all that this would happen.' She was raising her voice and I realised that she hoped to reach the ears of her clients down the passage. 'You must leave at once,' she shouted. 'I'm not having black babies here. At once, do you hear?'

'We're not staying a moment longer than we have to,' H.A. said. 'Bring us our baby and get out of here, you and your pack.'

We returned home physically exhausted and emotionally drained. The house was cold and unwelcoming, the fridge empty, the beds stripped. Our maid was away for a fortnight, the period I expected to spend in the nursing home. Sandra was with the Carnesons and H.A. would have been eating out with friends. Worst of all there were no napkins or any baby clothes; I was relying on getting these with the help of friends during my lying-in. H.A. put me to bed, wrapped the baby in a sheet and left her beside me while he went off to buy food. I lay there feeling sad and dispirited when unexpectedly Edna Uys arrived. She quickly took in the situation, made me comfortable and promised to return shortly. When she did she brought back a big roll of cloth. Out came H.A.'s Singer hand machine and Edna started sewing. In no time the napkins and baby clothes were piling up around her as she worked methodically and efficiently. Watching her deftness and calm self-assurance raised my spirits; I've always remembered her kindness.

WHEN Sandra was four I left her with Sarah Carneson – my old friend Sarah Rubin – whose daughter Lynn was the same age as Sandra. I had to go to a conference in Port Elizabeth and Sarah suggested that both children could go to Lynn's day nursery during my absence. It seemed a good idea and when I returned Sarah told me how well Sandra had fitted in. 'Why don't you enrol her?' she suggested. It was a Hebrew day nursery and Mr Avin, the headmaster, welcomed us warmly. 'By all means,' he said, 'she's happy here and we'd love to have her.' By the end of the school year Sandra came top in Hebrew and received the prize from Rabbi Abrahams whose own little girl came second. Rabbi Abrahams was the Chief Rabbi of Cape Town and Chairman of the School Board. A month later I received a letter from the school governors. 'We regret to have to ask you to remove your little girl from the school.' I found it difficult to believe. 'What does this mean?' I asked Mr Avin, and showed him the letter. He was equally incredulous. 'I have no idea,' he told me. 'This is the first I heard of it. I'll enquire, of course, but you mustn't think of removing the child.'

The next time I saw him Mr Avin was indignant and ashamed. He confirmed that the reason for Sandra's expulsion was the colour of her father's skin. 'I'd never have taken this post if I'd realised what sort of community I was going to serve,' he told me. He assured me that he meant to fight this issue, this was a matter of principle and he was staking his future on it. 'Sandra stays,' he asserted, 'and my staff is one hundred per cent with me.'

Sandra became a *cause célèbre* before she'd reached her fifth birthday. An article condemning Rabbi Abrahams and his committee appeared in a leading Israeli magazine and the Herzlia School parents divided themselves into two opposing camps. For us were the headmaster, his staff, and a small but active group of parents. Jean Bernadt and Sarah Carneson mustered a group of well disposed leading Jewish women who joined her in a deputation to the Chief Rabbi.

'Is it not true, Rabbi,' they put it to him, 'that in terms of Jewish law this child is Jewish, since her mother is Jewish?' 'That's as may be,' he prevaricated, 'but if it gets out that we have a coloured child in our school, the government may decide to withdraw our school licence. I'm not risking that for one child.' 'Rabbi, you do know, don't you, that the headmaster has said, "If Sandra leaves, I go too?"' The Rabbi considered for a while then came up with a proposal, 'Why don't they send the child to Israel? She'd have no problems there.' 'But the parents can't afford to send the child abroad,' the deputation objected. 'That's all right. The Jewish community of Cape Town will foot the bill,' the Rabbi told his surprised visitors. My friend Jean spoke up, 'But, Rabbi, the mother would never agree to part from her child.' The rabbi snorted, 'Lots of Jewish mothers have had to part from their children all over Europe.' 'He dismissed us,' Jean told me afterwards, 'without giving us a chance to enquire whether he really thought that what had happened in Europe could or should be relevant here.' It was the Rabbi's undeserved good fortune that other events intervened to determine our future and the decision was taken out of his hands.

M Y BEST friends are women. I always found among them the sisters I never had. They are strong, dependable, intelligent, sensitive and understanding to a degree that men somehow fail to reach. When I hear silly sisters declare, 'You can't trust a woman' I feel sad and sorry for them; they have missed out on one of life's great gifts – friendship.

I also like men and in Cape Town my world was full of men who were handsome, witty, fun to be with, kind, considerate, attentive. Being wholly committed to and in love with H. A. did not blind me to the attractions of other men and I basked in the pleasures of dancing, flirting, joking, debating, arguing with Moses, Fred, Jack, Yussuf, Tony, Rex, Brian, Sam and quite a few others. One night someone brought a visiting British journalist to one of our parties and he introduced himself as Basil Davidson. I was charmed by his cultivated good manners and his English self-assurance, a quality which sails through life disguised as modest understatement. He was also, as it turned out, a delightful dancer.

The Revd Michael Scott was another attractive man who once came to stay for several days. His thirst for tea was infinite and so was his appetite for talking politics. The discussions lasted into the small hours and were conducted with passionate commitment. I could barely participate; I was kept busy running to and from the kitchen bearing pots of tea and plates of biscuits. But I did notice Michael Scott's striking good looks. What a pity, I thought, that such a desirable man should be a priest. What a waste!

Yussuf Dadoo was a frequent visitor. With his easy, relaxed air, his engaging smile and flirtatious manner, he proved irresistible to many women and once or twice I detected a distinct note of jealousy from H.A. when Yussuf was around.

When Eddie Roux came to see us together with his wife, Winnie, and daughter, Alison, I fell once again under his spell as I had done when I was a young girl. Of course I argued with him – he was critical of Soviet policy – but I always saw in him the qualities I most admired in a man and I thought that Winnie was a lucky woman. Young Alison was already showing the artistic promise she was to realise in later life – I was impressed with her portrait of me. I was also grateful to the Rouxs for the two kittens we adopted from their mother cat. At first we said we'd have one only but when Eddie brought the two kittens and invited us to choose one he relied on the impossibility of separating the two fluffy bundles and of course we kept both.

One of the projects close to Eddie's heart was the spreading of literacy among the African population. To this end he promoted the use of basic English and, in partnership with Julian Rollnick, launched the African Bookman publishing house. The Sixpenny Library series proved one of the most popular, dealing as it did with a wide variety of subjects. My contribution at Eddie's request was No. 9 in the series, entitled *Famous American Negroes*, in which I could include my hero, Paul Robeson. Two years ago, at H. Festenstein's memorial meeting in London, my friend Paul Joseph told me that it was this modest little book that first introduced him to the Communist Party which he later joined and in which he subsequently played a leading role. At Eddie's gentle persuasion I also agreed to undertake an evening class, teaching English to Africans. Somehow I managed to fit it in with all the other activities that engaged us all; it proved to be far more rewarding than my first attempts at English instruction to Indian women in Durban.

EACH working day in the office was followed in the evening by committee meetings, general meetings, study groups, classes to teach and classes to learn, open-air meetings, *Guardian* sales. Yet, miraculously, we also found time for parties, dinners, swimming, mushrooming, climbing, and dropping in on friends without notice for a cup of tea and a chat. We all had children but it never occurred to me or, I daresay, to my friends that our hectic political and social life deprived our babies of our presence or our attention. If anyone had suggested that it did I would have replied that I had to work, my income was essential, and this was true. But it was equally true that I loved my job and if I'd been compelled to stay home I would have resented it deeply. My children's delightful prattle was not enough to keep me engrossed all day. How grateful I was for the invariable presence of the dependable nanny.

My friend Sarah once asked me: 'Don't you find the thought nagging at the back of your mind all day, "I wonder what's happening at home with the child?" ' I had to confess that it didn't. 'When I get to work,' I told her, 'I forget about home. My mind is concentrated entirely on the job. By the same token I don't give work another thought when I reach home. I switch off.'

I would rush home from work in the evenings to bathe the children, feed them and tuck them into bed after reading them my favourite poems, stories and nursery rhymes. Through them I discovered a whole new field of children's literature which was unknown to me in Lithuania when I was young: A.A. Milne, Beatrix Potter, Mother Goose and songs I loved to sing to them. H.A. enjoyed these hours with the children as much as I did and he never seemed to tire of entertaining them. 'He's great with babies,' I used to boast and then I'd tease, 'before they can talk back.'

Recalling his early years in the garment trade, H.A. used his Singer hand machine to design and sew dresses for Sandra. It gave him a great deal of satisfaction to see her in his creations and she loved basking in the compliments of our friends. It was at this time also that H.A. developed the urge to paint and although self-taught he produced pictures of remarkable quality. Our friend Gregoire Boonzaier, a professional artist, invited H.A. to accompany him on painting trips and offered useful tips.

We had good reason to be grateful for our lives: our days were filled with work, play, friendship and love. But always, just outside our circle, there loomed the chill winds of hate and prejudice.

In the Gardens suburb was a park with swings and a sandpit where Jean, Sonia, Celia, Sarah and I would sometimes meet to sit and chat and watch our children play. It was a pleasant way to pass the time of day and Sandra enjoyed these outings where she could meet her friends and play with them. But I had to give it up when H. A. came home one day and reported how Sandra, in the car beside him, had pleaded, 'Daddy, Daddy, take me to the swings.'

He parked the car and walked her to the park. At the entrance the park keeper confronted him. He pointed to the notice by the gate which read, 'For whites only.' 'Can't you read?' he sneered. 'It was bad enough not to be able to take her to the swings,' H. A. told me, 'but to be humiliated in front of the child was intolerable.'

For the same reason holidays were out and so were picnics. There were no places where both of us could go together with our child in public without fear of abuse or humiliation. Better to stay within the safe walls of our own or our friends' homes and make our own entertainments. Only once did we agree to go on a picnic when we joined the Carnesons, Buntings, and other comrades some miles out of Cape Town. It was a lovely summer's day and the secluded spot on the river bank was shaded by weeping willows. We spread our blankets on the grass and set out the good things we had brought to eat and drink. Tony brought his wind-up gramophone and some records. 'Try A Little Tenderness' sung in a crackling soprano on a worn old disc was my favourite. We were easy, relaxed, cheerful – all except H. A. who was tense and ill at ease. He felt exposed and vulnerable. He couldn't shake off the fear that any passing farmer or other white bigot might suddenly appear and demand to know what that 'coolie' was doing there. H. A. had not enjoyed the day. We did not repeat the experience.

Our friends did all they could to cushion our life. When the Buntings went on holiday they lent us their beautiful bungalow high on the slopes of Fourth Beach overlooking the sea at Clifton. We could not swim together or lie on the beach but it was marvellous to spend a fortnight within sight and sound of the ocean.

IN 1947 the South African Communist Party made history. Our candidate, Sam Kahn, was elected to the House of Assembly as Native Representative, a post he filled with distinction until his expulsion in May 1952.

The Houses of Parliament were close to my office at Union Buildings and I spent many hours slipping across to help Sam with his vast correspondence. I liked to be in the corridors of power, to watch the political manoeuvres, to listen to the questions and answers in the House and then to compare them with the informal exchanges outside. The Nationalist MPs who attacked Sam in the House would often come up to him afterwards to dig him in the ribs and congratulate him on his fine speeches. '*Ag, Sammy man, jy's 'n slim jong, eh!* Pity you're a Communist.' But when Sam pointed out in the House one day that a leading Nationalist MP who was arguing heatedly in favour of depriving the coloured people of their vote had himself a grandmother who was buried in the coloured cemetery, the other Nationalists felt that he was getting too close to the bone. They rallied to their colleague's support and threatened to *donder* Sam. The Nationalist MPs reacted so violently because they all felt threatened. It was known, though never publicly acknowledged, that most Afrikaners had some coloured blood. George Finlay, the Pretoria barrister, had recently published a book called *Miscegenation* in which he offered evidence that this was true. But this was something that most Afrikaners refused to confront. 'Now you've gone too far,' the Nationalists shouted at Sam in the House and he was warned not to step outside the safety of the Chamber until the gangs of pugnacious MPs had dispersed.

Every year some coloureds passed over the colour barrier into whitehood and some whites were pushed back into second class citizenship if their hair was found to be too crinkly or their skin too tanned. In factories which boasted that they employed white women only applicants for jobs were subjected to a leg test. It was believed that coloured women had marks on their legs which white women did not. No one could ever confirm that this belief was based on more than a superstition but the test was practised in a number of factories. The rewards and privileges of a white identity card were so disproportionately great that coloured families would be prepared to cut themselves off from any son or daughter able to break into that charmed circle. Parents, brothers or sisters would pretend not to know each other in public so as not to risk exposing the 'white' among them. Coloured mothers, seeing their offspring in the company of whites would cross the street to avoid them or pass by with lowered eyes so as not to embarrass their son or daughter or prejudice their chances of advancement. Among the coloureds, too, divisions and sub-divisions proliferated, based on dark, darker, darkest. At Sarah's one afternoon I watched her maid Selina help her best friend, Bessie, get ready for a dance. She pressed her dress and fussed over her necklace and earrings. 'Why aren't you also going to the dance?' I asked Selina. 'Oh no, madam,' she answered without rancour, 'I'm too dark. This is a dance "For slightly coloureds only".'

WHEN the Party nominated Joey Fourie as parliamentary candidate I became one of her active canvassers. My territory was the Cape Flats, a damp and windy stretch of land populated by coloured farm labourers and Afrikaner farmers whose vote we sought. We had no expectations of winning the white vote but it was considered a good opportunity to bring our message to Afrikaners whom we would not otherwise meet. I trudged from one farm to the next to be met by incomprehension, hostility and very often the threat of physical violence when I explained that I was canvassing for 'that Communist'.

One farmer's wife met me on her stoep, hands on hips, and when she understood for whom I was canvassing, said, 'You're lucky my husband is sick in bed or he'd set the dogs on you.' 'Let me speak to your husband,' I asked. 'Ag, no, go away,' she shouted, but from the back room I heard a man's voice demanding, 'Who's that?' 'It's about the election,' I called out and edging past her I made my way to the room where the husband was lying in bed. I introduced myself. 'I've come to ask for your vote for Joey Fourie, our Communist candidate.' 'What, me vote for the kaffir boeties!' the man was incredulous. 'God made the white man to be boss and the black man to be his servant and you think you can come here and interfere with his laws.' 'No,' I protested, 'God made all men brothers.' In no time at all I found myself embroiled in a theological disputation for which I was ill equipped. I felt sure that the Bible had something to say about brotherly love but I could quote neither chapter nor verse. 'Wife,' ordered the sick farmer, 'bring me the Holy Book and I'll show her.' He will, too, I thought. If he can find the quote to back up his prejudice, then I've lost not only the argument; I've lost a possible vote. I wished Father had let me attend scripture classes in school.

The wife came back with the Holy Book and the farmer proceeded to riffle through the pages, looking for the section that he swore was there. He had difficulty finding the page he wanted and while he persisted with his search I tried to steer the discussion into safer channels. 'You Afrikaners call yourselves republicans. Well, so do we,' I told him. 'We also want a free, democratic republic, without kings or foreign rule.' That was the truth, but not the whole truth. I omitted to mention that we also stood for votes for all, regardless of colour. I stilled my conscience by telling myself that I wasn't actually telling lies. 'Really!' said the farmer. He put aside the Bible and a wide grin spread across his leathery face. 'In that case you Communists and we Afrikaners should join forces. Together we could drive the kaffirs and the coolies and the Jews into the sea.' I didn't stay to ask if he'd vote for us. I fled.

Pinelands also lay within the constituency. In contrast to the Cape Flats this was a prosperous, white, middle-class suburb with leafy, well swept streets and cool, painted bungalows. We hoped that here the voters would at least give us a hearing and might even, just possibly, vote for us. We called a meeting in the main hall and it was crowded. Joey spoke with her usual brusque frankness and then I, as chairman, fielded questions which were relevant, intelligent and not unfriendly. I was in my element, tasting the heady wine of power, holding the audience in the palm of my hand, feeling them respond to my words, my phrases. I found I could make them nod, smile or share my indignation. It was a triumph, endorsed at the end of the evening by the vote of confidence carried by a large majority. As members of the audience came up to shake hands and congratulate Joey and me I felt that I could love the whole human race. Was this how politicians felt? And actors? As expected, we lost the election, but the campaign had proved to be well worth the effort and the cost. We'd made some friends and unblocked some prejudices.

ONE Friday evening we'd finished our meal, tucked the children in bed and were relaxing in our living room when we heard a knock on the door and I went to open it expecting some friends to drop in, as they often did. Instead I was confronted by two burly, thick-set men in black trilbies, unmistakably CID. They regarded me with cold, fish-eyes and pushed police identification cards in my face.

'We want to see Harry Naidoo,' the older man said.

'I'll get him,' I told them, wondering how they came to the unfamiliar 'Harry' when everyone called him H. A. I wondered what they wanted but I was not unduly disturbed. I had no way of knowing that these two unprepossesing little men had come to foreclose on our world, to shatter the life we had built for ourselves and which we naïvely believed to be safe. The detective looked puzzled when H. A. appeared.

'We want Harry Krishna Naidoo,' he said. 'You are not Krishna Naidoo.'

'No,' H. A. agreed, 'Krishna is my brother. Why do you want him?'

The detective ignored the question but we had no difficulty in guessing that despite our warnings, Krishna had failed to register as we had been urging him to do.

'His landlady said we'd find him here. Are you hiding him?'

'No, we're not. You can search the place if you must,' H. A. told them, and they did. They peered into cupboards and under beds; they woke the baby and set her crying; they woke Sandra who sat up in bed and gazed in dismay at two hostile strangers in her room. Finally they decided that we were after all telling the truth and turned to go.

'Krishna is an illegal immigrant in the Cape and when we catch him he'll be deported,' the detective informed us with grim satisfaction. He'd almost reached the door when his companion whispered in his ear. He swivelled round and faced H. A. 'And where is your permit to live in the Cape?' he demanded. 'I've been here for seven years,' H. A. told him, 'the police know all about me; I don't need a permit.' The policemen beamed, their journey had not proved fruitless after all. 'Oh, yes, you do need a permit,' they said. 'You're under arrest. You're coming with us.' They produced a pair of handcuffs and advanced upon him. I stepped between them, the baby in my arms. 'You can't arrest him,' I cried. 'He's not a criminal; he's not done anything wrong.' They weren't interested. 'At least let me call our lawyer,' I pleaded. 'Let him talk to you.' The younger man frowned but the older one agreed. 'He stays here,' he said, pointing at H. A. 'you can go and phone.' I handed the baby to H. A. and ran out to phone from Nancy's house, wondering what I would do if our lawyer, Sam Kahn, were not at home. At the gate I bumped into a visitor who was just stepping out of his car and dropping in to see us.

'Oh, it's you, Sam, thank goodness. What a stroke of luck!' The words poured out. 'They want to arrest H. A. They came for Krishna but now they want to take H.A. They weren't even looking for him.' 'Leave it to me,' Sam said. He entered the house and with his usual urbanity greeted the older detective: 'Why Officer, you wouldn't arrest a man on Friday evening when you know we can't apply for bail until Monday morning.' The younger policeman stuck his chin out belligerently but the sergeant shuffled his feet and looked down. 'Ag, Mister Kahn, you know that's the law.' Sam placed his hand on the policeman's arm and drew him outside where they conferred for a while, out of earshot. When they came back Sam announced, 'It's agreed then. I undertake to produce Mr Naidoo in court on Monday morning and in the meantime I will take full responsibility for him.'

When the two policemen left H.A. and I looked at each other in dumb disbelief. 'What's going to happen now?' we asked Sam. 'Well, I'll try to get you a week or two extension "to wind up your affairs" but then you'll be deported to Durban – I'm afraid that's almost inevitable.' 'Will he be able to get a permit to return?' I asked. 'I'm afraid that's most unlikely, seeing that he came here illegally in the first place,' Sam said. And that's how it turned out. H.A. was given a fortnight's 'grace' and deported – an illegal immigrant in his own country. He was warned not to return or he'd face a long prison sentence. It was the end of a dream, the expulsion from our fool's paradise. How simple we were to imagine that we'd be allowed to live peacefully, to raise our children in our own house. We knew and had accepted long ago that many of the things which our white friends took for granted were closed to us: holidays, outings, cinemas, restaurants, even parks and beaches; but we considered ourselves fortunate in what we did have; our work, our friends, our home and, above all, our children and each other. Now we, too, were about to be separated by the laws which tore apart wives from husbands, parents from children.

We'd have to return to Durban, to live in an overcrowded ghetto; we'd have to renege on our promise to my mother and father and cause them further pain and embarrassment; we'd have to lose our friends, our jobs, our beloved city, and forsake the house that we'd built, watching it grow. Each blade of grass in the garden had been planted by us; our grafted peach tree had rooted and would soon begin to bear, the little oak was thriving and we were still searching for a worthy name for our dream house. No doubt there would be plenty of political and trade union work in Durban also but our lives would be circumscribed, secretive, fettered. But we had no choice. If we wanted to remain together, we would have to return to Durban. In the meantime, with only one salary, I could no longer afford to repay the mortgage so Nancy invited me and the children and Doris to stay with her. We placed our house on the market and I had to listen to prospective buyers finding fault with its size, its lack of pretension, its beautiful simplicity, the very qualities which endeared it to us. 'What,' I heard them mutter, 'no garage!' or, 'Only one bathroom!'

In Durban, meanwhile, H.A. spent weeks trudging round the Indian areas, searching for a house or a flat. He found nothing. The best offer was two rooms in his cousin's overcrowded flat at the end of Grey Street where we'd have to share a kitchen and a bathroom with his cousin, his wife and their four children. No, we agreed, it was out of the question. Then H. A. had a bright idea. Why didn't we find a smallholding, outside Durban, where we could build ourselves a house with a garden and grow fruit and vegetables? It was not a life that immediately commended itself to me. I would be isolated in the country without friends, having to adapt to a rural existence of which I knew nothing. I had always lived in the city. Could I put up with the blackness of the nights, the heavy silence, the moths and mice and cockroaches? I grew up totally divorced from all things rural. For me flowers had but two names: they were either roses or cornflowers, and – as for birds – I couldn't tell the difference between a swallow and a crow. But, if there was no choice, I could persuade myself that living in the country was something I could grow to love. I weighed up the advantages, the freedom, the privacy from prying neighbours, the good fresh air, perhaps even a pony for the children, lots of fresh fruit and vegetables . . . Before long I was weaving fantasies; I could visualise a neat bungalow with a broad stoep, a small orchard with bananas, mangoes, pawpaws, avocados and a wide lawn in front of the house. I could even see myself on the lawn, pouring tea for Mother, Dad and Maurice. Mother and Dad are leaning back in their deck chairs, relaxed and happy, drinking in the sight of Maurice romping on the grass with their grandchildren. There was also, I told myself, a good deal of consolation to be drawn from the fact that H. A., back in his old environment, would regain his enthusiasm and vitality.

M Y HOPES of a reconciliation with my parents soared when H. A. wrote to tell me that Father had called him to his hospital bed where he was recovering from a minor heart attack. It was their first meeting since our marriage and Father shook his hand warmly. 'I want you to know,' he told H. A. 'that I opposed your marriage not because I dislike you. On the contrary, I have the highest esteem for you and your integrity and I can see what my daughter sees in you. But I still think that in this country, at this time, it was a misguided decision. All the same, I wish you both happiness.' H. A. was clearly moved when he wrote to me about this encounter, and I felt that at last I had been granted my father's blessing in the traditional, biblical sense.

I never saw my father again. A few days later Nancy came running to call me to the telephone. At the other end was my brother, Joe, calling from Durban, to tell me that our father had died. In accordance with Jewish custom the funeral was held immediately afterwards and he was already buried. 'Why didn't you tell me he was dying?' I cried. 'Why didn't you call me before he died? I wanted to see him and now I never will.' Joe tried to soothe me, 'It happened suddenly.

We thought he was recovering but his blood pressure rose and he had another heart attack. You couldn't have come in time; there was nothing you could do.' Joe was right of course, but that didn't assuage my bitterness. I should have been there at my father's bedside, at his graveside. I felt guilty and angry and desolate and I wept bitterly. It's so unfair, I raged. All his life had been a struggle against poverty, illness, stress, disillusion. He had such dreams when he was young, such magnificent hopes not only for himself, but for humanity; he never settled for second best, not in his material possessions nor in his ideals, and life failed him on both counts. He wrote poetry and reached for the stars but all he could grasp was a stultified, graceless existence in a strange land and a foreign tongue which never served him. His fine ideals came crashing down on his head and from me, his only daughter, he had no joy. It was not fair, not just. He was not an old man, only in his middle fifties and now he was dead and we had never had the long talk I'd rehearsed in my mind for almost as long as I could remember. And now we never would. There were so many words left unsaid between us, so many pardons unasked, so much unforgiven. Years later, when I discovered Dylan Thomas, I found the lines that he might have written specially for me and my father.

> Do not go gentle into that good night,
> Old age should burn and rave at close of day:
> Rage, rage against the dying of the light.

O NE day I returned from work and entered Nancy's house where we were now staying, to find Sandra and Doris bursting with news. Before they could explain H.A. emerged from the back and stood there grinning. I was delighted to see him but frightened out of my wits.

'How did you get here?' I demanded. 'Don't you know the risk you're running? If they catch you they'll lock you up for years!'

I rushed to draw the curtains and lock the doors and when we'd calmed down H.A. explained that a Malay friend had bought his rail ticket in Durban and lent him a turban for the journey. Indians were confined within the provincial borders but Malays were not bound by this restriction. He'd left the train before it reached Cape Town and made his way to us by bus and on foot. The risk was worth it, he'd decided, for he had to see us and he felt sure that if we were careful he could hide here for a while.

We explained to five-year-old Sandra and to Doris that if anyone knocked they must give H.A. a chance to retreat to the back bedroom before they opened the door. If anyone asked for H.A. they must say firmly that he was not at home. If anyone wanted to know where he was they must say they did not know. If anyone insisted on coming into the house, they must phone me at work immediately.

'Of course it's wrong to lie,' I tried to explain, 'but in this case it's necessary to do so because there are bad men who want to take Daddy away.'

The news from Durban was not good. H. A. told me how miserable he had felt there, and how unsuccessful had been his search for a home. The movement was once again in the doldrums and political activity was at a low ebb. A number of the old comrades had turned their backs on the the Party and were concentrating on making money. H. A. also brought me the distressing news that the African Commercial and Distributive Workers' Union which I'd launched in such high hopes had disintegrated after the new secretary had run off with the funds. Unfortunately this had also happened in a number of other trade unions. 'Of course,' said H. A., 'there will be a new upsurge one day, but who can tell when.' Our private ambition of finding a smallholding was proving to be a pipedream. The few that were available were not very attractive and were, in any case, out of our financial reach. Then to top it all H. A. had collapsed one day in the street, while he was out looking for a flat. The doctor who'd examined him could find nothing physically wrong and had expressed himself baffled. 'It's just emotional stress,' he guessed.

W HEN the Nationalists came to power in 1948 some of our comrades, fearing the worst and with memories of Nazism in Europe still fresh in their minds, packed their bags and hopped across the border to Rhodesia. Most of us sat tight, determined to stay. This was our country and we would carry on the struggle. In 1950 the Nationalists introduced the Suppression of Communism Act under which they appointed a Liquidator who published a list of 'named' persons. Those who were 'named' became non-persons. They could be ordered to leave their jobs, be told where to live, be made to resign from any club or organisation. The Minister of Justice assumed the right to decree with whom a 'named' person might communicate and he could imprison people in their own homes. The Communist Party was declared to be an illegal organisation but the Party pre-empted the government's plan by disbanding. However, it was deemed sufficient to have been a member of the Party at any time in the past to be banned, detained, banished, or placed under house arrest. As a Central Committee member H. A. was among the first to be 'named' and it was a matter of pride to me that after the Central Committee I was next in line to be so 'named'.

We continued working while we waited for the axe to fall. We knew that it was only a matter of time before we were ordered to leave our jobs and confined to house arrest or worse. If we were banned from working and confined to house arrest what were we going to do? Whether in Durban or in Cape Town our future looked bleak. H. A. had returned to Durban but he just seemed to be marking time. I called on Moses Kotane, our General Secretary and a very good friend. I had come to rely on his wisdom and his loving concern. 'Moses, what shall we do? It looks as if we can't live in Durban and we can't stay here.' Moses considered my question, taking his time before answering. 'I think,' he said, 'that it would be a good idea if you and H.A. and the children left this country.'

The thought of leaving South Africa, our work, our comrades, was not something I had seriously considered before, certainly not since coming to Cape Town. Lately, as our situation became more desperate and I began to feel hemmed in, I had started to fantasise about how life might be in – say – England, but I didn't believe in it as a practical possibility for us. Now, suddenly, here was Moses in whose judgement I trusted absolutely, proposing just such a solution. I looked at him blankly in mute surprise, then a doubt crept in, 'Do you think the Central Committee would agree?' 'I'll put it to them and let you know. After all,' he went on, 'we all know that it's only a matter of time before you're banned from holding any office. The Party will have to go underground but well-known Communists like you two will have little part to play in an illegal organisation. As I see it, if anyone has a good reason for leaving, you two do.'

A week later Moses called me to his office and said, 'We all think you should leave. There's an important job to be done overseas: people there need to know just what's happening here. You two could help to spread the word.' I flung my arms round his neck and kissed him. We would not have contemplated leaving without Party permission but now we were free to seek a new life overseas. Here indeed was Communism with a human face! Here were comrades who cared not only for the big principles and abstract ideas and the working class in theory; these comrades concerned themselves with the human needs of individual men and women. Once again we had good reason to congratulate ourselves on the calibre of our leaders: just how special they were in the international Communist arena we were not to discover until later.

As SOON as we had the go-ahead from the Central Committee, we applied for passports, H.A. in Durban, I in Cape Town. After a month of waiting and hoping, the answer came to each of us: 'Your application for a passport has been refused.' Although we had braced ourselves for this possibility, it nevertheless came as a crushing disappointment. What to do now? H.A. had come to visit us from Durban for the second time and he was living secretly with us in Nancy's house. We decided it would be best to get him out of the country first and then I would follow with the children. As long as he remained in Cape Town there was the ever-present risk of his discovery and arrest.

Sandra had become so used to denying his presence that all unfamiliar callers were told as soon as they appeared, 'My Daddy's not here,' before they even asked. One day I arrived from work to find Doris and Sandra in a state of agitation, their eyes wide with fear.

'Daddy's gone,' Sandra announced as soon as she saw me. She was bravely trying not to cry.

'What do you mean?' I demanded. I had visions of H. A. being dragged away in handcuffs.

Doris took over. 'Two men came and they asked for the master. We told them he's not here and they said they'd be back.'

'Where is H. A. now?' I asked. 'Is he in the back room?'

'No,' they told me. 'He jumped over the back fence and ran away. We don't know where he is.' I stood there wondering what to do. H. A. could be anywhere but I knew I could not telephone friends – we took it as a matter of course that our phones were tapped. He might have been captured already – a possibility I tried to dismiss from my mind. Keep cool, I told myself, feed the baby, make supper. There's nothing you can do but wait.

I was sitting in the back room breastfeeding Karen when I heard a tap-tap-tap on the window. I looked up to see the reassuring face of Wolfie Kodesh. He beckoned me outside. 'H. A.'s all right,' he whispered. 'He's safe for the time being.' 'Where is he?' I asked. For answer Wolfie placed his fingers to his lips and mouthed 'Shshsh . . .' 'What do you mean "Shsh . . ?"' I wanted to shake him. 'H. A.'s my husband. I'm entitled to know where he is. Don't you trust me?' Wolfie, the solid, trustworthy comrade, tried to reassure me but I also detected a lurking, little-boy delight in this real life adventure, this *Boys' Own* game of cops and robbers in which I had no part. 'If you must know,' he conceded grudgingly, 'I've hidden him in a hut up the mountain and no, you can't see him, it would be too risky.' He'd provided H. A. with food and blankets and we'd have to decide later where to go from there. Before I could question him further Wolfie scaled the back fence and disappeared as mysteriously as he'd come.

I returned to feeding Karen and had no sooner finished than there was a knock on the door. Sandra rushed in, shaking with fright. 'Mummy, Mummy, those bad men are back. They want to take my Daddy away. Don't let them in.' 'It's all right,' I tried to pacify her. 'They won't hurt us. I'll talk to them.' I opened the door and there they were: two thickset men in raincoats and dark trilbies, the unofficial CID uniform. If they weren't so sinister they'd be ridiculous.

'Can we interest you in a new system of water heating that has just come on the market? As we're in the area we thought we'd call on you and show you how it works.' No, I was not interested, and no, they could not come in to demonstrate, despite their clumsy attempts at persuasive charm. When Nancy came home she confirmed my suspicions. 'Hm,' she snorted, 'water heating indeed! Salesmen don't walk around in trilbies and dark raincoats and never in pairs.'

This incident brought home to us that H.A. had to get out of the country as quickly as possible. The question was, how? Ilse Dadoo thought she had the answer. She knew a disbarred lawyer in Pretoria who boasted that, for a fee, he could get a passport for anyone. She invited me to come to Johannesburg and she drove me to Pretoria. Mr X turned out to be as shady as his reputation. He looked at me with hard, lack-lustre eyes. 'Whether I win or lose it will cost you £180; but I've never failed anyone yet,' he assured me. He wanted cash and he was not disposed to enter into any negotiations. 'Take it or leave it. Trust me.' £180 was a lot of money but if it stood between us and freedom, what choice was there? I raised the sum and handed it over. Two weeks later I received a message from Ilse. 'He says the answer is no. They told him that if his client was an ordinary criminal, a robber or a murderer, he'd get the passport but they're not getting mixed up with politicals, meaning Communists. I'm sorry,' she added, 'I'm afraid that's your money down the drain.'

At the shipping office the agent was quite adamant. 'Without a passport you'll get no ticket.' I tried to convince him that it was not illegal to travel without a passport but he countered, 'I know it's not illegal for you to leave without a passport but you wouldn't be allowed to land anywhere and then we'd have to bring you back at our expense.' 'But we're British subjects. We have a right of entry into Britain,' I argued. 'I'd want to hear that from them,' the man told me, 'in writing.' The airlines adopted the same policy. The British embassy was not interested in my dilemma. 'It is not our custom, . . .' they began and followed with a good deal of pompous verbiage which, stripped down, meant 'no.' They were not prepared to give us written assurance of our right to land in Britain. The Israeli ambassador was no more sympathetic. 'I'm Jewish. I'm entitled to go to Israel with my family,' I told him. 'Won't you please give me a document to say so in order to satisfy the shippers.' The ambassador agreed that we would certainly be entitled to enter Israel once we found ourselves there. 'What's more,' he added, 'public opinion would be on your side. But I'm not going to make it easy for more Communists to come in. We have enough of those already.'

India was the third country on which we had a claim. 'Yes,' said the consular attaché, 'we have to accept any Indian who wishes to go to India but are you prepared to make it your permanent home?' Once there we would find it very difficult to leave. 'I'm far closer to Britain than I am to India,' H.A. confessed to me. 'I find I have more in common with the British than I do with the Indian Indians, culturally, socially, and in every way. I doubt whether I'd fit in in India.' This confession appeared to embarrass him; I tried to re-assure him. Even a first generation immigrant like me, I explained, can become completely integrated in the life of her country and regard it as much more her own than the land of her birth; how much more so must this apply to a third generation immigrant like him. Both of us knew much more about Queen Elizabeth I and

Shakespeare than we ever suspected of the history and literature of India or Lithuania. His language and mine was English, not Tamil or Hindi or Lithuanian or Yiddish, though this did not mean that either of us had to deny our roots or to value them less, or to apologise for them. No, we agreed, we did not want to settle in India. We wanted to reach England, where we felt we belonged.

AFTER two days in the mountain hut, Wolfie hid H.A. in various safe houses and then he brought him back to the room in Nancy's house where Sandra and Doris resumed their protective surveillance over him. It was becoming daily more urgent that he leave Cape Town, but for overseas, not for Durban. There was no alternative but to leave illegally, perhaps to stow away. But how to set about it? It was a field in which we had no experience.

Someone suggested that Lascars on one of the small cargo steamers plying between Cape Town and London might agree to hide H.A. If only one could find a sympathetic crew and make it worth their while to take the risk, a stowaway could make a get-away. I began to haunt the Cape Town docks. With Nancy at my side to bolster my courage and lend moral support, we loitered in the area, accosting passing sailors to test their reactions to our propositions. The first sailor listened open-mouthed to our story and said, 'You should come to speak to the captain. He's not a bad sort. He might help.' He led us on board a small, unkempt vessel, and knocked on the captain's door. We heard a gruff 'Come in.' and entered to find the captain sprawling on his bunk, a half empty whisky bottle at his side and the cabin befogged by liquor and cigarette fumes. He regarded us with disfavour. 'I don't allow women on my ship,' was his greeting. 'What do you want?' I decided to be equally direct. 'Would you consider taking a passenger to England if we made it worth your while?' 'Hm. A criminal, I suppose, running away from the law.' 'Well, no,' I said, 'he's not a criminal. He's a political who hasn't got a passport.' 'Politics,' he bellowed. 'I'm not getting mixed up in any of that. Off! off! Get off my ship!' Two nights later when Nancy and I drove down to the docks we saw police patrolling the area. We stayed in the car, drove through the docks and away.

During the following weeks Nancy and I kept a careful look-out for the harbour police. We did not relish the thought of being picked up as prostitutes and having to explain why we were not. We learnt to steel ourselves to the many insults and abuse from tipsy sailors; of course they took it for granted that we were soliciting – what else would bring two women down to the docks? Some threatened to become violent when we rejected their advances and I marvelled that any woman would choose this kind of danger and degradation to make a living. Early one evening we struck lucky. Two Lascars listened politely to what we told them and said, yes, they might be interested. We arranged to pick them up the following night to take them home and explain exactly what we wanted. With Wolfie as escort, we turned up the next night, to find eight Lascars instead of two and all were coming to the house. We brought another car and drove them all to Nancy's house where H. A. was waiting to meet them. After treating them to tea and cakes, wine and brandy, we got down to business.

Their English was limited and we had difficulty in making ourselves understood. Fortunately our friend Seedat was in town and he spoke their language. We called him in to translate and with his help we finally reached an agreement. For the sum of £300 to be divided amongst them, as well as six chickens and a crate of brandy, they would hide H. A. on board and look after him until the ship was out of the harbour. Once the ship was far enough out of port to make it impractical to turn back, H. A. was to give himself up and throw himself on the captain's mercy. They, the crew, would deny all knowledge of him. The ship was due to sail at three o'clock next day so it was agreed that early in the morning Wolfie would drive H. A. down to the docks, hidden under a pile of rags and blankets, together with the chickens and the brandy. Once they reached the ship Wolfie would walk up and down, whistling 'It's a long way to Tipperary,' and await their signal to transfer the loot and the stowaway on board and to hand over the cash.

'I must have whistled that blerry tune for half an hour,' Wolfie told me, 'and then I began to wonder if they recognised the song: I'm actually tone deaf, you see.' When he was beginning to wonder whether he shouldn't turn back the signal finally came to board the ship. They were hustled below deck to the headman's cabin and H. A. was quickly bundled into a smelly bunk where he was again hidden under a pile of blankets; he wondered how he would breathe. Just as Wolfie was handing over the cash a man was dragged into the cabin and 'our' Lascars proceeded to beat him up. They set about him with fists flying, not caring where their blows landed, on the head, chest, stomach, legs. 'What are you doing?' Wolfie cried. 'What's he done?' The headman brushed aside his protests and told him not to interfere. 'He belongs to another village and he found out about the stowaway. Now he wants a share of the money and threatens to tell the captain if we don't pay. We'll show him what'll happen if he talks.' Not wishing to add to my anxiety, Wolfie kept this incident from me until after H. A. had landed in England.

While these exchanges were taking place I kept out of the dock area but I watched for Wolfie's return at a pre-arranged spot at the bottom of Adderley Street. 'Is it all right? Is he safe? Will he get away?' I demanded of Wolfie as soon as I saw him. He took my arm. 'He'll be all right,' he assured me. 'If we go to the top of Woolworths building, we'll be able to see the ship pull out. Once they're beyond the harbour entrance he'll be safe.' The two of us slipped into the back entrance of Woolworths and taking care to avoid being seen we climbed to the top. We found our way to the roof from where we could see the ship in the harbour and we settled down to wait. For the rest of the morning we kept our eyes glued to the gangway of the ship, fearing to see H.A. being ignominiously ejected. Twelve o'clock came, then one and two and finally it was three o'clock. Nothing happened; the ship hadn't moved. 'Oh, Wolfie, they must've found him. They'll throw him off and hand him over to the police.' Wolfie gripped my arm. 'If they do, we'll see him coming off. Look, look,' he called out in excitement. 'They're pulling up the gangway and he's still on board. It'll be all right.'

We watched tensely as the ship pulled away slowly and made its way through the harbour entrance, into the wide, open Atlantic. We waited until the light faded and the ship disappeared from view. Then we left the roof top as unobtrusively as we could and made our way home. It was still possible, though unlikely, that if H.A. were discovered the ship might turn round and come back. There was also a chance that a vindictive captain might transfer his stowaway to a South African-bound ship at Madeira, their first port of call. To forestall such a calamity I waited a day and then sent a cable to Walter and Vera Saxton, our friends in London, together with a bank transfer for £250, asking them to go to the shipping office in London and pay for H.A.'s first-class passage. Please explain to them, I asked, that H.A. didn't stow-away to avoid payment but as the only way of getting out of S.A. When they did so, the shippers expressed surprise at such an unusual procedure, but were quite happy to accept the fare money.

H.A.'S account of his departure began with his anxious wait for the boat to pull out, hidden in the dank cabin. For him too, three o'clock came and went and no-one explained the reason for the delay but at five past three a flustered Lascar rushed in and ordered him out of the cabin. 'What do you mean?' H.A. demanded. 'Where should I go? I don't know my way around. You've just taken my money and promised to look after me and to hide me.' The Lascar boss explained that he'd intended to do so but that the situation had changed. The rival group of seamen, those who were not from their village, had not been deterred by the beating-up of their spokesman and were still threatening to expose them to the captain. He had given them some money but did not trust them. If H.A. left his cabin they could not pin it down to him. 'But where am I to go?' H.A. demanded. He'd never been on board a ship and certainly knew of no hiding places. With bad grace the Lascar rushed H.A. to the deck and bundled him into an empty oil-drum. 'You stay there for a couple of days,' he ordered and disappeared.

H.A. was not a small man and the drum was not large. By nine o'clock the next morning he was so stiff and cramped that he could endure his confinement no longer. With a great effort he toppled the drum to its side and crawled out, trying to straighten his limbs. A white officer strolling on the deck caught sight of H.A. as he wriggled his way out of the drum and gazed at him in astonishment. 'What on earth are you doing there and who are you?' he demanded. 'Please take me to your captain,' H.A. said. 'I'm a stowaway and I want to give myself up.' 'That's not so simple,' the officer replied. 'The captain is still sleeping and he hates to be woken up before he is good and ready.' On the other hand he might get into trouble for not reporting an incident such as this immediately, and on balance the officer decided to risk the captain's ire. He led H.A. to the captain's cabin and knocked timorously on the door. In reply came a flow of curses and abuse which did not augur too well but now there was no turning back.

'Reporting a stowaway, Sir,' the officer announced and H.A. found himself standing before a red-faced, irascible, middle-aged man who was still in the throes of his hangover. 'How dare you come on board my ship without my permission?' the captain roared and H.A. knew that this was no time to explain the political intricacies of the South African situation. 'Well you see, Sir,' H.A. started explaining, adopting a broken English which did not come naturally to him but which he felt would fit in with the image he was trying to project, 'I want to go to England to study and I have no money.'

He had decided to adopt Bernard's advice and to play the innocent; it offered a better chance of acceptance than laying bare the whole truth. Had they decided to search him they would have found the bundle of legal documents which set out who he was, why he was leaving and why, as a British subject, he should be admitted to the United Kingdom. Fortunately the captain was content to continue ranting for a while longer and then ordered him to be put to work, scrubbing the deck, 'to earn his passage'.

This H.A. willingly undertook and he scrubbed away for the rest of the voyage. After a while the news spread that a stowaway was on board and the few passengers diverted themselves by coming to catch a glimpse of him. One elderly Afrikaner sidled up one day and pushed a half-crown into his hand. 'Take this,' he told him. 'You'll need it when you get to the other side.'

When the ship docked at Southampton the captain, officers and passengers stood on the deck and gawped in amazement as H.A. was met by the Saxtons, a lawyer, a representative from the Civil Liberties Association and various immigration officers. They came on board to interview him, studied the various documents which he produced, and eventually agreed that he had a right to land. When the shipping company realized that their tame stowaway was a leading South African Communist they took fright. Very likely under pressure from the South African authorities they returned the money which we'd paid them for his fare and brought charges against him for unauthorized trespass of their ship. It was H.A.'s first experience of the British legal system, and he was amazed at the docility of his lawyer and the rudeness of the magistrate. Walter Saxton, a retired school inspector with a long and distinguished career in India, came to court to speak on H.A.'s behalf and was introduced by his correct title of 'Professor'. The magistrate sneered at him. 'Professor! Where did you pick up that title?' The lawyer tried to explain but the magistrate shouted him down and all the lawyer could mutter was 'Yes, your Honour.' 'Believe me,' H.A. told me afterwards, 'our South African lawyers would not have buckled under such bullying.' He was found guilty and fined £300. The proceeds from our house sale were fast diminishing but he'd arrived. He was in London – an acknowledged subject, though not yet a citizen of the United Kingdom.

AS SOON as news reached us of H.A.'s safe arrival, I began to plan our get-away. With two children stowing away was out of the question, but how to persuade a company to sell us tickets without a passport was a problem that exercised our minds night after night. Several friends came up with schemes which were dangerous, hare-brained, or just impractical. One said, 'Why don't I drive you to a deserted beach, put you and the children into a small boat and you row out to sea. You are bound to be picked up by a passing vessel.' I recalled this suggestion when I read about the Vietnamese boatpeople, and it was borne in on me how desperate to get away these poor folk must have been to undertake such a dangerous means of escape. I had nightmares in which my boat overturns in heavy seas; I'm trying to save my two children, each one crying out for me from opposite ends of the boat; or I'm watching helplessly as our stocks of water disappear and the children plead for a drink. These images haunted me even in waking hours. Bribery and disguise were also mooted and one friend even offered to help me hijack a plane. As time wore on the suggestions grew more bizarre and fantastical and as often as not we'd end up on the floor, rolling with laughter. But no one could think of a realistic way out.

It was clever Bernard Herzberg who finally came up with a plan which was feasible, safe and legal. 'Find a woman,' he told me, 'of about your age who qualifies for a British passport, a patrial, someone whose parents or grand-parents were born in Britain. She'd be less likely to have it withdrawn for helping you than if she had a South African passport, but she must be prepared for police harrassment when the story leaks out, as it's bound to do. This friend then applies for a passport in her own name and you give her a letter authorising her to enter your children's names on her passport. You explain that you want her to take your children to England because you want them brought up and educated "at home". This good friend then buys the tickets for herself and the children and goes through Customs and Immigration. You go on board with them, ostensibly to see them off. At the last minute she changes her mind about going so she disembarks, taking her passport with her. You then take her place on board. When you get to England you apply for entry as a British subject and they will grant it, as they did with H.A.'

Like all bright ideas, the scheme was so simple and obvious. Why hadn't I thought of it? Finding a friend to help me proved to be the easiest part. Joan Robinson qualified for a British passport because her grandfather was born in England. When I explained my request to her she didn't hesitate. 'Of course I'll do it,' she said even though she knew that by helping me she would be drawing a lot of unwelcome police attention to herself. Joan's subsequent arrest and detention during the Emergency of 1960 was directly linked to her act of friendship; the police admitted as much when her father intervened on her behalf. Our plans were working smoothly and with mounting excitement I awaited our day of departure. Joan obtained her passport with my children's names entered on it and she booked their passage on the *Pretoria Castle*. As the date of my departure drew nearer my feelings grew mixed: I wanted to go but I hated to leave. I longed to be re-united with H. A. but I knew I would miss Cape Town desperately. The night before our ship sailed I couldn't resist throwing a farewell party, to say goodbye to my closest friends who had worked so tirelessly to help me although Bernard had warned me to keep my plans secret. I told only a few friends who were close as clams but the party nearly proved to be my undoing. Owen Williams, a journalist friend of Joan's, got wind of it and published a news item in his gossip column speculating about where Miss Podbrey had gone. He reported that he'd enquired for me at my office but no one could or would tell him my whereabouts. There were rumours, he wrote, that I had left for India, or was it England? Had I gone to join my husband? Were my children with me? This alerted the police but by then we were three days out to sea.

It was a late afternoon in mid-July 1951 when Joan, the children and I went up the gangplank of the Union Castle liner and I watched as Joan passed through the Customs and the Passport control. She presented her ticket at the barrier and was waved through, together with the children. I walked up with them. When the call came for non-passengers to go ashore I said goodbye to Joan and she left, as arranged, taking her passport with her. I took the children below and kept out of sight until the ship left the harbour. Our friend Sonia Bunting, on her way to an International Youth Festival, shared our cabin and she and I both tried to explain to Sandra why she now had to call me Joan, not Mummy. By now our six-year old Sandra was becoming used to bizarre requests and she tried to comply for the rest of the voyage but every now and then 'Joan' was forgotten and 'Mummy' slipped out. 'Oh, I'm sorry,' she'd giggle so that everyone present would turn to look at her. 'I don't mean Mummy, I mean Joan.'

Before Cape Town dissolved entirely in the evening mist I felt compelled to get a last glimpse of my beloved city. I went on deck and watched as the distance widened between me and Table Mountain. These last seven years, I told myself, were the best years of my life and I'll never see their like again. I recalled the words of Queen Mary Tudor, 'When I am dead and opened, you shall find "Calais" lying in my heart.' On my heart you shall find 'Cape Town'. My sense of loss persisted well beyond the length of the voyage. It took me seven years to conquer the nagging, aching, emptiness inside me. Not a day passed without my thoughts turning to Cape Town with longing and a sense of despair. And then the day came when I woke up in London and realized that Cape Town belonged to a world which was dead and gone for ever. Even if I went back the next day, I knew I would not find again my old life, my work, my home. By then most of our friends had also left. Enough of this pointless, sentimental nostalgia, I berated myself sternly. The past is over. Live in the present.

On the third day out at sea a steward arrived with a message from the purser. 'Would Mrs Robinson kindly present herself to him.' Sonia became agitated. 'They've found out,' she said. 'What will happen now!' I tried to reassure her. 'They won't throw me overboard.' The purser was polite and formal. 'May I see your passport, Mrs Robinson?' 'I'm not Mrs Robinson,' I told him. 'My name is Mrs Naidoo and I have no passport.' 'No passport!' he looked at me in amazement. 'But everyone has a passport.' Starting at the beginning and as honestly as I knew how I told him my story not omitting the politics, the mixed marriage, the fruitless efforts to get a passport. The man heard me out and then to my delighted surprise he chuckled. 'I've got a cable here from the Cape Town police. They've caught up with you, but they're too late. As far as I'm concerned, you've paid your passage and you've broken no law. Welcome on board.' I thanked him and as I rose to leave he added, "Er . . . one more thing. If you don't mind, would you continue as Mrs. Robinson, just for our records.' In high spirits I went below and told Sonia the good news. 'We can now begin to enjoy this trip,' I told her. And we did. We swam and danced and played deck games; we made friends and laughed a good deal. It was on this journey that I first saw Danny Kaye in *The Secret Life of Walter Mitty*, and even now, about twenty viewings later, I still find it hilariously funny. That first time on the boat I turned enthusiastically to a middle-aged white couple as we were leaving the cinema and burst out, 'Wasn't that wonderful?' He pulled a face and so did she. 'Such silly nonsense,' she said and he agreed. It made me feel better about leaving South Africa.

It was a dull, misty afternoon when our boat docked at Southampton. H. A. was there to meet us, accompanied by a lawyer and a press photographer. When I tried to disembark I was held back by an immigration official who'd come aboard, 'You'd better wait here,' he told me. 'There's a slight problem.' By now the rest of the passengers had departed and I was left alone on deck, holding Karen in one arm and grasping Sandra's hand with the other. Our lawyer and the official engaged in a long and heated dispute and I wondered what would happen if our lawyer lost the argument. Would they send us back? After some time H. A. was allowed on board and as we hugged each other we wondered whether it was possible that all our efforts could now come to nothing. Many hours passed and finally we were given permission to land. The Customs officials at the dockside looked at us suspiciously. They pointed to our crates stacked up on the now deserted tarmac containing our household goods so meticulously packed by our friend Etel Mittag.

'Will you open these crates please and let us examine them?' I couldn't believe they were serious. The crates were big and well nailed down; the children were cold and tired and hungry. It was dark and the last train for London had left a long time ago; we didn't know where we would sleep that night. 'We'll tell you where we're placing the crates in storage; you can examine them there,' we pleaded. 'You can't make us off-load them here!' I had visions of my pots and pans, sheets and plates spread out on the ground all around us, the children growing hungrier, worn out and fractious and us watching helplessly as these stony-faced officers continued to dig into our personal belongings, searching for we knew not what. After a good deal of argument they eventually agreed to let us off and then, as if to prove that they were still in charge, I was ordered to empty my handbag. When I did so they pounced on a bit of old newspaper on which I had rolled up a length of black cotton and through which I had pinned a needle, just in case I had to sew up a hem or mend a lining on the journey. With great care they removed the needle and unwound the thread. Then the paper was carefully smoothed out and examined, first one side then the other. When they were satisfied that it contained no dangerous codeword or secret message the paper was meticulously rolled up again and the black cotton re-wound on it. I was grinning but Sonia was indignant. 'H'm,' she snorted in disgust, 'do you call this British democracy?' 'Never mind,' I told her, 'we've landed, we're here.' I was grateful to be here and relieved; I could overlook the silly irritations but the irony of the situation did not escape me. Here was I claiming and winning rights of entry and citizenship through my marriage to H. A. who was himself disfranchised in his own country of birth.

We found rooms in a guest house for the night and the next morning we set out for London. As I gazed out of the train window in happy anticipation my eyes rested on mile upon mile of dreary, dank streets, wilting lines of washing and square, squat chimneys on top of peeling, shabby houses. How sad and unbeautiful it all seemed! When we reached London we found a city pockmarked with bullet holes, rubble everywhere and people who looked tired and careworn. It was August Bank Holiday weekend when we arrived and the whole town seemed to be deserted. We started telephoning the friends who had promised to help, only to find that they had all left town for the long weekend. The boarding houses were either full or not prepared to accommodate children. We were becoming desperate. Eventually we succeeded in tracking down an English comrade who had once passed through Durban and enjoyed our hospitality. Diffidently he offered to let us sleep on his floor that night and we accepted gratefully.

THE next day we decided that we might as well turn our dilemma to good advantage. We would take our first family holiday and go away somewhere nice by the seaside for a week or so. With our friend's help we booked a room in a boarding house in Broadstairs, described as a 'fine seaside resort'. Everything was new to us. Going on holiday together was a 'first' in our lives, exciting and thrilling. When we reached Broadstairs we stepped off the train and waited for our luggage to be off-loaded from the guard's van. We had no reason to suppose that the procedure here would be any different from South Africa where attendants see to the luggage. When it dawned on us that the train was pulling out with our luggage still on board, I ran to the driver's cabin and waved frantically to him, 'Stop, stop, we want our luggage,' I called to him. The driver didn't hear my words but he saw me waving and he waved back cheerfully as his train gathered speed and disappeared. The station master was sympathetic and telephoned down the line but he could promise nothing. With a bit of luck we might get our luggage tomorrow or it might take longer, he couldn't say.

Then, instead of heading for the seashore, as I'd confidently expected, our taxi dropped us off at a gloomy, semi-detached house in the suburbs. It could have been anywhere. This was no 'fine, seaside, holiday resort'; there was no glimpse of the sea. The landlady welcomed us without much enthusiasm and showed us up three flights of stairs to a cluttered room. The tiny window and the sharply sloping roof of the attic in which we found ourselves induced claustrophobia rather than romance and its musty smell testified to its infrequent use. They clearly deemed it good enough only for couples with children and in this boarding house there weren't many of those around. 'Dinner's at 6.30,' our landlady announced as she turned and left. We had with us one spare napkin and the baby's bottle. I changed Karen's nappie, washed it out and hung it over the back of a chair to dry. We then washed our hands and faces and descended to the dining room. The other guests were already seated and all looked up as we entered. They watched us silently as we made our way between the tables until we reached an unoccupied one in a corner of the room. When we made as if to sit down, a fellow diner at the next table leaned forward, 'Oh, I wouldn't sit there if I were you,' she informed us with considerable satisfaction. 'That's Miss Freemantle's table.'

We retreated hastily and waited until the elderly waitress agreed to see us and lead us to another corner, deeper in the shadows. She served us a putty-coloured soup which was followed by two wafer-thin slices of overdone beef, lumpy mashed potatoes and soggy cabbage. The pudding was something unrecognis-able hidden under watery custard. H. A. and I looked at each other and then at

Re-united in London, 1951.

London, 1951.

our fellow-guests. They seemed to be tucking in without complaint and at the end of the meal each one carefully rolled up his or her napkin and ceremoniously inserted it into the napkin holder. We retreated to our bedroom, put the children to sleep, and sat and looked at each other. 'Is this what they call a holiday?' H. A. wanted to know. The next morning when we came down to breakfast the news had got round that our luggage was missing and this seemed to stimulate everyone into a great good humour. Suddenly everyone was friendly and chatty and full of consoling words. 'I had a friend who lost her luggage on a train once, when she was travelling to Scunthorpe,' one elderly lady volunteered. 'But she got it back — six weeks later. I'm sure yours will turn up eventually.' Her companion could beat this, 'My friend also lost her luggage on a train but it went to Stockholm before they returned it,' she added triumphantly. A third guest also had a friend who lost his luggage, 'But he never got it back.' We spent the day telephoning the railways and wondering what we should do. It was too far to walk to the beach and anyway, the weather was dull and cloudy. The following morning our lost luggage reappeared and with great relief we settled our bill and caught the next train back to London. So ended our first family holiday in our new country.

D URING the following six months we moved house five times. From a room in an Ealing boarding house we went to a flat in Finsbury Park and then when the owner of the flat returned from holiday, we moved to another lodging house in Manor House. After a fortnight the landlady called me aside. 'This arrangement wasn't meant to be long-term,' she told me. 'We don't normally have children here and you have two.' She said this accusingly and I felt guilty for my presumption in having two. 'I'm sorry,' I apologised. 'We are trying very hard to find a flat and it shouldn't be long now.' Then came an unexpected leap into upper-class luxury. It happened when our wealthy South African friend, Minnie Bodenstein, invited us to use her elegant flat in Park Lane while she went to stay with friends in the country. For two weeks I pushed a dilapidated pram up and down elegant Park Lane and we spent hours in Hyde Park, listening incredulously to the rude things some of the speakers said about some of Britain's most hallowed institutions, such as the Church and the Royal family, as well as to the speakers who preached sensible, left-wing politics. It seemed to us as if sense and nonsense was handed down in equal proportions from these platforms.

When Minnie returned and we had to vacate her flat, a friend of a friend from the Friends of the Soviet Union arranged for us to rent a flat in Fulham belonging to an absent Irish professor. There was only one condition, that we leave one room free for his son whenever he wanted to stay there. The son, a charming young man, would turn up from time to time with another young man and I would say, 'You've only one narrow bed in your room, so why doesn't your friend sleep here on the sofa – he'd be much more comfortable?' 'No, that's all right,' I'd be told, 'we're used to it,' but I, in my ignorance, wishing to be helpful, would persist. I had no concept of homosexuality nor, it seems, had H. A. for he didn't try to stop me from interfering or trying to persuade them how and where they would be more comfortable.

Budapest

IMMEDIATELY after arriving in London we reported to the Party head office in King Street. Comrade Bob Stewart received us, an avuncular, round-faced man whose lack of pretension and friendly Scots burr encouraged confidence. 'I've read about your arrival in the *Daily Worker* and seen your picture there,' he told us. 'Your General Secretary, Moses Kotane, has written to us about you,' he added. 'He gives you good references and speaks highly of both of you. You, H.A. Naidoo, were on the Secretariat of the Central Committee and Pauline, your wife, was a member of the Cape Town District Committee.' He was reading from the letter before him and peering at us over his spectacles. 'I expect you'll be looking for work now.' We confirmed that we needed jobs, a permanent place to live, a school for Sandra and a nursery for the baby. We'd be grateful for any suggestions he could offer. Bob gave us a benign smile. 'I think I might be able to solve all your problems,' he said. 'How would you like to live and work in Hungary, broadcasting for Radio Budapest in English? You would of course be provided with accommodation, schooling and everything else you needed. They'd look after you pretty well.' We looked at each other in disbelief. The thought of living and working in a socialist country excited and thrilled us! In our dreams we'd never hoped for such a privilege. To experience at first hand the struggles and achievements of building socialism, to share in the life of a people engaged in this historic task, to be part of their movement to create a workers' paradise; it all seemed to us too good to be true.

'We'd love to but we know nothing about broadcasting,' H.A. blurted out. Bob brushed this objection aside. 'They'll teach you all you need to know once they've accepted you,' he assured us. 'That is the least of your problems. The main thing is for them to give you positive vetting. They've already rejected a number of our previous recommendations but your credentials should satisfy even them. You're the highest-ranking Party members we've put forward. I'll send in your names and let you know.' Clearly political reliability mattered far more than technical or professional skill. 'Anyway,' Bob assured us, 'you, Comrade Naidoo, are an experienced journalist. You'll soon learn the ropes.'

When we called back a week later, there was no reply from the Hungarians, but, as Bob remarked, 'You can't rush these things. And since you're here,' Bob continued, 'let me introduce you to Comrade Palme Dutt.' Judging from his respectful manner it was obvious that this was an honour not granted lightly. Palme Dutt was the internationally recognised interpreter of Marxism/Leninism, a leading theoretician whose name was well known to us from his writings on theory and practice. One didn't so much read Palme Dutt as study him. At the Empire Party Conference H.A. had heard him speak and been introduced, but formally, distantly, and he now welcomed what he thought would be an opportunity of getting to know the great man better. Bob led us into Palme Dutt's office and I saw a tall, gaunt man, bent over a pile of papers on his desk. He barely raised his head as Bob introduced us and he muttered a greeting. It was clear that Comrade Palme Dutt was too immersed in ideological problems to waste time on people. He seemed to resent the interruption; we did not stay long.

The next day we rang the bell of the heavy door at the Hungarian Embassy in Eaton Place, expecting a warm, comradely greeting, but our reception was disappointingly cool. A severe young woman in grey woollen skirt, buttoned-up flannel shirt and thick, flat shoes – a combination I was later to identify as received Party wisdom in female attire, almost a Party uniform – informed us that before any visas could be issued to us many inquiries would have to be made and this would take time. 'Come back in two weeks' time,' she instructed and walked us to the door.

A fortnight later there was still no news, nor a fortnight after that. We complained to Comrade Bob who looked pained and assured us that he was doing all he could but clearly his influence was limited. When three months had passed and our bank balance was shrinking by the day I suggested to H.A. that perhaps he should get a job. He explained that it wouldn't be easy for a journalist to find temporary work and this seemed reasonable enough so I registered with a secretarial agency while he looked after the children. For the next three months I typed and clerked my way round a succession of London offices but despite my wages we still had to dig into our savings. At the beginning of December we called on Comrade Bob and presented him with an ultimatum. 'Unless our visas come through within the next two weeks,' we told him, 'we'll call the whole thing off.'

The uncertainty and insecurity of our existence was becoming too much of a strain but what also hurt was the thought that we weren't trusted. What else could account for this long-drawn-out investigation into our bona-fides? Before the fortnight had elapsed Comrade Bob called to tell us that our visas had been authorised and all would now be plain sailing. At the Hungarian Embassy we found that the former chill had been transformed into a warm, genial welcome. A smiling consul presented us with travel documents, visas and tickets and we drank a toast in Tokay Aszu to our life in Budapest. 'As you have no passports,' he told us, 'we thought it would be safer for you to travel through friendly socialist countries and so we have arranged for you to go by boat to Gdansk in Poland. There you will catch a train to Prague, spend a night in a hotel and then fly to Budapest. From now on you are our guests and our responsibility and we shall look after you,' he assured us, his arms round our shoulders.

The British passport officer who checked our documents at the London docks before we embarked on the Polish vessel looked at us in amazement when we told him that we had no passports. 'But we're entitled to leave with these travel documents, aren't we?' 'Oh yes,' he said, 'there's nothing to stop you from leaving but do you realise what you're doing, going behind the Iron Curtain without passports, and with young children? You'll be completely at their mercy.' I dismissed his comments with disdain. 'Of course we know what we're doing,' I informed him haughtily. 'We're going to a Socialist country.' A country, I might have added, where we expected warm friendship, hard work, equal sharing, enthusiastic commitment and the privilege of playing a part in the building of a bright new future.

We weren't long enough in Gdansk to look around, but when we reached Prague and checked in at the sombre hotel, we took a walk before supper. What we saw was a beautiful city but a sad one. It lacked vitality; it seemed downcast. Instead of a confident, purposeful people we found men and women who kept their eyes on the ground as they hurried past, dejected, morose. Back in the hotel the waiters pretended to be hard of hearing and the receptionist gave every indication of hating people.

'I think,' said H. A. 'that the Czechs are by nature a rather dour people. Don't you think so?' I agreed that it must be so and then I recalled the party we had in Cape Town when Harry and Beryl Bloom turned up after spending some years in Prague where Harry had worked as a press correspondent having abandoned his legal practice. Rumours had reached us in Cape Town that the Blooms were critical of the Czech Party leadership after the fall of the Benes government. We were given to understand that they were under a political cloud. For us, the Party faithful, that was enough. We cold-shouldered our old friends that evening and made it clear that as far as we were concerned, they were *persona non grata*. We didn't give them a chance to explain; if our Czech comrades were critical of them, they must have erred. Now, as we went to sleep in our cold room in Prague, I wondered secretly whether perhaps, just by chance, there was something wrong here. Should we not have given the Blooms a chance to tell us? By the time we reached Budapest I'd managed to banish these seditious thoughts.

IT WAS a cold day in early January 1952 when we stepped off the plane and were formally greeted with flowers by Comrade Kati Gal on behalf of Radio Budapest and °Comrade Szusza on behalf of the Hungarian Party. With them was Leon Griffiths, the young head of the English section whose term of office had now expired and who was waiting impatiently to initiate H. A. into the job before returning to England. They took us to a building in Museum Utza where most of the foreign radio workers were housed in a large apartment on the second floor. We were allocated two comfortable rooms with our own bathroom and introduced to the housekeeper, Comrade Marika, who would cook and clean for all of us. We shared this apartment with the Italians, French, Turks and the rest of the English section, all of us employees of the foreign section of Radio Budapest.

Leon was a talented journalist with a sardonic manner and, as we soon learnt, an air of deep disillusion with the workings of the system which he, too, had initially come to serve with dedication. He was careful not to influence our judgment, preferring to let us find out for ourselves. Then there was Isobel Pepper, a former actress from Unity Theatre who squinted at the world through a haze of blue smoke from the cigarette which always dangled from her lower lip. She was proud of her working class origins and determined to keep calling a spade a spade. Dora Scarlett joined our section a month or two later. She was older than the rest of us, and she had the tough, self-centred independence that characterises so many English spinsters. She had no previous experience of broadcasting or of journalism, but her credentials also must have proved acceptable. The last to join our section was Graham Heathcote, a lanky ex-*Daily Mirror* man who had thrown up a good post in Fleet Street for a job which he considered would be more worthwhile and morally rewarding. Graham regaled us with anecdotes of life in Fleet Street which he recounted in a dry, understated manner. How very English, I thought admiringly.

Our secretary, interpreter, translator and guide, was Yudit, a well-built young woman with chiselled features and a soft, gentle voice. She had an excellent command of English and could also interpret fluently from French and Italian and a little more hesitantly from German and Spanish. This was a great asset at our multi-lingual, Babelish departmental meetings when all seventeen foreign sections got together, huddled round their own interpreters.

Kati was the official go-between us and the rest of the department. She it was who carried our complaints, requests and comments to the higher echelons in the Radio and the Party, either to be dealt with or, as was later disclosed, to be recorded in the debit side of our secret files. We were encouraged to regard her as our friend and we did so. In many ways she was our friend, and where possible, she did her best for us but she also had, understandably, a great sense of self-preservation and whenever this conflicted with her loyalty to us, we naturally came second. Who could blame her! Kati had learnt her survival techniques the hard way. She was 18 and her sister was 17 when both girls were rounded up by the Nazis and deported to Auschwitz. Like everyone else who survived the death camps, Kati was reticent about her experiences. She had a naturally cheerful disposition and a practical, pragmatic approach to life. Circumstances had tossed her into the role of party *apparatchik*; she would have better filled the part of contented suburban housewife, enjoying a gossip and a grouse with the neighbours, caring for husband and son and creating for the family a safe and comfortable haven. Much later, when I got to know her better, I asked Kati about her Auschwitz experiences.

'LUCKILY for us,' she told me, 'my sister and I were both young and fit, so we survived. We were put to work building an airstrip. We had to leave our huts when it was still dark to trudge to the site carrying our spades. On winter mornings it was bitterly cold and many women suffered from frostbite.' It was a grim memory but suddenly Kati remembered something else and burst out laughing. 'Do you know the best way to warm your toes when they're dropping off with frostbite?' she asked me. 'It's a useful hint to keep in mind. You put them between someone's legs, right up here, in the crotch. It's the warmest part of the body, did you know that? That's how my sister and I warmed each other when we got back at night, to stop our toes from falling off.' She remembered something else. 'One day my sister came running to me in great excitement. She'd seen a notice posted on the wall inviting blue-eyed blonde women to volunteer for lighter duties. We were both blonde and blue-eyed so she was all for it. 'Let's go,' she urged me. 'I can't take the back-breaking digging much longer.' 'Did you volunteer?' I asked. 'No we didn't, fortunately for us,' Kati answered. 'I told my sister that I didn't trust those Nazi swine. At first she argued but in the end she reluctantly agreed.' 'Did you ever find out what those lighter duties were?' I asked her. 'Yes, I did, after the war, when I met a girl who served as a medical orderly in that camp. The Germans needed blood for their troops on the Eastern front, when their losses multiplied. They were so desperate that they even took Jewish blood for their transfusions, but they stipulated that it had to come from blue-eyed blondes, you know, the Aryan ideal. So the poor, foolish girls who thought they'd be given lighter work had their blood sucked out and then were left to die.'

ANNA Peterne was one stage higher up in rank. She was an American married to an Hungarian who had returned to his homeland after the liberation and he now held a lofty, mysterious post in the Party hierarchy. Anna was small and trim with a taste for smart clothes which set her apart from the rest of the Party sisterhood in their drab, shapeless grey. She atoned for this deviation by outdoing the rest in her protestations of Party loyalty and by always managing to be one step ahead in knowing and promoting the correct new Party line. Maybe her husband's influential insider position gave her an advantage. She was the bossy head of the North American section and, in addition, was charged with the responsibility of monitoring the work of the English section. After Kati had checked the accuracy of the translations from the Hungarian, the material was then submitted to Anna for 'lecting', a strange, deformed word which aptly described the manner in which she went through all we had written, searching for the naughty word or phrase, which here, at Radio Budapest, could consist of many more than four letters. She was as diligent as any Catholic inquisitor in pouncing on a deviation from the official Party line or what she deemed to be so. When, as frequently happened, a dispute arose between us, the item in question had to go a stage higher for a ruling. It had to be submitted upstairs to Comrade Istvan.

Istvan was a nervous, bespectacled man who could and did arbitrate on the finer linguistic and semantic meanings of words and phrases in 14 languages. He confessed that he was fluent only in six but he claimed, with justice, to have a good working knowledge of the other eight languages. He was responsible for the foreign language broadcasts, answerable only to the chief of the department. His absolute devotion to the Party and its edicts was rooted in a firm conviction that no matter how stony the path at its end lay Utopia, and in order to achieve it no sacrifice was too great. It is not always easy to distinguish between the idealists and the time-servers, the true believers and the merely ambitious, because, combined with power, the effect is the same. I think that Istvan was probably sincere in his loyalty but when we confronted each other over matters of policy or terminology he became part of the 'other side', the ruling class.

About Comrade Szusza, the Party secretary, we had no illusions. No one could accuse her of sincerity or even good intentions; she lurked in the shadows of the hierarchical maze, drab, stooped, humourless, intense and, as we soon came to realise, all-powerful. Like a grey spider Szusza would emerge from her dingy office in the nether regions to admonish, castigate, punish, always, of course, for the good of The Party and therefore for the good of the entire working class, the people, the country, International Peace, and the Soviet Fatherland; higher than that one could not go. '*Servus!*' she would greet you when meeting in the corridors, in what she believed to be a comradely gesture, and on the sunniest day your spirits would sink.

BUDAPEST is a beautiful city on the banks of the Danube and the Hungarians are a talented, witty, life-loving people, but in January 1952 we could only glimpse the ghost of the gay and romantic place it once was. The wide streets were still flanked by graceful, well-proportioned buildings but these were pockmarked by shell fire and mortar fire, discoloured, not unlike London. 'The Germans blew up all our seven bridges before they were driven out,' Kati informed us, 'and we have already managed to rebuild them all,' she added proudly. True enough, there was construction work going on all round the city – with women labourers sharing the tough, physical jobs with the men. This was something I had not seen before. I admired their endurance and respected the obvious sexual equality this demonstrated, but I also wondered, would I be prepared to undertake such back-breaking labour? At midday the men and women labourers produced thick hunks of bread and lumps of pork fat for lunch which they consumed there and then on the building sites, out in the cold, sometimes perched on girders high in the air.

I searched the faces of passers-by for signs of eager, enthusiastic commitment. Where were all those happy, determined men and women, marching forward in triumph, with red banners held high? Where were the models for the people who'd inspired me on all those Soviet posters? The strong, rosy-cheeked women, the determined, confident men? Were these dejected, suspicious citizens the builders of the glorious future?

'You've got to remember,' Anna explained when I broached the subject, 'Hungary had 25 years of Horthy Fascism and the remnants of the old regime don't like to be dispossessed of their privileges. Naturally they're dissatisfied, but the majority, the workers, are now much better off and grateful to the Party.' The backwardness, repression and exploitation of the '25 years of Horthy Fascism' became a recurring theme in any explanation of present-day shortcomings and, together with my colleagues in the English section, I was only too eager to accept it. All the same, it would have been good to meet more of those happy workers in whose name the Party ruled.

When I announced in triumph a few weeks later that I'd met and made friends with a Hungarian who was an enthusiastic supporter of the new regime and that he'd invited H.A. and me and the children to his house to meet his family, I expected Anna and Szusza to be delighted; instead there was all-round consternation. 'Where did you meet him?' Anna demanded. 'He's one of the soldiers in the forecourt of the Radio,' I told her. There was a permanent detachment of soldiers guarding the entrance to the Radio building who checked our passes before we were allowed through, no matter how many times a day we went in and out. I had argued with one of these guards when he tried to insist that seven-year-old Sandra also needed a pass. Finally, when I presented him with her official dispensation, signed by the Party secretary – after a long argument – he grinned with apparent relief. It was clear that he had not relished having to enforce such a silly rule, and he and I became friends.

'You musn't trust just anyone you meet,' Szusza lectured me. 'You don't know who might be an enemy. After all, we've had 25 years of Horthy Fascism.' 'But this is a soldier, our guard,' I protested. 'Surely he's been vetted for security.' Szusza pursed her tight lips. 'You can't take anything for granted. You must never again go to a private house unless it's been arranged through the Party.' Our soldier friend must have been transferred for we never saw him again and so ended our one and only attempt to establish friendly contact with an ordinary Hungarian family. Their small, neat, crowded flat was the only private home we visited during our stay in Budapest – apart from Anna's house. He was also the only Hungarian we met in our three-and-a-half years' stay who was an enthusiastic supporter of the regime, but it didn't seem to help him keep his job.

Just before leaving Budapest for England we managed to strike up a friendship with a Hungarian journalist. What a pity, we said, that we hadn't met sooner. Why indeed had he not approached us before, I demanded, considering we all worked for the Radio and he spoke such good English. He then told us that they had been warned about us as we had been about them. 'Don't mix with these foreigners; you don't know who might be a spy.'

Kati found a local school for Sandra and a nursery, set among the leafy gardens of Buda, for Karen. Every morning a school bus picked her up and it delivered her back in the afternoon. She seemed to like her new surroundings and was happy to go there. Sandra, too, enjoyed her new school and was made much of by her teacher and fellow pupils. Within three months her Hungarian was fluent and she walked away with the language prize at the end of her first year. 'And what did you have for lunch today?' I would question her. 'Today we had soup and bread,' she'd announce, or, 'Today we had pork and bread.' I went to the school and saw for myself that the child was not fabricating. I stormed in to Kati. 'Is this the way to feed children? Isn't it disgraceful? We have good food in our canteen. Why can't they?' Kati sighed. 'I'm sure they're issued with good food but someone must be selling it on the black market and stealing the cash. I'll look into it,' she promised. A few days later she told me: 'I've arranged for Sandra to eat her lunch with us, here in the Radio. It's only a short walk from her school.' She looked pleased with herself and I was grateful for my child. 'But Kati,' I asked, 'what about the other children? What are you going to do about them?' Kati patted my back tolerantly, 'Oh, Comrade Pauline,' she laughed, 'you can't take the troubles of the world on your shoulders. Just be pleased that your child is all right.'

WHAT'S gone wrong here, I wondered miserably. This is not socialism! How can they turn their backs on the theft of food from children and pretend it isn't happening? Was it inefficiency or corruption? Where was the hue and cry over the scandal? The exposure, the steps to clean it up? As the weeks went by we came across more and more examples of injustice that battered our consciences and caused us distress but we kept on trying to find explanations, if not excuses. H.A. took it particularly hard. 'Is this,' he anguished, 'the cause to which I dedicated my life?'

The five of us from the English section would meet in a coffee house after work, away from our office, in an old-fashioned partitioned cubicle which offered a sense of privacy and there we would agonise over 'What has gone wrong?' We wanted to believe Dora when she reminded us, 'After all, they have lived for 25 years under Horthy Fascism, they don't know the meaning of democracy.' 'But the Party should be teaching them,' Isobel said, 'and setting an example. Democratic centralism indeed,' she snorted, quoting Lenin's famous dictum. 'They know all about centralism but precious little about democracy.'

'Well, they know a lot about football,' Graham offered and we all laughed gratefully, relieved to turn our backs on politics, if only for a while. As our sports commentator Graham covered the only field to which the whole nation was dedicated, where national unity was patently manifest. The first things that greeted us on arrival in Budapest were banners, flags, posters, shop displays, even cakes in patisserie windows, all decorated with the numbers 8–3. Not being football fans, we had no idea what this meant. When strangers heard us speaking English they would shout gleefully, 'EIGHT THREE!' 'What does it mean?' we asked Kati and she looked at us in astonishment. 'Don't you know that we beat your English team 8–3? It's a great national victory.'

In the coffee house H.A. brought us back to the serious subject under discussion. 'What bothers me,' he said, 'is that all the Party people seem to be on the make. Where are the good, devoted, honest comrades with whom we grew up? Where are the people who belonged to the Party before 1945, when it was a dangerous thing to do? All these people climbed on the bandwagon after the Party came to power and they're reaping benefits from their Party membership, material benefits.'

'I think,' I suggested naïvely, 'that Comrade Rakosi doesn't know what's happening in the Party. If only he could be told I'm sure he'd do something about it; after all, he's been to prison for his beliefs and he's spent 16 years in exile in the Soviet Union. He's a real Communist.' I wasn't alone in my artlessness; we all believed it because we wanted desperately to believe it. We could not imagine that a man who had suffered imprisonment and exile for his convictions could be anything but upright and honest.

Five months later, during a visit to the Houses of Parliament, it was arranged for H.A., Isobel and me to meet Comrade Rakosi, the Secretary of the Party, and the boss of the country. It was impressed upon us that we were greatly favoured and we were warned that the great man would not have too much time to spend with us. My first impression of the unattractive figure who came to greet us, arms outstretched and watermelon smile, was the absence of a neck. His outsize head seemed to rest directly on his shoulders and his arms appeared too long for his short, squat body. 'Welcome, welcome to Budapest,' he beamed at us. 'I hear you're doing a great job. I only wish I had more time to spend with you.' And with that he was off. We were left open-mouthed, in mid-sentence. Our Hungarian friends, our guide, our interpreter, and the guards apparently felt that our visit had been a great success. They clapped us on the shoulders, offered congratulations and tried to get near us. We had, if only for a moment, basked in the aura of greatness and maybe some of it would rub off.

This was the second head of government I had met and this interview turned out to be even less satisfactory than the first. That had taken place in Cape Town when, with a group of woman trade unionists, I was ushered into the presence of General Jan Smuts whom we had come to petition over trade union legislation. He, too, beamed at us encouragingly when we walked in. We'd barely finished our prepared speeches when he stood up, patted us on our heads and told us, 'My children, you can leave this matter with me. I know how you feel and you can trust me to do what I can to help.' We were not reassured by his patronising manner and events that followed proved us right. Now, with Comrade Rakosi, I again realised that we had gained nothing from the interview except, possibly, enhanced prestige with our fellow workers. 'I suppose he is a busy man,' Isobel said, 'but he might have given us a chance to say a word or two.' 'What we have to tell him would take more than a word or two,' H.A. said, and we laughed ruefully.

It had not taken H.A. long to catch the whiff of corruption in the air. The day after our arrival in Budapest Kati had taken us on a tour of the city in a chauffeur-driven limousine. She pointed out with pride the lovely streets and houses of old Buda and took us past the fortified villa where lived Comrade Rakosi, the leader whose name was mentioned in awe. 'Does Comrade Rakosi live in the best house in the best street?' H.A. asked. 'Of course,' Kati said. 'Why shouldn't he?' 'Because he is the Party Secretary,' H.A. muttered to me. 'But I suppose he's got to live where the Party instructs him.' The following night H.A. had a dream which he found very disturbing. 'They were taking us round Budapest,' he told me, 'and showing us all the big new buildings which, in my dream, rose to the sky, mile after mile, as far as the eye could see and they all looked alike, the same height, the same colour, the same shape. The Comrades kept nudging me, 'Pick one, pick any flat you like, it's yours.' But I pointed to a decrepit little house which was standing apart from the rest. 'I'd like that one,' I told them. They laughed at first then they became angry, and they were about to throw me out of the car when I woke.'

Crossing the wide street between our apartment building and the road leading to the Radio was a constant hazard. The street was intersected by tram lines and in order to reach the safety of the paved tram stop in the middle of the road we had to dodge through the rude, impervious traffic. There were not many cars on the road but those that were there behaved towards pedestrians with utter contempt. 'Why can't they instal some pedestrian crossings?' I demanded of Kati. 'Pedestrians also have some rights.' 'But, Comrade Pauline,' Kati explained with tolerant patience, 'these cars are all on government business. Naturally they have priority.'

IN SPITE of the restrictions imposed from above Leon had succeeded in devising a half-hour daily programme which was lively, interesting, and well received abroad, judging from the listeners' letters which reached us from England, Scandinavia, Holland, and even from as far afield as South Africa. The English section received more letters than all the other sections put together. We were proud of it and resolved to maintain the high standard and distinctive character of the programme. After Leon left and H. A. took over, he was summoned to Comrade Istvan's office. 'Leon was a good chap,' Istvan said, 'but he was a bit young and self-willed. Now you, Comrade Naidoo, were a member of your country's Central Committee so I'm sure we'll have no problems in getting along. You are a responsible comrade and I'm sure you appreciate the importance of Party discipline.'

He collared me in the corridor one day and demanded, 'What class would you say you come from?' 'Well,' I considered, wishing to be absolutely truthful, 'my father was a bookkeeper so I suppose you could say I'm lower middle class.' It was not a question that had ever exercised my mind before. 'Hm, pity!' he snorted and hurried away. 'You're silly, you should have said working class,' Isobel upbraided me. 'It'll all go down in your file and working class is the only thing to be around here.'

At our first weekly section meeting, Anna spelt out the guide-lines we were to follow. The Section Leader, Comrade H. A., must draw up a quarterly plan of work and submit it to Comrade Istvan for approval. Then he must draw up a monthly plan, a weekly plan and a daily plan for the section which she, Anna, would supervise. We would also be required to submit our personal plans to her and at our weekly section meeting these would be checked to make sure that no deviations occurred. We looked at each other in disbelief. 'But this is absurd,' we protested. 'We'll be spending all our time drawing up plans. When are we going to put out our programme?' 'Those are your directives from above,' Anna pronounced. They were clearly not open to debate. Fortunately, we soon found that before many weeks had passed, this mountain of bureaucracy was quietly swept aside and we continued to concentrate on the work in hand – until a new avalanche of red tape would descend from above. Then the same wearisome, time-wasting procedure would be repeated, argued, protested, followed by the inevitable submission and then relegated to the rubbish bin. But not all orders were so easily circumvented.

'Every news bulletin must include at least one minute of anti-Tito news,' came the order from above as the tension between Yugoslavia and the rest of the Socialist countries hotted up. 'But most of the anti-Tito news that you provide is nonsensical rubbish,' we protested. 'Give us real news and we'll include it.' That wasn't easy as we soon discovered. In the absence of any real news two Yugoslav comrades were set to work next door to us manufacturing items of 'news' intended to show up Tito in a bad light, which explained such items as:

> In the Yugoslav village of So-and-so the members of the local co-operative found that all their cows were dying. They soon tracked down the man responsible for feeding poison to the cattle. He confessed that he was working on orders from the renegade Tito and his American and British imperialist bosses. It was their aim to discredit the socialist system of workers' co-operatives and to restore the capitalist system of private ownership by the Kulaks.

When we told the Yugoslavs what we thought of their efforts their only response was, 'All right, you're so clever, you think up something better.'

If a news item came from Tass, carrying a report of a speech by Comrade Stalin, no matter how indigestible the English translation, it had to be broadcast verbatim, with no deletions and no alterations; even commas and full stops were sacrosanct and it had to be the leading item. One day a seven-minute speech by Comrade Stalin was handed to us with the usual directive. 'Here it comes,' said Isobel, 'the snappy little item from our catchy little paper with its perky little title, *For a Lasting Peace, for a People's Democracy.*'

The printed speech was, as usual, a tract full of clichés and slogans and the translation into unlikely English had not improved it. Moreover the speech was at least five days old, but, coming as it did from the official organ of the Communist International, it had to be broadcast verbatim. 'Let me try a bit of subbing and judicious cutting,' H.A. said. 'Perhaps we'll get away with it this time.' But we had underestimated Anna's gimlet eye. Furiously she stormed into our office, waving our script. 'What's the meaning of this?' she demanded. 'This is a speech by Comrade Stalin; you have changed it.' 'I've only tried to put it into reasonable English,' H.A. told her, 'and to make it easier to read. I haven't changed the meaning in any way.' 'You can't do that with a speech by Comrade Stalin,' Anna proclaimed. 'It's got to go out without any changes.' Isobel pushed her glasses up her nose and drawled, 'I suppose next time Comrade Stalin sneezes that too will have to go out in full.' We all laughed but Anna did not. She marched out of the office and a few minutes later H.A. was summoned upstairs. 'You are the leader of the Section,' Istvan pointed at him, 'and yet you joined in the laughter about Comrade Stalin. It showed disrespect; it is no laughing matter.' 'Oh, come on Istvan,' H.A. tried to chaff him, 'don't take it so seriously.' But Istvan's face muscles didn't relax. He stood up and waved H.A. away. 'That is all, Comrade Naidoo, there is nothing more to discuss.'

Kati confided to me how she, too, had earned a bad mark and all because of me. It seemed that in one of my live reports I'd used the seemingly innocent phrase, 'the tractor belonging to the co-operative farm.' What's wrong with that?' I demanded. 'You may well ask,' Kati said. It seemed that tractors were not owned by co-operatives, they were hired out to them by the state farms, and Istvan had demanded to know how it was possible that Kati should have allowed such a heresy to pass unnoticed. It's bad enough that foreigners don't know these things, Istvan had lectured her, but you, a Hungarian, you should know better.

FROM time to time visits were arranged for us to factories, farms, parks, and other places of interest to make 'live', on-the-spot reports. Special interpreters would accompany us to double up as guides and 'political responsibles'. These trips, though carefully chosen to depict the best of life under socialism, merely confirmed the disappointment we felt about this country. Despite all the efforts of our guides to show us only that which they thought would impress us, we came face-to-face with peasants and workers who were resentful, angry, fearful. We knew that our interviewees were hand-picked and we could see that their responses to our questions were mechanical; they sounded as if they had been rehearsed. 'Have you always worked on the land?' I'd ask a weather-beaten peasant who refused to make eye contact. A stream of Hungarian followed and the interpreter would take over: 'He says that he's always worked on the land and before Liberation he could hardly make enough to feed himself and his family. He owned no land but was a migrant worker, travelling from farm to farm to look for work from the Kulaks.' 'And now?' 'Now life is much better. After the Liberation, when the land was distributed, he was given a plot and he joined the collective. His children now go to school and thanks to the Party and the example of the glorious Soviet Union, they have enough to eat and a roof over their head.' I was hungry for good news and only too eager to incorporate the man's testimony in my report. Surely the land distribution programme of the government was one of the more positive acts of the regime! But when I tried to find out exactly how the Soviet example had been followed, I was told that the comrade peasant had to return to his milking.

On another occasion, when we visited a shoe factory where the windows had been washed and the floors swept prior to our arrival, the local Party secretary produced the shop steward to be interviewed. 'Our production has gone up by 15%,' he intoned, 'thanks to the modern machinery and equipment which our glorious Soviet brothers supplied to us.' As we were leaving a middle-aged man sidled up to me and spoke in English so that only I could hear him. 'Ask them why 500 shoes had to be destroyed last month?' he whispered, and then he supplied the answer. 'Because they were all for left feet.' Is this some kind of bad joke, I wondered. Anna had explained to us a long time ago that we were bound to get a wrong impression of the country if we only communicated with people who spoke English. 'Anyone who speaks English,' she pointed out, 'must come from the dispossessed middle classes and they are bound to be resentful. They have lost their previous privileges.' This man spoke English. So could one dismiss his hostility to the new regime and was there no substance to his story?

IT WAS to Eva Vertes that I turned with questions like that. Eva worked for the Hungarian Radio and we'd struck up a friendship in the coffee bar. She was a lusty, statuesque young woman with an engaging laugh and no illusions about the propaganda which she was disseminating to the country with great skill and panache. 'Of course it's true,' she told me. 'The waste and mismanagement in the factories is well known but it's never published and the managers are not accountable to anyone provided they fulfil their plan. If the plan says they must produce 500 shoes in a day or a week it doesn't matter if all the shoes are for the left foot. They've met their target. Just last week,' she went on, 'I heard of one manager who ordered a new desk for his office and a valuable antique desk was delivered to him. But it was too big to go through the door so it was left in the garden for months until it was completely destroyed by the rain and the snow. Nobody feels responsible and nobody gives a damn.' She spoke without bitterness or indignation, merely reporting facts, almost with amusement, sardonically. 'Are you sure, Eva?' I asked. 'Isn't this just hostile propaganda?' 'My fiancé is a factory manager,' she answered. 'He knows what's going on. I wish it were just propaganda.'

Eva's sense of priorities, of what really mattered, had been determined eight years before, when she was 14. Together with thousands of other Hungarian Jews Eva and her mother were deported to Auschwitz and there Eva came face to face with the infamous Dr Mengele. It was he who stood on the station platform as the train with the deportees pulled in and it was he who, with a casual wave of his gold-tipped stick, determined who should live and who should die immediately. 'How old are you?' he barked as Eva stood before him. She hesitated, wondering desperately whether to tell the truth or pretend to be younger – or older. Some of the Polish prisoners, who had boarded the train as cleaners when they reached Auschwitz, advised the mothers of young babies to leave them with the grannies. It was a kindly gesture, meant to save the mothers the agony of having the children torn out of their arms, for the Poles knew that the babies and the grannies were destined for the gas ovens immediately. Eva didn't know it at the time but had she told the truth, Mengele would have pointed to the left and instant, gruesome death. Fourteen was the arbitrary dividing age between adults and children. As she hesitated, Mengele pointed right and Eva was reprieved. She was sent to work in a factory. In the factory a wire fence separated the men from the women but Eva could look across and see a young man, probably not much older than herself, gaze at her with a look of longing in his eyes. One day, when he thought the guard wasn't looking, the young man threw a piece of bread over the wire to Eva, a gift of courtship that meant more than wine or roses or diamonds. The guard saw him, grabbed him by the collar and dragged him away. Eva didn't see him again and couldn't even ask about him afterwards as she never knew his name.

NOT long after we arrived I was dismayed to find myself pregnant. I told Kati that I wanted an abortion. She shook her head. 'That is not possible, Comrade Pauline,' she told me. 'Abortions are strictly illegal.' 'Never mind about that,' I told her, 'I've had illegal abortions before and I'd have thought that in a Socialist country women had the right to decide what to do with their own bodies.' Kati promised to take it up with Szusza, the Party secretary who then came to see me accompanied by Anna. Patiently they set about trying to persuade me to accept the inevitable. 'It's not always possible to put one's personal desires above the imperatives of the Party and the State,' Szusza pontificated. 'We need children, we love children and we guarantee them a good future.' 'Be that as it may,' I told them, 'I want an abortion and if you can't arrange it then you must send me back to England. It's illegal there also but I'm sure I'll manage.' A week later Kati informed me that the Party had arranged for me to have the operation. She accompanied me to the hospital where a covey of eminent gynaecologists and psychologists solemnly testified that in their learned opinion it was essential for me to have an abortion on medical grounds. There was no pretence of examining me; they'd received their instructions and acted on them.

Three days later I presented myself at the same hospital where I joined three other women, equally privileged, in a dingy waiting room. One young woman trembled with fear. 'Does it hurt?' she asked me. 'It's not pleasant,' I told her, 'but it doesn't hurt and it's a great relief when it's all over.' I'd had two abortions before but nothing prepared me for the indignity to which I was now subjected by this doctor and his nurse. Neither of them glanced at me as they strapped me into a reclining chair and tilted it back, my legs spreadeagled above my head. They might have been working on a corpse for all the attention they paid me. Did their cold indifference signify boredom, overwork, or moral disapproval? It was difficult to judge but it was humiliating and degrading. When it was over the doctor, still without looking at me, motioned the nurse to take me back to the waiting room. 'You can wait here for a while before you go downstairs,' the nurse told me as she led me out, stumbling and crying. The next patient who had asked for reassurance before now looked at me accusingly. 'So it did hurt,' she said. 'You're crying.'

I tried to explain that my tears were from anger and humiliation, not from pain, but the language barrier was too great and I was too distraught. I slumped into a chair and sat there for about ten minutes. Then I groped my way down the three flights of stairs, fearful of falling and resting on the landings. H. A. was waiting for me and I lurched sobbing into his arms.

Later, back at work in the Radio, I tried to explain to Kati how unnecessarily cruel I considered my treatment to have been. 'You don't know how privileged you've been,' Kati told me. 'Do you remember young Lydia, the typist in the American section? She couldn't get a legal abortion like you so she arranged to have one illegally at great expense. Well, somehow she was found out. She's now in prison for six years and her doctor is serving a 20-year sentence.'

I felt ashamed to be benefiting from such a hypocritical system, one in which abortions, like other prizes, were at the disposal of the privileged, like me. The class differences of other countries seemed trivial by comparison. Did Lydia, I wondered, feel about me as I felt about the Russian women who shopped in their exclusive store? From the outside one couldn't tell that this gracious old house was now a discreet shop for Russian officers and their wives; not until one happened to see them and their chauffeurs emerging with loaded baskets full of oranges and other products unavailable to ordinary citizens. Like wealth, privilege, too, is relative. I could get an abortion but I couldn't buy an orange for my children, not even when the doctor told me that they needed extra Vitamin C. 'Your children are not used to our harsh winters,' he said when both Karen and Sandra seemed wan and debilitated and kept catching one cold after another. 'They need Vitamin C.' 'Where,' I asked him, 'can I get that?' 'Oh, you foreigners,' he said, 'have access to goods which we can't get.' I realised what he meant when I discovered what the house across the road was. He'd confused me with the Russian foreigners, but I had no access to this shop. The Hungarians in the Radio were amused at my indignation over such a trivial deprivation, as it appeared to them, but to me it again proved the inequalities of the system, and was not to be accepted lightly.

THE children kept falling ill one after another. Karen caught hepatitis and was removed to an isolation hospital where we could only talk with her through a closed window. She seemed cheerful enough as she pressed her little face against the pane, thanking us for the food we brought. I wished I could hold her in my arms. 'You should give the nurse a tip,' Kati advised. This had not occurred to me. 'Surely you don't tip nurses? Won't they be insulted?' I asked. Kati laughed. 'On the contrary, they expect it and you make sure your child is not neglected.' I found out that not only did one tip the nurses but relatives were

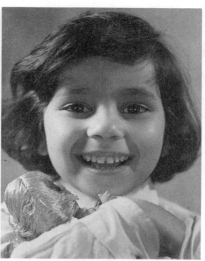

The children in Budapest.
Sandra *(L)*; Karen *(R)*; Jennie *(below)*

With Sam and Pauline Kahn in Budapest.
Barry Kahn and Karen Naidoo in front.

Budapest snapshot.

expected to bring food and a change of clothes for the patient. So this was why the nurses were so surly the previous month when Sandra was taken in for observation. Nobody had warned me to tip at that hospital. Sandra was diagnosed as suffering from a heart murmur and the doctors prescribed a six-weeks' stay in bed at home. After three weeks she insisted on getting up and as she seemed to be perfectly well, I let her. When we returned to London and she was examined by a heart specialist, he dismissed my fears. 'There's nothing wrong with her heart,' he assured me.

Karen was left with great big scars on her back where they had injected her with an outsize needle. Then she started getting earaches and the doctors advised that the boils inside her ears had to be lanced. I sat in the surgery holding her tight on my lap while they performed this excruciating treatment; I could do nothing to share her agonising pain. Two weeks later it happened again and the same ghastly operation was repeated. The third time, as I carried her round the corner of the street where the hospital was, she started struggling and fighting in my arms. 'Is there no other way you can treat my child?' I begged but the doctors insisted that was all they could do. When we returned to England and Karen again developed earache, she was given penicillin and the trouble cleared up. Whatever supplies of penicillin existed in Hungary were not shared among the ordinary people in the local hospitals. It was all reserved for the Central Hospital which catered for the Party hierarchy. I discovered this too late to spare my child but some months later H. A. collapsed one day while shaving and the doctor advised that we take him to hospital for observation. I insisted he be sent to Kutvoldgy, the Party hospital.

'But Comrade Pauline,' Kati objected, 'that place is for the very top people, the Central Committee, and that sort.' 'If H. A. won't be sent to Kutvoldgy,' I told Kati, 'then he stays in the house, and you, the Hungarian Party, will take the responsibility if anything happens to him.' Then I brought out my ace. 'Or you could of course send us back to England.' The argument continued for several days but I remained adamant. If the rotten system was based on privilege then my husband was as deserving of it as any of their jumped-up *apparatchiks*. While we argued H. A.'s condition did not improve; he lay like a log in his bed, staring blankly at the ceiling, with no appetite for food and no interest in life around him. He seemed to be drowning in his own unhappy thoughts and I found it impossible to get through to him. The doctor declared himself baffled and admitted that he was unable to identify the cause of the illness. The Party secretary Szusza came in every few days to check on his condition and after another week passed without improvement, they gave in. H. A. was removed to the modern purpose-built hospital on the hill with its spacious wards, attentive staff, à-la-carte menus and no lack of drugs. 'What your husband needs,' the Kutvoldgy doctor informed me after he'd examined H. A., 'is the latest Soviet treatment: sleep, simply sleep.' He pointed to the patients lying in the surrounding wards. 'These are all Stakhanovites, heroes of Labour who have over-fulfilled their norms; they arrived here exhausted and depressed but after a couple of weeks' treatment, they'll be as good as new. So will your husband.'

And so it proved. For two weeks H. A. slept. He would be woken at intervals to use the lavatory, wash and eat. Then he would take his sleeping pills and sink into unconsciousness. By the end of a fortnight his depression seemed to lift and he returned to work.

O N 5 March 1953 we were summoned to an urgent meeting upstairs. When we were all gathered in front of °Comrade Szendru, he announced in a tone of doom that he had very serious news to put before us. Comrade Joseph Stalin was dead. I was thunderstruck. Stalin dead! A world without Stalin! For all my recent doubts and disillusions Stalin still represented the rock around which our faith clung; he was the great war hero who had led his country to victory over Nazism and so saved the world for all humanity; the friend and saviour of oppressed peoples everywhere. Stalin was the Daddy of all my dreams, the pivot of my ideals for as long as I could remember. In losing him I'd lost my youth, my childhood. I burst out crying, tears of sadness and regret.

When I lifted my head and looked around I was amazed to find that everyone else was dry-eyed. Was I the only mourner present? I, who could fairly be described as a critic and a doubter? One may criticise a father and even quarrel with him but that doesn't mean you stop loving him. Anyway, I harboured a conviction that Stalin, like Rakosi, was unaware of the evils perpetrated in his name. He was good and kind and dedicated; how could he possibly know what the shabby little men around him were doing? I sometimes wove fantasies in which I looked into Stalin's twinkling eyes and heard him invite me to be frank, be open. Tell me what you really think should be done? By dying he'd robbed me of a world of dreams. I felt bereft.

S HORTLY afterwards I again fell pregnant and we decided, after much debate and heart-searching, to have the baby. It was more than a reaction from undergoing another abortion; now I was ready for another child and wanted her, urgently. As ever my pregnancy went by easily, healthily, without a break in my working life. Although unplanned this coming birth came more and more to be desired; it had a sense of rightfulness and inevitability, of completeness. Once a person had managed to break through the cordon which surrounded entry to Kutvoldgy he and his family were entitled to return there and so it was that when Jennie was born I found myself in a ward overlooking the park and ordering strawberries for lunch in the middle of winter. The staff were kind and attentive and I basked in the unfamiliar luxury. Kati was with me in the labour ward when Jennie was born. The matron agreed to break the rules about not letting strangers in the delivery room when Kati persuaded them that I might need an interpreter. To me she confessed that she knew the doctor spoke English pretty well but she wanted to witness a birth, something she had never seen before. When my labour pains grew fiercer I was offered an injection which I refused. The nurse then attempted to press an anaesthetic over my face and I pushed it aside. 'But Comrade Pauline,' Kati urged, 'they are trying to ease your pains; why do you not let them?' 'Tell them to leave me alone,' I gasped. 'I'm concentrating. I'm trying to relax.' Kati turned to the nurse and doctor and spread her palms: 'These English,' she marvelled, 'even at a time like this they do not lose their sense of humour.' It transpired that at this leading Hungarian gynaecology ward nobody had heard of the natural childbirth method.

I'd always joked that three children was the ideal number, one for Mummy, one for Daddy and one for the country. When our beautiful Jennie was born, and H.A. was told that he was the proud father of a baby girl, he appeared to be somewhat subdued: 'Oh,' he murmured, 'another girl!' But in no time at all he was as besotted with this new baby as he had been with his other daughters. He was a good father, particularly of babies, and he had patience and skill. As for me, I can honestly say that I neither expected nor longed for a boy. I always knew with utter conviction that my baby would be a girl; I could not imagine any other outcome.

We had decided months before to call our daughter Shanti. Shanti Naidoo had a lovely soft lilt and besides I'd discovered the word in a delightful song by Rabindranath Tagore and I was told it meant 'peace'. How appropriate for a child of ours. Then it occurred to us that in South Africa, where we hoped one day to return, 'Shanti' would be mispronounced 'Shanty' and that word did not have a happy association. To be on the safe side we agreed to add the pretty name Jennifer and then she'd have a choice. I believed then, and I still hold fast to my conviction, that all children should come when they are wanted, longed for, loved. A child is too important to be an 'accident', a 'mistake', a 'tragic consequence'. And certainly it is up to the woman who will bear and rear the child to decide when and if she wants one. She is the one who will be called upon to make the life-long commitment and to devote her best years to the child's imperious needs which should always come first.

ANNA Peterne was often called upon to act as intermediary between us and the higher orders in the mistaken belief that as an American she could explain problems to us in a tongue we could understand. She was held in great esteem by Szusza, the Party secretary, and when she rose to speak at meetings we were all expected to pay respectful attention. Anna's method of delivery was slow and deliberate. She would hesitate between sentences, spreading her arms and casting about with her eyes, persuading her listeners that her words were not merely regurgitated slogans but were dredged out of an inner conviction and a well-digested wisdom, thus gaining in weight what they lacked in spontaneity. For all her homilies about making sacrifices and making do, Anna and her husband Peter lived in considerable style, even in luxury. Peter's position as some kind of superior *apparatchik* entitled them to a spacious apartment with shiny wooden floors, high decorated ceilings and large windows overlooking a green, well-trimmed garden. This wasn't one of those cramped, crumbling, seedy modern flats that we were expected to praise in our broadcasts as one of the great achievements of Socialism; this was a residence built in the old days, solid, comfortable and undeniably middle-class. Anna also enjoyed the full-time services of a housekeeper who cooked like a trained chef and kept the furniture and silver in a permanent state of gloss. An invitation to dinner at the Peters was an event to be savoured and Christmas dinner with the Peters was not to be missed: succulent turkey and mouthwatering chestnut stuffing. Neat, trim, prosperous and more elegant than any of her colleagues, Anna held sway in her small world with every appearance of contentment and self-satisfaction. When the news reached her that I was expecting another child she came into our office and said, 'If the baby is a girl you won't want her, will you? You've got two already; what would you do with three girls?' I laughed. 'Oh definitely, if it's another girl I'll give her away.' Anna wasn't laughing but I assumed she was trying to be funny. 'Give her to me,' she said and I answered, 'Sure, you can have her.' I never gave this nonsense exchange another thought until Shanti Jennifer was born and Anna and Peter came to visit me in hospital.

'We've come for our baby,' Anna beamed at me as she presented me with a big bouquet of flowers. 'We've got her room ready and we've ordered a cot and a pram. Lena will make a wonderful nanny; she's had three children herself.' I stared at Anna and Peter in disbelief and H.A., sitting next to me, gulped in amazement. 'But Anna, dear Anna,' I pleaded, 'you surely didn't think I was serious. You didn't really believe that I'd give away my baby!' Anna's face crumpled and her 5′2″ frame seemed to shrink. It was sadly obvious that I had under-estimated her longing for a child and over-estimated her sense of humour. She tried to tempt me with promises of a good home for the child, an abundance of love and material things and finally, as if that were the ultimate inducement, an undertaking to send Jennie to Moscow University when she grew up. Eventually when I convinced her that our baby, even though she was a girl, was not for disposal, Anna's face resumed it's cool, calculated look and her body its upright bearing. She became again what she always was, tough, brisk and bossy. Never again did she allow her inner desperation to surface or her longing to show.

B Y THE end of 1953 we were told that a new block of flats had been built to house the foreign workers in the Radio and in due course we were moved to our own apartments. It was pointed out to us that we were among the privileged members of society and when we compared our living standards and salaries with those of our Hungarian colleagues, we could see that this was so. Our interpreter, Yudit, her mother and her young brother lived in one room and had to share a bathroom with their neighbours. We paid no rent, ate subsidised lunches, enjoyed free schooling and nursery care and were even sent on holidays to Lake Balaton. Our furnished flat was small but neat and well-equipped and it overlooked a large garden at the rear. We enjoyed the services of a daily cleaner and tolerated the presence of a full-time concierge at the entrance. It was his job to monitor our comings and goings. Visitors were not encouraged and if any came they had to sign in on arrival and sign out when departing.

We were grateful for our tidy new apartment but we missed the camaraderie at the big table in Museum Utca and the badinage with our colleagues in a babel of French, Italian, Turkish, English. We missed Sundays in Museum Utca, when it was Marika's day off, and each section used to take turns to provide dinner for all of us. We enjoyed watching the Frenchmen spend hours preparing mayonnaise: Andre would mix the eggs while Charles, with tongue tip showing and narrowed eyes would concentrate on adding the oil, drop by drop. The Italians left all their cooking to the women. Big, slow Assunta and small, nervous Patrizia would rise at dawn and start kneading and rolling the pasta. By the time we got up and came to the kitchen for breakfast, the pasta would be draped all over the furniture, paper thin and drying. Then it was lovingly rolled up and expertly sliced to be dropped into boiling, salted water. The Turks made kebabs and flaky, spicy rice which they stuffed into vine leaves. It was mouthwatering.

Then it came to our turn. 'I'm no cook,' Isobel was quick to declare and Dora confessed that neither was she. 'In any case,' Isobel said, 'what do we give them? Roast beef and Yorkshire pudding? A fine chance we have of finding that here. What about a typical South African dish?' They turned to me. I looked at H. A. 'There's bobotie, the Cape Malay dish,' H. A. suggested, 'but we haven't got the recipe.' 'Tomato bredie would be nice,' I suggested, 'if only we knew how to make it.' 'A curry is something I could make,' H. A. announced, but where would we find curry powder?' Hungarians had never heard of curry; they used paprika. We racked our brains trying to find a dish that was typical, available and within our limited prowess; they were all too few. The meal that we eventually placed before our colleagues consisted of a big roast of beef which proved to be tough and leathery, roast potatoes which were underdone and boiled vegetables which were overcooked. We added nothing to the reputation of English cuisine and we were never allowed to hear the end of it.

After that, by common consent, the English section was excused from Sunday dinner catering. Instead, we were allowed to do the washing-up.

On one of his trips to the country H. A. found himself sitting opposite a young Soviet soldier in the train. When he discovered that H. A. came from South Africa the young man grinned happily. 'I know about South Africa,' he told H. A. through the interpreter and promptly burst into song about the brave Boers defending themselves from the British Imperialists. 'That was in the Boer War,' H. A. told him, 'a long time ago. Today it is the Boers who are oppressing the black people and we have to defend ourselves from them.' The young Russian would have none of it. 'My grandmother taught me this song,' he said, 'and she wouldn't lie to me. The Boers are freedom fighters.'

W E HAD postponed our return to England when we knew we were expecting another baby. In London we had no home, no job and very little money – it had not occurred to us to arrange for part of our salaries to be deposited in an English bank as the other English comrades had done. We decided it would be easier to have the baby in Budapest but then the question arose, what nationality would our Jennie have. Could there be problems when we wanted to leave? Could they argue that since she was born in Hungary, she had Hungarian nationality and they were then entitled to withhold her exit permit as they did to their other citizens? I lay in bed worrying and imagining the worst. When H. A. came to visit I demanded urgently, 'You must register her birth with the British Embassy. We mustn't risk any problems about her nationality when we leave this country.'

When we first arrived in Hungary we were warned, among all the other prohibitions, never to visit any foreign embassies. 'It is best you are not even seen in the same street as the embassy,' the Party secretary told us. 'It is for your own protection,' she explained. 'You might be kidnapped and held in a foreign embassy where we could not gain access and so could do nothing to save you.' 'After all,' Szusza added, 'we are responsible for you to your national parties.' So when H. A. went to see Szusza and told her he had to go to the British Embassy, she threw up her hands in horror. 'Out of the question,' she asserted. 'Don't even think of it.' H. A. duly reported this back to me and I felt my hackles rising. 'You tell Szusza,' I said, 'that if we don't get Party permission I will go to the embassy without permission as soon as I'm discharged from here before I return home.' H. A. warned Szusza that I meant it. 'You'd better let me go,' he told her, 'and if you don't trust me send someone with me to make sure I don't pass over any secrets.' Szusza was immune to irony. 'It's not you we don't trust,' she purred. 'It's the British. We don't know what they will do once you're inside their territory.' In the end, after appeals to higher bodies, permission was finally granted. 'But don't give them your address,' Szusza instructed. 'What address should I give, they're sure to ask?' H. A. asked her. She thought for a while. 'Give them your old address in Museum Utca.'

When H. A. eventually reached the British Embassy he wondered what to expect. 'Am I about to enter a forbidden fortress? Will they be hostile, inquisitive, menacing?' In the event his reception was so matter-of-fact and businesslike that he could hardly believe it, used as we were to the tight security measures of the Radio and all other official and semi-official buildings. At the British Embassy reception desk a clerk directed him to a room on the second floor. H. A. stood and waited. He waited for a pass, a guard to accompany him, a phone call from above, permission to go ahead. To his surprise none of this happened. 'The stairs are over there,' the clerk pointed, and alone and unaccompanied he walked upstairs and knocked on the door. The woman consul invited him to enter and greeted him serenely. 'Oh yes, you are Mr Naidoo,' she said. 'We know all about you. You work for Radio Budapest. We wondered when we'd get to meet you.' 'She helped me fill in the necessary forms and we got through all the formalities with so little hassle that I felt ashamed to lie about my address,' H. A. told me. He laughed as he continued. 'As I left the building I almost waved to the portrait of the Queen. I felt as though I were walking on air.'

A S H. A. stepped outside the embassy he almost bumped into another Indian. The two men stopped and stared at each other. To meet a fellow-Indian was surprise enough, but suddenly they also realised that they knew each other. They had met at the United Nations sessions in New York and now his acqaintance was Ambassador in Moscow and Hungary was part of his constituency. As happens when two people meet by chance far from home they greet each other like long-lost friends even though they barely know one another. 'You must come for dinner,' the ambassador declared, clapping H. A. on the shoulder. 'I'll send you an invitation. What is your address?' Just in time H. A. remembered that as he'd left a false address inside the British embassy he'd have to keep up the pretence with the Indian ambassador. 'I felt mean and silly,' H. A. told me, 'but I gave him our old address.' 'Does that mean that we won't get the invitation to dinner?' I asked, sadly disappointed – it would have made a delightful break in our prosaic routine. 'I'm afraid so,' he told me.

A week later, as we sat down to dinner in our flat, we heard a knock on the door and there stood a uniformed chauffeur with a formal invitation from His Excellency the Indian Ambassador. 'How did you find us?' H. A. blurted out. 'Well,' said the chauffeur, 'You made a mistake, you left your old address but when I went there they told me that you now live here.' 'So much for our security,' I laughed when the man had left. 'Oh do let's go,' I pleaded. 'Let's not ask for permission; they don't need to know.' But H. A. was cautious. 'We'll have to get Party permission,' he said. 'They'll know about the invitation from the porter at the entrance.' 'They'll never let us,' I predicted and I was right. This time there was no concession. Permission was refused and H.A. did not feel that this was an issue over which we could make a stand. As for me, I felt as Cinderella would have felt if she'd lost her invitation on the way to the ball. Yudit was directed to phone the Indian consulate and make our apologies. 'The Naidoos have been called away to the countryside on urgent business,' she had to lie. My disappointment was so acute it shamed me. Why did I so long for an evening of relaxed good manners and good food? Of easy, good-humoured conversation about non-political topics? Why did I yearn for sparkling glasses, damask cloths and candlelight? These were the trappings of privilege and a good Communist should not be seduced by them. And yet, and yet! Could not a good Communist also appreciate gracious living? I had to face it; a break in our grey, proscribed existence was something that I craved. But it was denied me; I had to accept the prohibition from above and agree with H.A. that it would be unseemly to make a fuss over this issue.

A PLACE was found for Jennie in the Radio crèche and I was entitled to time off at four-hourly intervals to nurse her. So every three and three-quarter hours I dropped whatever I was doing, ran down the three flights of stairs in the Radio building, hurried down Brody Sandor Utca, round the corner to the next street and then climbed four flights of steep stairs to the crèche. Not surprisingly my milk soon dried up and from overflowing with it in the hospital where I nourished half the ward, I soon had not enough milk to feed my own baby. After six weeks Jennie had to be put on the bottle and I felt very remiss – my other two had been breast-fed for nine and ten months.

D YURIE was thin, dark-eyed, intense and in charge of the music department. His encyclopaedic knowledge of music and musicians was a constant source of wonder and we relied on him to provide us with signature tunes, musical interludes, programmes of 'listeners' requests'. His commitment to Communism was so total that he refused to speak English properly, although he had a good command of the language, on the grounds that it was the tongue of the imperialists. It was all right, apparently, to speak English as long as it was pronounced phonetically; that was a gesture of defiance which satisfied his conscience. It became a game which we were quite happy to play most of the time but every now and then it could become an irritation when something was urgently needed but Dyurie persisted with his nonsense. 'Hoveh areh youu?' he would drawl and we'd reply, 'Tank youu, very vell.' He came into the office one day when Isobel, Dora and I were talking about anti-Semitism. 'Are you a

Jew?' Isobel asked him. 'Oyjam a Hungarian,' he answered. 'He says,' I offered, 'that he is not a Jew.' Dyurie's pale face turned pink. 'Oy did not saa-eh dat,' he said as he turned on his heel and left the room. It was a dilemma that confronted many a Party member: how to be a good Communist and yet not to deny one's ancestry. I was amazed to hear in 1956 that Dyurie and his wife were among the first to get out of Hungary during the uprising, as soon as the borders were opened.

It was during the Slansky trial in Czechoslovakia that the Jewish question became a topic of conversation. Until then it was not much talked about although it did occur to me that quite a few of the leading comrades were Jewish. I firmly believed that anti-Semitism was one disease that Socialism had cured so I reacted indignantly to the reports in the western press that the Prague trials had anti-Semitic overtones. I wrote commentaries denouncing Slansky and his fellow-accused as traitors which I firmly believed them to be. To prove that there was no anti-Semitism in the Socialist countries I proposed that I do an interview with the Chief Rabbi of Budapest in his synagogue. 'What a good idea,' Anna drawled. 'We must arrange it.' But the weeks went by and nothing was arranged. When I persisted in my request I was finally informed that the Chief Rabbi declined to be interviewed.

In one of my commentaries I used the expression 'world Jewry'. Anna put her blue pencil through it. 'Why?' I demanded. 'Because there is no such thing as world Jewry,' she said. 'Jews are part of the country in which they live and their interests often diverge from each other.' 'True enough,' I conceded, 'but there are certain issues on which all Jews agree, and one of these is denouncing anti-Semitism.' As usual we appealed to Istvan and not surprisingly he concurred with Anna. 'You see,' he explained, 'the expression "world Jewry" has a certain connotation. On the one hand . . . on the other hand . . .' As he developed his theme it struck me for the first time that Istvan too was Jewish. This kind of Talmudic disputation had only one source — the *cheder*, the Jewish religious school for boys. In that case why was he, also, so coy about his origins?

Not long afterwards, on his way to the coffee bar one morning, H.A. saw Istvan clocking off at 11 a.m. 'This is not like you,' H.A. teased. 'Skiving off, are we?' Istvan walked away without answering or looking back. He slipped through the door and disappeared as though he'd never existed. Overnight he became a non-person, a never-was person, and we could find no one who could tell us what had become of the man who had dominated our working lives for so long. A few weeks before we left Budapest H.A. and I bumped into Istvan in Vaci Utca. He looked shabby and down at heel. 'Whatever happened to you?' we demanded. 'We kept asking people but no one seemed to know.' 'I was sent to work at a factory,' Istvan's tone was expressionless. H.A. and I gaped at him. 'You, Istvan, you were always so devout and faithful! Whatever did you do to deserve punishment?' Istvan removed my restraining hand on his arm. 'You must excuse me,' he said. 'I have an appointment.' He turned and walked away briskly, leaving us staring after him.

This was the post-Stalin era. This, we were assured by the Party, was the new dawn of openness, of free discussion, of real criticism without fear of repercussion. No more informers, no more tittle-tattle and, what's more, we were promised that all those secret files which had been accumulated on each and every one of us, were being destroyed, abolished, consigned to the dust-heap. This lie was not exposed until 1956, when control of the Radio was taken over by the Workers' Council and all the files were found intact. Only then were they destroyed. We never did discover what heinous crime the faithful Istvan had committed but rumour had it that he had failed to confess to a bourgeois Jewish merchant father when applying for Party membership and he'd compounded the sin by visiting his exiled brother in Vienna during an official Party mission.

F ROM the time of our arrival until our departure, regular departmental meetings were called to boost our morale, stiffen our resolve and make us acquainted with the Party line. Each section would huddle round its interpreter to listen to the speech of Comrade Szendru, the head of the Radio as he analysed the current political situation and pointed out the correct policy for the coming weeks. One of his more memorable dictums remains imprinted on my mind for its crass contradiction of what a Marxist should be, 'There is only one yardstick of a good Communist,' Szendru told us. 'It is his attitude to the Soviet Union. This is our Soviet Fatherland and it must be supported always, unquestioningly, obediently, loyally.'

Then, to prove our fealty, we were all instructed to listen to Radio Moscow's foreign language programmes and to follow their example in all respects. Each member of the department had to undertake at least five hours' Moscow listening per week and to make detailed notes. We were then to report back to the next meeting what we had learnt and how we intended to apply it to our own section. At the following section meeting we listened in growing disbelief as Mario, on behalf of the Italians, Françoise for the French and then the Turks, Greeks, Spaniards and all the rest solemnly recited how much they had learnt from Radio Moscow and how they were going to apply their new-found wisdom to their broadcasts from Radio Budapest. Then it came to our turn. Our Section Head, H.A., stood up and reported that in his section all the members had agreed that the English language foreign broadcasts from Moscow were lamentable. They were presented in a dull and uninteresting way and had no appeal whatsoever to any but the most devoted Party members. 'Is that what foreign broadcasts are for?' H.A. asked his incredulous audience. 'To preach to the converted? We do not believe,' he went on, 'that Radio Moscow attracts anyone and we feel that our broadcasts are far more interesting and professional. Moreover,' he continued, 'we would recommend that comrades listen to their own language broadcasts from the BBC and take some tips from them. Now that,' he told them warming to his subject, 'is a successful and clever way to spread propaganda, while seeming to be impartial and objective.'

Our fellow-broadcasters gasped at us in various languages and were quick to dissociate themselves from our blasphemy. 'That is what is wrong with you,' Comrade Szendru said, more in sorrow than in anger. 'You have fallen victim to British propaganda. I suggest that you do not listen to the BBC any more. Concentrate on Radio Moscow.' We understood that the seemingly fraternal tone of Comrade Szendru's 'advice' was intended – and succeeded – to convey an unmistakable threat. We continued to listen to the BBC but preferred to do so in the absence of our Hungarian comrades. The BBC World Service became a lifeline for news, for interesting features, for the lovely sound of the English language.

THREE months later came a triumphant vindication from an unexpected source. The leading Turkish poet, Nazim Hikmet, exiled from his country for his Communist sympathies, came to visit us from Moscow, where he now lived. 'Our guest today,' Comrade Szendru announced, 'is the revered holder of the Stalin Prize. He also broadcasts regularly from Radio Moscow so listen carefully to what he has to tell us.'

Nazim Hikmet was a handsome bear of a man and as he swept into the room our spirits rose. His eyes sparkled and he exuded an aura of infectious vitality. He was larger than life-size but his stature, far from diminishing others, only served to enhance one's appetite for life. 'Now there's someone who could leave his shoes under my bed any night of the week,' Isobel said *sotto voce*, while Yudit looked pained and Dora tut-tutted in disapproval. But it wasn't only his magnetic personality which enchanted us. Here was a Stalin prize-winner, one of the privileged, the chosen, the élite, straight out of the Moscow inner sanctum, and what was he telling us? He was declaring in public what we had tried to say, using almost the same words.

'If you want to be effective propagandists,' Hikmet said, 'listen carefully to the way the BBC operates. Don't copy Radio Moscow. I know, I work regularly in the Turkish section and I can tell you, Comrades, we are boring, long-winded and unimpressive.'

Comrade Szendru did his best to hide his chagrin and the Italians looked at us and grinned, acknowledging our triumph. Nazim Hikmet's visit restored our good standing within the section – no one could now accuse us of being imperialist dupes; nor could they pretend that our bulky mailbox was of no consequence. However, before long we were in trouble again.

A DIRECTIVE arrived from upstairs which decreed that criticism and self-criticism was a good thing and it should be encouraged. Comrade Szendru called us together and spent the whole meeting impressing its importance upon us. 'This is the way in which good Communists examine their own and their comrades' mistakes and take steps to correct them,' he told us and he urged us to search our consciences and prepare our contributions for the next meeting. In due course the next meeting was called and one speaker after another stood up and offered examples of 'criticism and self-criticism'. The technician, Julia, confessed to us all how wrong she was to rush off home after work instead of staying behind to attend the prescribed classes in Marxism/ Leninism. 'Of course my children need me at home but I'm convinced that they will benefit more in the long run by having a mother who is ideologically sound.' She sat down to applause, looking uncomfortable.

Georgy from the editorial department confessed that he had failed to carry out his monthly plan in which he had undertaken to write five political commentaries a week. Last week he'd only written three and the week before that only four. However, he promised to mend his ways in future. Applause. The comrade chairman was gratified to get such full and frank admissions of faults and errors and he invited more contributions from the floor. 'Those were good examples of self-criticism,' he beamed, 'but you mustn't forget criticism, Comrades, even of the highest.' Margarita, a cleaner, stood up and swallowed hard. 'Just the other day,' she told us, 'I met Comrade Szendru on the stairs as I was going down and he was coming up. I said, '*Servus*, Comrade,' but he ignored me completely and just walked past me. I don't think that was very comradely of him,' she ended lamely and sat down. Comrade Szendru jumped up. 'I apologise, Comrades,' he said. 'It was very wrong of me to ignore Comrade Margarita. I must have been preoccupied and thinking about other things. I promise it won't happen again.' The audience clapped and the chairman smiled. 'It is very good to get these things out into the open,' he told us. 'You can see how important it is to discuss all these matters and to practise criticism and self-criticism.'

Some time later, at one of our infrequent trade union meetings, Isobel raised the question of the quality of the news that was handed down to us daily. 'Lots of important international news gets no mention at all and some silly, inconsequential items get reported at length,' she complained. She also pointed to the lack of political understanding in the choice of some items and offered an example. 'Yesterday we were asked to broadcast a report which boasted that among other products, the consumption of bread had risen by 8% and of potatoes by 11%. Doesn't it occur to them that if bread and potatoes are consumed in greater quantity it doesn't signify a rise in the standard of living? It points to the opposite; it indicates a fall in living standards. People who are better off don't eat more bread and potatoes, they eat more meat, or vegetables, or cakes.'

There was a ripple of laughter in the room but it was quickly stifled when the chairman, with a stern countenance, rose to conclude the proceedings of the meeting, ignoring Isobel's contribution. We were left in no doubt that the open season for criticism and self-criticism was over. As we drifted out into the corridors, several Hungarians sidled up to us. 'I'm so glad you said it; it needed telling.' Rosie, herself a member of the editorial department told us how much she agreed with us. We turned on her, angry and contemptuous. 'Then why didn't you support us in there?' She smiled wanly, shrugged her shoulders and walked away. Ferenc, a senior translator, told us, 'That was very brave of you.' 'It had nothing to do with bravery,' Isobel retorted. 'It's true, as you well know. Anyway,' she added, 'if they don't like it they can send us back to Britain.'

We were foreigners, guests of the State, emissaries of our Party; we felt safe and inviolate. What we failed to understand was how exposed and vulnerable the Hungarians were. The worst they could do to us, we reckoned, was to send us back. Well, let them. By now we were ready to end our terms of office; we longed to return to Britain. All the same, it was hard to jettison the ideals of a lifetime. In our reluctance to face the unpleasant facts we persisted in seeking various explanations. This sorry state of affairs, we told ourselves, must be peculiar to Hungary and its Fascist past, its lack of democratic traditions, its ignorance of Socialist practice, it's dearth of experienced Communists. 'Yes,' Graham said, 'I'm sure it's quite different in Czechoslovakia, or Poland, or Rumania; they had active and experienced Communist parties and a sophisti-cated working class.' We clung to this misguided belief.

Our false sense of security from retribution was also based on a misconcep-tion which only emerged after the 1956 uprising, when we were already back in Britain. It was only then we realised that our foreignness was no guarantee of immunity, nor was the fact that we were representatives of the fraternal British Communist Party. What none of us knew during our Hungarian sojourn was that Dr Edith Bone, who had also been sent to Hungary officially, by the Communist Party *Daily Worker*, had disappeared in mysterious circumstances. In response to the British Party's repeated inquiries about her whereabouts the Hungarian Party swore, with hand on heart, that Dr Bone had boarded a plane to Yugoslavia and all enquiries should be directed to the infamous Tito. They disclaimed all knowledge of her. It wasn't until the jails were emptied during the 1956 uprising that Dr Bone was discovered and released from her cell where she had survived eleven years of solitary confinement. One method which this indomitable woman had evolved to retain her sanity was to pluck the hairs from her head and use them to knit with. Her crime had been to be critical of developments in Hungary – and to reflect this criticism in her dispatches to the paper.

It appeared that because Dr Bone was born in Hungary the Hungarian Communist Party felt entitled to treat her with the contempt they reserved for their own citizens. How lucky I was that I was not a Soviet citizen! I could have been. After the war news reached me in South Africa that all those born in the Baltic Republics, now part of the Soviet Union, could apply for Soviet citizenship. The prospect of being a citizen of the Soviet Fatherland captivated me; it would be marvellous, I thought, to join the ranks of Mayakovsky's privileged band, holders of red passports.

I discussed it with Moses Kotane but he did not think it was a good idea. 'They already accuse us of being Soviet agents,' he said. 'How would it look if it turned out you were a citizen of that country? They'd want to know where you stack your Moscow gold.' We laughed at this hoary old jibe but I had to agree that it would not be a good idea to seem to be owing first allegiance to a country other than your own. And anyway, it was to South Africa that I was committed.

Although I was born there, Lithuania was now a distant memory without any emotional pull. The Soviet Union was a dream of Utopia common to right-thinking persons all round the world, the Fatherland to which we all owed allegiance for moral, ethical and ideological reasons. But South Africa was my country; this was the place which sang to me, where the desert air filled my lungs with perfumed breath and on whose beaches I trickled golden sand through my fingers. I loved South Africa, its streets and mountains, its fruit and flowers, its snakes and stars and thorn trees; above all I loved its people, black, white, brown and it was with them that I felt inextricably bound. The notion of taking up Soviet citizenship was never a serious proposition, merely a passing romantic surmise.

Before the next trade union meeting was held in our section, we received a visit from our Party secretary, Comrade Szusza. She shuffled her feet and cleared her throat. 'Comrades,' she began, 'perhaps it would be better if you did not take part in the discussions at this meeting. If you wish to talk at the following meeting then it would be advisable for you to come to see me a few days before and tell me what it is you want to talk about.' We stared at her. 'But, Comrade Szusza,' we protested, 'this is a trade union meeting, surely we can speak freely at our own meeting? We know that the function of trade unions under socialism is not only to concern themselves with the welfare of the workers but also to improve the standard of the work and to raise productivity. That is what we're trying to do.' 'And anyway,' I added, hoping to corner her, 'weren't we all directed to criticise and self-criticise?' Szusza rewarded me with her arid little smile. 'That was at the last meeting, Comrade Pauline.' When she left we walked across to Anna's office and confronted her. 'Do you mean to tell us,' we demanded, 'that we need prior permission to raise an issue at a trade union or party meeting?' Anna explained that indeed we did. Not only to speak; we also needed guidance on how to do so. 'It's a question of Party discipline,' she added unctuously. 'Comrade Szusza will approach you and tell you if she'd like you to say something at a meeting. It's better left to her.'

*H*UNGARY was the title of a big, glossy, English language picture magazine modelled exactly on its Soviet counterpart, *Soviet Union*. It mirrored the Soviet magazine in layout, display, print, but whereas *Soviet Union* publicised Soviet achievements, *Hungary* boasted its own national progress in the cultural, industrial, political fields. The other difference was that every article in *Hungary*, irrespective of its subject matter, ended with the incantation, 'This great progress was achieved thanks to the brotherly help and the good example of our glorious Soviet allies.' Isobel and I were deputed to edit the English text of the magazine and as this brought us in some extra money we were quite happy to oblige. In conformity with general policy the overall impression projected by the magazine was of a country which, before liberation, was industrially bereft, agriculturally backward, politically Fascist. I had no reason to doubt this general picture but the magazine's sycophancy to the Soviet Union, in attributing all progress to 'the glorious big brother' became wearisome and boring. Even football, a field in which Hungary excelled, and which was introduced to the country not by a Russian but by an Englishman, ended with the same tired cliché. 'But this is patently untrue,' I remonstrated with Ilona, the editor. 'Do you think your readers are fools?' I recalled the jubilant 8–3 posters that decorated the streets of Hungary when we arrived, celebrating the victory of the Hungarian football team over their English rivals. 'Do you think the English readers are unaware of this, or of the fact that the Russians never managed to beat them at football whereas the Hungarians did?' Ilona, stony-faced, replied, 'The article stays as it is.'

'But Ilona,' I argued, 'this touches the very core of Hungarian national pride.' As a non-believer I had watched with amusement the rapt faces and agonised expressions of the true football worshippers as they listened to Sepesi, their sports reporter, commenting on an international football game. '*Dyerekek*, children,' he'd plead into his microphone, 'you're not at home now. Go, go, go, pick up that ball,' and his listeners at home would hang on his every word, wringing their hands in anguish and tensing their muscles as if their lives depended on it. During the elimination games of the European football championships people could be seen praying that Hungary didn't draw the Soviet Union in the first round. 'If we do,' Eva explained, 'we have to lose and drop out of the game.' 'You're a Hungarian,' I now said to Ilona, and, I might have added, a die-hard Party member who would sacrifice good English rather than risk infringing the Party line. 'Doesn't it upset you to pretend that you're worse at football than the Russians, when everyone knows that's a nonsense?' Ilona turned on me with a ferocity that was as unexpected as it was startling. I had always regarded her as bereft of emotion, a female Party automaton, a tramcar running on Party lines, looking neither to left or right. Suddenly I was confronted with a flesh-and-blood woman with blazing eyes and flushed cheeks. 'Don't you tell me how Hungarians ought to feel,' she exploded. 'I'm a

Hungarian and I know. Don't you think I'm ashamed and humiliated at having to write such rubbish? One would think we were a backward tribe that had just come out of the trees when the Russians came and that they dragged us into the 20th century. Well we weren't. We were and are a civilized, cultured people very much part of the European mainstream, with an advanced industrial system even before they built Stalinvaros, that potty tintown where the houses are already crumbling away.' She glared at me challengingly, as if waiting for opposition. When I remained silent she went on: 'Our Tokay wine was famous all over the world. It was like liquid gold and what's happened to it now?' she demanded rhetorically. 'The vineyards have been allowed to fall into decay because we've got to become "industrialized"'. She spat the word out with contempt. 'Our theatre and opera were as good as anything you could see in any other capital but our greatest playwright, Imre Madach, is never performed because his marvellous play, *The Tragedy of Man* is considered subversive.' I could only stare in amazement at such a passionate outburst and I waited for her to continue. She paused long enough for the colour to fade from her cheeks and for her eyes to regain their hard, dead, look. 'But what can one do?' Ilona shrugged. 'The article stays as it is.'

TO ORDER a coffee in Hungary one asks for a *simpla* or a *dupla* depending on whether one wants a single or a double helping of the concentrated extract of the coffee bean. One could also get a coffee if one simply ordered a *fekete*, meaning black. '*Ne'zd ott egy fekete*,' children would whoop gleefully when they saw H.A. in the street. 'Look, there's a black!' As far as we could gather H.A. was the only black man in Hungary and his appearance on the streets never failed to create a stir, sometimes leading to near accidents as drivers craned their necks to catch a sight of him. There was no hostility, only curiosity – open, incursive, unashamed, as little boys would retrace their steps in order to pass him for a second time, pretending to whistle unconcerned as they peered at him sideways. *Fekete* was one of the few Hungarian words we had come to recognise and when it was voiced loudly at a table next to ours in a restaurant one night, H.A. pushed his chair away and stood up, ready to do battle. 'I've had enough of it,' he announced. 'Why can't they leave me alone? I'm going to tell them what I think of their rudeness.' I leaned over and held him back. 'For goodness' sake, sit down, do. They're only ordering a coffee.' We looked at each other and burst out laughing. We'd come pretty close to making fools of ourselves.

Poor H.A.! There was no end to it. The very next day he was accosted by a group of gypsies as he was crossing the street. 'Where you come from?' their spokesman demanded in broken but recognisable English. 'From South Africa,' H.A. told him. The gypsy grasped his sleeve. 'Oh, sir,' he begged, 'take me back with you to your land. I want to be with my own people, with black people, like you and me.' 'But in South Africa,' H. A. tried to explain, 'the black people have a bad life, they don't have equal rights with the whites, they suffer from discrimination and prejudice.' 'Same as here, same as here,' the gypsy nodded, 'but I want to be with my own kind. Please take me with you.' 'I had a hard time shaking him off,' H. A. told me, 'and he wasn't even black, just a sort of dark tan.' Our only previous contact with gypsies had been in restaurants, listening to their seductive, soulful melodies or foot-tapping to their wild, abandoned, exciting strings. Were they really an oppressed minority? 'Nonsense,' Anna retorted. 'We offer them homes and schools and jobs if only they'd settle down and lead normal lives like everyone else.' 'But what she didn't tell you,' Eva said afterwards, 'is that it's twice as difficult for a gypsy as it is for a Hungarian to get a job or a house. Of course they're not treated equally. People taunt them and insult them and consider them inferior, *untermenschen*. *Tzigan* is not a compliment in Hungary; it's a term of contempt.' So Socialism doesn't change people. They still cling to their prejudices and their hates. There goes another article of faith, I thought.

WE WERE sitting in our favourite coffee bar, indulging in another of our interminable discussions as we listened to H. A.'s account of his exchanges with the gypsy. We felt depressed. 'Come on,' Dora said, trying to cheer us up with her best no-nonsense, hockey-mistress directness. 'You've got to allow time for people to change. What's seven or eight years when you're talking about deep-seated prejudices, hundreds of years old.' She was right and we were all pleased to grasp at it. 'We've also got to take into account the fact,' H. A. offered, 'that the Hungarians didn't have a revolution to gain their freedom. It was offered to them on a plate.' Graham agreed. 'And that's why there are no Communists of pre-war vintage, only the Johnny-come-latelies who jumped on the bandwagon after the liberation.' 'Yes,' Isobel added, 'the sort of people who associate membership of the Party with privilege, not with struggle.' 'Do you realise,' Dora mused, 'that we don't know a single person here who belonged to the pre-war, illegal Party. A veteran Party member here is one who joined in 1945, after the Russians marched in. We must be the oldest Party people here.' 'Then they have the cheek to tell us what Communism means. They forget that we joined the Party from conviction, not from opportunism.' I told them about Janos, our young interpreter who had refused to translate for me what an irate peasant woman was shouting during a recent report at a collective farm. ' "It is not interesting, Comrade," the pompous little ass told me when I asked what she was saying. I confess I lost my temper. "I'll decide what's interesting, not you," I told him. Janos must have joined the party all of 12 months back.' I who had been in the Party since the age of 16 felt entitled to consider myself a veteran. I didn't need instruction on Party ideology from a pipsqueak like Janos.

B OOKS continued to be one of my main diversions and since the classics in English were the only ones available, it was a great opportunity to fill the gaps in my literary education. I caught up on Shakespeare, Jane Austen, Charlotte Brontë, Thackeray, Fielding, Dickens; I discovered at least two great books, the Hungarian classic, *The Tragedy of Man* by Imre Madach and the Danish novel, *Ditte, Daughter of Man*, by Nobel prize-winner Martin Anderson Nexsoe. Of contemporary novels only the Russian writers were freely available in English translations and most of these were mechanical, propagandist and altogether third-rate. A modern American novel that came my way was *The Cross and the Arrow* by Albert Maltz, one of the Hollywood Ten, the group of writers who were hounded by McCarthy during the notorious American witch-hunt of the fifties. The book is set in Nazi Germany and describes the daily life and love affair of a peasant woman and a factory worker. He, the worker, becomes aware of the horrors around him and feels compelled to act by committing an act of sabotage. I was riveted by the story but appalled at the similarities of daily life in Nazi Germany and Communist Hungary. In Germany, too, the grim Party secretary was undisputed boss; she monitored the comings and goings of the people in her area. There too, she was hated and feared; there too the slogan, the cliché, the poster became the substitute for argument and debate. But to link Nazi Germany with Communist Hungary! Even to posit such a comparison seemed to me blasphemy. I discussed it with no one and tried my best to banish the hateful thoughts from my mind.

W HEN our friend Sam Kahn phoned from London to say that he was coming to visit us, he asked what he should bring us. Of all the shortages we experienced one thing stood out; I missed it greatly and it was unknown in Hungary. 'Please bring me Tampax,' I asked him, 'as many packets as you can manage.' Sam arrived in Hungary and was treated respectfully as a VIP – he was a Communist MP from a fraternal Party. Nevertheless, he was obliged to submit his luggage for inspection by Customs and they came upon the packets of Tampax. 'What are these?' they demanded curiously. Sam tried to explain that they served a feminine purpose but, unusually for him, he was beginning to stumble over words. His translator also was finding difficulty and the colour was rising in her cheeks. Far from being re-assured, the customs officer was becoming more and more suspicious. Then he burst out: 'If these are something special for women, why are you carrying them?' When he finally managed to pass through the barrier Sam was trying hard to restrain his laughter. 'Don't ever ask me for these wretched things again,' he warned me.

The next time Sam came to Budapest he was accompanied by his wife Pauline and their young son, Barry, who was the same age as Karen. The three of them had spent a holiday at Sochi as guests of the Soviet Union and had stopped off at Budapest to see us on their way back. I was delighted to see my old friends again and to enjoy Budapest through their eyes. The Hungarian Party welcomed them generously; they provided an interpreter, transport and facilities to see the sights. Together we went to the opera, visited Margit Sziget and took trips on the Danube.

This was the heyday of Hungarian football. The Hungarian team, under their world-renowned captain, Ferenc Puskas, had just won the European Cup and they basked in the fame and acclaim of the entire nation. Nothing was too good for these god-like figures; they were above the law and beyond criticism. People chuckled with approval as they related how the city streets suddenly sprouted an abundance of consumer goods after the team's trips abroad. Little stalls selling ribbons, laces, chocolates, cosmetics, nylons and all sorts of other goodies suddenly appeared on street corners, strictly illegal, of course, but never interfered with by the police. All knew these were the footballers' perks. Apart from official Party functionaries, they were the only Hungarians to be allowed foreign travel and they brought back so much contraband that the authorities laid on extra coaches on the trains for their luggage.

'Wouldn't it be a good idea,' Sam suggested one day, 'to get the Hungarian team to autograph a football for me to take back to Cape Town. I'd present it to the coloured teams in Cape Town; it would make a wonderful trophy, the envy of the white teams who exclude them.' Hesitantly I broached the subject with Sepesi, Radio Budapest's popular sports commentator. 'Do you think it could be arranged?' I asked him. He promised to try and came back triumphantly to say, 'It's been fixed!' We arranged to go with Sepesi to the sports grounds where the team practised and when we arrived were introduced to the great man himself. Puskas laughed when we tried to explain to him how precious the trophy would be and threw the ball playfully to Barry. Then, as the players ran past us to enter the grounds, Sepesi stood at the gate with a pen and stopped each one; 'Sign here, my friend,' he said and they did. 'I'd like to explain to them about apartheid in South Africa,' Sam said but Sepesi assured him he would be wasting his time. 'They don't know and they don't want to know,' he assured him. 'They're not interested in politics, football is all they care about.'

THEN a new woman came to work in the Radio hierarchy and she turned out to be a 'real' Communist, a member of the 'old guard' who had spent years in exile in Moscow before the war together with Rakosi, Nagy, Kadar and the rest of the old stalwarts who had to escape from Hungary between the wars.

Vera Horvath was a grey-haired, smooth-skinned woman in her sixties, with a tranquil manner and a kindly smile. She could not have been less like the brash, strident *apparatchiks* who made up the bulk of the Party functionaries. She, too, argued for the Party line, but she did so from a base of logic and national necessity, not from ignorance or opportunism. I spent many hours in Vera's office, savouring the opportunity of dialogue with an honest adversary, one I could respect. 'Vera,' I appealed to her, 'how can you, a true old Bolshevik, justify the corruption all round us? Everywhere one looks, one sees Party members who are on the make, sycophants, hypocrites. And these are the very people who get promotion, who climb to the top, the ones who can mouth the acceptable slogans. Not only is the system bad but language, too, has become corrupted. Words no longer represent thought; they often mean the opposite of what one hears. People dare not say what they think, only what is expected.' Vera sighed. 'I am very disturbed at what I see around me,' she told me, 'but I can't opt out, I've got to try to change things from within. This is my home. I've had enough of exile.'

FERENC from the Editorial Department stopped me in the passage one day. 'I've just got to ask you,' he said. 'Why does the *Daily Worker* follow the Soviet line as slavishly as we do? After all, we risk everything if we deviate but you British won't lose your homes or your jobs if you criticise the Soviet Union. So why don't you ever do so?' It was a question I was hard put to answer. 'Perhaps they don't know the real facts,' I muttered. When Comrade Bob Stewart from the British Party came on his next official trip I tried to enlighten him. 'Do you know what's going on in this country?' I asked him when we had a few moments alone. But Comrade Bob would not be drawn, he was evasive and embarrassed and he changed the subject. It was not until the following year, when we were back in Britain and, in his office, I returned to the subject that he gave his reply.

THE time had come to leave Hungary. Our original two-year contract had now expanded to three and a half years without any indication that life would be easier and work more rewarding. The weight of our oppressive surroundings was taking a marked toll on me and even more so on H. A. who seemed less able to bear it. We knew that we faced a tough existence in Britain and a struggle for survival, without a home, jobs or money. All the same we deemed it preferable to the oppressive dishonesty of our present surroundings.

The children were ill too often and we could not provide them with the necessary drugs or even with vitamin C supplements which were freely available to the Russians and the Hungarian top brass. We also realized that they were growing away from us. The language barrier was separating us from our children even more divisively than it had alienated my brothers and me from our parents. I could foresee a time, if we remained in the country, when conversation between us and our daughters would become as stilted and imprecise as it had been in my family or for that matter as it had been between H. A. and his mother. Already Karen needed an interpreter when she wanted to tell me something – Hungarian was her first language – and Sandra's English was beginning to falter as her Hungarian was growing daily more fluent.

When we'd first arrived the Hungarians offered to supply me with a language teacher but after a few lessons I quickly realized I would never master the impossible tongue. I reckoned we'd be there for only two years anyway and I decided to concentrate on brushing up my German which I thought would be more useful in the world outside.

The Hungarian comrades were nonplussed when we declared our intention of leaving. 'But Comrade H. A.,' Szusza protested, 'if you're not happy with your flat you should let me know and I'll see what I can do. Or do you think you should get a rise in salary?' She seemed genuinely perplexed that anyone as privileged and secure as we were should want to return to the capitalist hell-hole that we'd left behind. 'What if the British don't accept you?' Anna demanded. 'After all, they know you've served our government.' 'In that case,' H. A. told her, 'we'll return to South Africa.' 'You mean,' Anna was incredulous, 'that you'd rather live in racist South Africa than here?' 'Yes,' H. A. told her, 'at least there I have the possibility of opposing the system, of forming genuine trade unions, of resisting.' Anna and Szusza looked at each other and by mutual accord turned on their heels and left the room.

The Naidoos go to vote for the first time in their lives, London 1956.

The family in London, 1956.

Postscript

IT WAS raining when we returned to London, and we wondered where we would sleep that night. The captain of the Polish vessel that brought us from Gdynia heard of our dilemma and offered to let us stay on board while his ship remained in the London docks, a maximum of two nights. We started phoning boarding houses but one after another turned us down. It was the same objection we'd met before when we first arrived in London, only this time our sins were compounded. 'What! Three children!' Eventually we managed to contact Leon Griffiths and he and his wife Lily very generously offered to accommodate us in their Hampstead home until his mother returned from Scotland. Leon and Lily made us welcome and they put up with damp napkins draped in front of the fire, baby's bottles in the kitchen and the presence of five strangers in their midst. Then our friends Eileen and Percy Denton announced triumphantly that they'd found a boarding house near them in Manor House which had agreed to take us in. We moved in gratefully and stayed far longer than we'd intended, searching for a flat we could afford. The landlady of the boarding house, not unkindly, reminded me from time to time, 'This was not intended as a permanent arrangement.' When eventually we found a flat in Highbury New Park we didn't care that we had to share a bathroom with the tenants in the flat below; it was such a relief to have a place of our own.

What did upset me was the presence of mice in the kitchen. It meant that if I wanted to make a cup of tea at night I had first to send in one of the family to chase the mice away even if it did involve using my little girls as advance troops. It was a great relief to discover that whereas I had inherited my mother's abhorrence of the harmless small beasts – an irrational and overwhelming repulsion I have never managed to overcome – my children can laugh at me for it. I'd lurk outside the kitchen while one of the little ones would be inside shouting at the mice, 'Go away! Mummy wants to put the kettle on.'

My mother was a woman of great courage. She proved it many times in her life confronting murderers, escaping floods, outwitting invading armies. But one event above all others impressed itself on my memory and demonstrated very graphically just how brave she was. It illuminated for me her will-power and nerve. We were at a *datcha* in Lithuania – my mother, brother and I – and our home was a barn on the side of a lake in the midst of deep forest. We slept on a bed of hay under the sloping roof, my mother in the middle with Yossele and me on either side of her. One night mother felt something stir at the foot of the bed. She jumped up and was horrified to see a mouse entangled in our bedclothes; it had apparently fallen from the rafters. Mother didn't scream or panic; without even waking us she shook the blankets to rid us of the invader and quietly went back to sleep. I can imagine my consternation under similar circumstances and I can appreciate what it must have cost my mother to exercise such calm self-control so as not to frighten the children.

'ARE we going to rejoin the Party?' I asked H.A. and his answer was a categorical No. He was unhappy and depressed but quite positive that he wanted nothing more to do with the Party even though it felt as though he were losing a limb. 'But H.A.,' I argued, 'the British comrades have no way of knowing what's going on in Hungary. It's our duty to tell them.' He was adamant in his refusal so I joined the local branch of the Party on my own. But first we had to report back to King Street and I persuaded H.A. to accompany me for a meeting with Bob Stewart who had sent us to Hungary three and a half years earlier.

'Comrade Bob, do you know what's going on in Hungary? You've visited the place. Were you taken in by the stage-managed tours and the meaningless slogans? Could you see the corruption, the cynicism, the opportunism? And if you know about it how can you collude in the lies that the Party here is spreading about Hungary?' Bob sank wearily back in his chair and held up his hand to stem the torrent of our words. 'Of course I know about it,' he said. 'I'm not a fool. And don't think it's only in Hungary. It's also true of the other Socialist republics and even of the Soviet Union.' He then confided to us the story of his daughter who had married an editor of *Pravda*, the official Soviet Communist Party newspaper. 'I knew him well,' he said of his son-in-law. 'He was a good chap and a devoted Communist but one day the secret police arrived and took him away and we haven't heard of him since. We don't know if he's dead or alive or what he's been accused of. You can imagine my daughter's feelings.' He spread his hands helplessly. 'But you're a high official of a fraternal Party, couldn't you do something?' I demanded. 'No,' Bob sighed. 'There's nothing I can do. I can only hope that they're going through a bad phase and that things will improve.'

We were angry and bitterly disappointed as we walked out of Party headquarters. 'Now you see why I want to have nothing more to do with them,'

H.A. said as we walked down the Strand. But I still couldn't agree. 'All the more reason to open the eyes of the ordinary members, to make them see.'

The local branch secretary of the Party in Green Lanes was Vi Strachan. She was warm-hearted, generous, humorous, and managed to care for her infirm mother-in-law as well as her own family without ever turning away an appeal for help from her neighbours on the large housing estate where she lived. Night and day they came knocking on Vi's door with problems that ranged from disputes with the rent department to violent husbands. Always they were received with patience and courtesy and offered tea and practical advice. I marvelled at Vi's ability to cope and was equally impressed by the devoted support she received from her trade unionist husband. It was Vi who helped me place Karen and Sandra in good local schools and who advised me against leaving Jennie with an unsuitable baby-minder. When she took me to the local Party branch I looked forward to meeting a group of people who were cast in her mould but it soon became clear that Vi and her husband were not typical of British Communists.

'Comrade Pauline,' Vi introduced me, 'worked for Radio Budapest as a broadcaster and she can give you first-hand news of the country where she's lived for three and a half years.' The ten or twelve members present regarded me with interest and waited to hear the glad tidings of life in a Socialist country. As it dawned on them that what I was telling them was the opposite of what they wanted to hear, their interest turned to embarrassment and then to hostility. They heard me out in silence, asked no questions and turned with relief to the next item on the agenda. The following week I tried again. 'It's no good pretending that everything is rosy there just because you want to believe it,' I told them. 'You must be honest, you must face facts.' There were unfriendly mutterings from the members. 'You must give the comrade a chance to speak,' Vi urged and for the next ten minutes or so I related some of my personal experiences to a stony-faced audience. The third week, determined to persist even though I realised that I might as well be talking to a brick wall, I once again asked to take the floor. A grim-faced, tight-lipped female comrade objected. 'We've wasted enough time listening to these stories,' she said. 'It's time we got down to the important work of deciding who's going to sell the *Daily Worker* next week.'

So ended my attempts to educate from within and to spread the truth. I realised that my wilderness voice would never succeed in persuading my erstwhile comrades. They didn't want to know. They refused to know. They preferred to believe that I was telling them lies rather than confront the flimsiness of the foundation on which their faith rested. Old friends and fellow expatriates continued to invite us to their homes and offered help in practical ways. Gradually we learnt to talk of other things, not always easy to political animals such as we. We knew that our good friends wished we had not become 'reactionaries', but they continued to value our friendship. Others could not forgive what they regarded as betrayal and they dropped us socially.

Some refused to listen and accused me of treachery. 'Why, you've become a reactionary,' Joe Slovo said to me at a party in London, as if that epithet absolved him from any further discussion. Intelligent people persisted in their delusions just as I had done in the years before Hungary. These people knew I was no liar but they looked for excuses and explanations for 'what has gone wrong', or 'the mistakes'.

There was also the unwarranted assumption that to denounce the evils of Communist states, proletarian dictatorship, Stalinism or whatever name it went by, led inevitably to embracing capitalism. The old slogan which I had so blithely disseminated in the past was now used against me: those who are not with us are against us. That capitalism bred its own set of evils was not in question nor was the role of the United States government in world politics an honourable alternative to the Soviet hegemony of captive states. I did not feel called upon to defend one when I denounced the other. But it was significant that when comrades were confronted with the blunt question of where they'd rather live, in Russia or in England, no one pretended that they'd choose the Soviet Union.

One person whose good opinion of me mattered more than most was my old friend Moses Kotane, Secretary of the South African Communist Party. On his return journey after attending the Bandung Conference of unaligned nations, Moses passed through London. He was enthusiastic about the Conference but he also told us how disgusted he was that Israel, which wished to attend, was excluded at the insistence of the Arab states.

When I tried to explain how our opinions had changed since our Budapest experience it seemed to me that Moses became impatient with me. This upset me and I wrote to him on 11 September 1963, reaffirming that 'I have changed my beliefs and opinions on many matters – not, of course, on South Africa.' I asked if that meant I was losing his friendship. On 19 September 1963 Moses replied, 'I do not know how I was impatient and cool towards your views in 1955. However, it may be better and profitable if we forgot the past and paid attention to the present and the future.' He signed it, 'With love, Mo.' I must have needed further re-assurance because on 25 December 1964 he included in his letter the following, 'By the way, who said that I was cross with you? You may rest assured that as far as I am concerned there is nothing of the kind, I have never been.' This time he signed the letter 'Moshe'.

ONE day an American knocked on our door. He appeared to be quietly nondescript but at the same time there was something mysteriously sinister about him. His face merged into his grey overcoat and seemed to disappear. He explained that his organisation was interested in background news of Hungary and anything H.A. could tell him would be appreciated. It would also be well rewarded financially.

We asked whom he represented and the American hummed and hawed.

'You're working for US intelligence, aren't you?' H.A. confronted him and when his visitor didn't deny it, he asked him to leave. 'I may be disillusioned with Communism,' H.A. said, 'and I certainly could use the money but that doesn't mean that I'm ready to sell out to American imperialism.' A couple of years later, when H.A. was working at India House he gave a similar brush-off to the person who approached him for information on behalf of a Soviet agency in return for a monthly stipend.

IN OCTOBER 1956 the Hungarian people rose against their Communist masters and demonstrators throughout the country demanded independence and an end to Soviet domination. The news filled us with great excitement and we sat glued to the radio and television set. Could this be the dawn of a real Socialist society? Suddenly people were eager to hear our first-hand reports of life in Hungary. At a gathering of friends in the Routh's home in Hampstead someone said to me after hearing me out, 'Why didn't you tell us this before?' I asked him, 'Would you have believed me if I had?'

AT BUDAPEST Radio a workers' committee threw out the old guard, including Comrades Szusza and Anna, and took control. Two emissaries from this committee were sent to see us; they invited us to return and work for the new Hungarian Radio. They told us that they planned to abolish all but four of the foreign language broadcasts and they wanted H.A. and me to take charge of the English section. 'All the things you criticised,' they said, 'have now been put right, and you'll have a free hand to run the section as you think it should be done.' They also told us that when the workers' committee took over they found all the personal dossiers which the Party had assured them had been destroyed during the period of liberalisation. 'In your dossier, Pauline,' they told me, were inscribed the words, 'A premature anti-Stalinist.'

We were greatly tempted. It meant throwing up our jobs and uprooting the children once again but the prospect of working for a real Workers' State rekindled all our old hopes and enthusiasm. We were still debating the pros and cons when the Russian tanks rolled into Budapest and set about crushing the will of the people. On 5 November we listened on the radio to the last despairing words of Hungarian Premier Imre Nagy appealing for help which he knew would not come. The words were muffled, the radio crackled. And then it was cut off. I burst into tears.

GRAHAM Heathcote, our former colleague on Radio Budapest, was also back in London. He'd married Yudit, our attractive interpreter and brought her out of the Budapest turmoil, together with her mother and young brother. Graham came to visit us in Highbury and gave us a graphic account of events during the uprising. He described inspiringly how the workers' committees functioned. 'Suddenly they knew all about democracy,' he told us. 'Remember how we used to criticise them?' We listened entranced to his account of real workers' power, the exercise of proper elections, freedom of expression, enthusiasm. The spread of democracy among the people brought with it a burgeoning of creativity; suddenly poems appeared on doorways, pictures and paintings were hung out for all to see, there was music and dancing on the streets. 'This really was a people's revolution,' Graham said.

I tore myself away from his fascinating story to make tea. When I returned with a loaded tray I heard Graham say: 'The Russians were right to march in. The Fascists were preparing for a take-over.' It seemed such a volte-face that I nearly dropped the tray in astonishment. We continued arguing heatedly for many hours and just before he left us Graham revealed that he'd accepted a post with one of the Eastern news agencies. I never did find out which came first, his offer of a job or his change of opinion.

I'D LOST my God many years ago but then I found the Party. Now I was stripped of my Party and it left me feeling naked and bereft. There was a gaping hole where my faith had rested, my centre of certainty. What was left? Where to find a moral base to live by, a code of decency? I knew that H. A. felt even more abandoned than I and his groping for a way out was as doomed as mine. But I could not help him and he could offer me no comfort. This was something each of us had to solve for ourselves. He seemed unable to 'pull himself together', as well-intentioned friends advised; he became apathetic and depressed, a complete contrast to the man he was. At first gradually, and then more rapidly, his mental health declined. Tragically he didn't live long enough to overcome his bitter disappointments and to forge for himself a new life. He never came to terms with his past.

As I went about my business, making a home, earning a living, caring for my unhappy husband and our three children and studying for a new career, I too, was bitter at having been so duped. Why was I so naïve, so eager to worship? Oh yes, the theory was fine, the words were inspiring.

From each according to his ability, to each according to his need.

What finer aim had humanity ever evolved? Nor did I regret the years of my life devoted to the cause in South Africa, the trade union work, the struggle against race discrimination. That was a part of my life I could be proud of – the South

African Communist Party was the only organisation which stood for total equality – and I would do the same again. But life under a Communist regime had opened my eyes to the evils inherent in such a system. More than that, it had made me question the theory underlying the system and to wonder whether it did not inevitably lead to corruption, inefficiency and suppression.

When challenged to find a solution to the world's problems I must confess that I cannot. All I can and must do is to resist injustice wherever I find it, to detest racism in all its forms, to uphold the virtues of socialism and democracy and to try to be true to my principles. This is not as easy as it might be. Getting older does not necessarily make one better or wiser. But I'll keep on trying.

Index

The sign ° denotes an invented name.